Blackbeard's
SUNKEN PRIZE

D1597491

Blackbeard's SUNKEN PRIZE

THE 300-YEAR VOYAGE OF *Queen Anne's Revenge*

Mark U. Wilde-Ramsing & Linda F. Carnes-McNaughton

The University of North Carolina Press [CHAPEL HILL]

Designed by Kimberly Bryant and set in Miller and IM Fell types
by Rebecca Evans

Manufactured in the United States of America

The University of North Carolina Press has been a member of the
Green Press Initiative since 2003.

Cover illustration: *Under the Black Flag*, by Jack Saylor (2007).
Courtesy of the North Carolina Office of Archives and History.

Library of Congress Cataloging-in-Publication Data
Names: Wilde-Ramsing, Mark, author. | Carnes-McNaughton,
    Linda F. (Linda Flowers), author.
Title: Blackbeard's sunken prize : the 300-year voyage of Queen Anne's
    Revenge / by Mark U. Wilde-Ramsing and Linda F. Carnes-McNaughton.
Description: Chapel Hill : The University of North Carolina Press, [2018] |
    Includes bibliographical references and index.
Identifiers: LCCN 2017048511| ISBN 9781469640525 (pbk : alk. paper) |
    ISBN 9781469640532 (ebook)
Subjects: LCSH: Excavations (Archaeology)—North Carolina—Atlantic
    Coast. | Underwater archaeology—North Carolina—Atlantic Coast. |
    Queen Anne's Revenge (Sailing vessel) | Shipwrecks—North Carolina—
    Atlantic Coast. | Teach, Edward, –1718. | North Carolina—Antiquities.
Classification: LCC CC77.U5 W55 2018 | DDC 930.102804—dc23 LC record
    available at https://lccn.loc.gov/2017048511

TO
Dina & Kirk,
OUR FAVORITE

PIRATES

Contents

Maps

Graphs

Tables

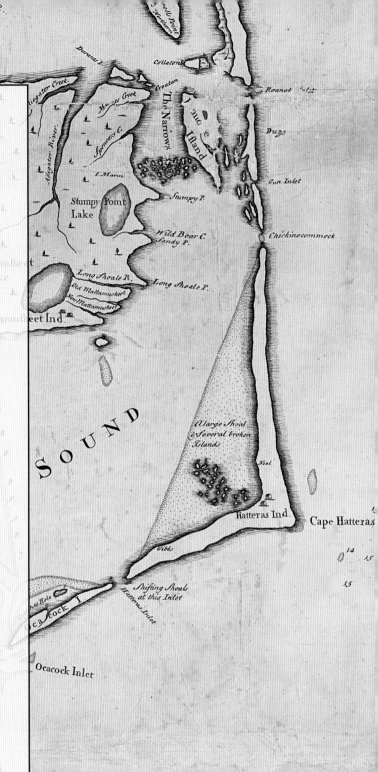

Vignettes

PART OF THE

Preface

Three centuries ago a wooden ship ran aground on a hidden sandbar about a mile off the North Carolina coastline. What transpired on that day changed the course of many people's lives, then and now. For this was not just any ship that wrecked; it was *Queen Anne's Revenge* (*QAR*), the flagship of the notorious pirate captain Blackbeard. The day of the ship's grounding was on or near June 10, 1718. From that moment forward, the tale of the vessel and what it contained took on another life of its own, as the ship slowly rotted on the ocean floor, out of sight and out of mind. Indeed, it was mostly forgotten in history, though the infamous pirate's life was subsequently embellished and frequently appeared in print and memory for years to come. Even today, the name Blackbeard conjures up a fierce scoundrel and his historic, outlandish actions. His life has been the major storyline of many books, poems, legends, and action movies. Blackbeard personifies the word "pirate."

What went down with this shipwreck, notwithstanding the few useful or valuable things the crew could retrieve as they scrambled to get off alive, remained hidden for a very long time. The fact that so little was known surely contributed to the rise of the Blackbeard legend. But then, all that was lost was found, and much of it was brought to the surface—to be examined and marveled at, to be cleaned and put on display, but mainly to tell us the story of that ship and its former occupants. Just as its sinking was serendipitous, so was its discovery. A licensed salver company, focused mainly on finding another shipwreck and its Spanish treasure, came across the cannons and anchors of an early eighteenth-century battleship. The leading candidate for its identity, actually the only shipwreck that it could possibly be, was *Queen Anne's Revenge*. It didn't hold much treasure in strictly monetary terms but, rather, an immensely valuable, historic haul of artifacts that has since drawn popular interest and excitement that seem to be endless. Much to the amazement and delight of the Intersal discovery team and North Carolina state archaeologists, November 21, 1996, the day of discovery, was a dramatic moment that changed so much for them. It too was a dramatic moment for the pirates on that fateful June day in 1718 when their ship went down.

Needless to say, much has transpired in the past two decades since *Queen Anne's Revenge* resurfaced, and that is at the heart of this book we teamed up to write. One of us led the archaeological investigations, literally diving deep into the shipwreck, while the other played a leading role in investigating and interpreting its artifactual evidence housed at the conservation laboratory, all the while searching archives on both sides of the Atlantic for clues. It has been a good union of our expertise, talents, and temperament, which stretches back years before we tackled Blackbeard's booty. We worked together on excavations of various land sites across the state—some frontier outposts, others Civil War coastal fortifications—and we shared a common appreciation of ceramics from all parts of the world. Our interests united several times as we each pursued our common passion for the past. Mostly, though, our collaboration has involved the many times when one of us, a "bubble-head" from the N.C. Underwater Archaeology Branch, brought up curiosities (at first ceramics) from sites under the water and offered them to the other, the N.C. State Historic Sites archaeologist and "jughead," who would glean the full extent of cultural knowledge from them.

As the *Queen Anne's Revenge* Shipwreck Project got under way, it was only natural for us to build upon our working relationship in order to shed light on the days of pirates in colonial North Carolina. Our paths would cross on the deck of the *QAR* recovery vessel, R/V *Shell Point*, during underwater excavations at the wreck site near Beaufort and, at other times, during analytical work sessions at the *QAR* Conservation Laboratory on the campus of East Carolina University in Greenville. As evidence built, we began to write up our separate research on different aspects of the shipwreck site and its artifacts for in-house publications and scholarly journals. Eventually we found our collective voice in a piece on glassware and bottles written for the project's online *QAR* Technical Series (2008).[1] We followed that with a more expansive article for *Pieces of Eight: More Archaeology of Piracy* (2016), titled "Blackbeard's *Queen Anne's Revenge* and Its French Connection."[2] We liked how those turned out, and thus when the 300th anniversary of *QAR*'s sinking began peeking over the horizon, we hatched the idea of writing this book.

The prospect was exciting, because while a vast amount of media coverage, popular and scholarly articles, and documentaries had covered nearly every aspect of the *QAR* project, there had not been a successful effort to bring the collective findings into a single, comprehensive read. Setting out to write, we wanted to walk a line between a deeply researched and factually accurate text and an accessible narrative that shared stories of our work offshore and in the conservation lab alongside tales from the days of the pirates. In doing so, we knew at times it might feel like we were walking the plank, rather than the line, but we continued to venture forth. It was a wonderful lift to our confidence when the editors at the University of North Carolina Press caught our vision and agreed to publish this work.

While we were not naive in this undertaking, having engaged the public with numerous articles, interviews, and programs relating the science and intrigue of archaeology to a wide audience, this book has required a lot of time, persistence, patience, and perseverance. Thankfully, our long-standing working relationship has given us the foundation to meet the many challenges. Interestingly enough, one of the more difficult aspects to navigate was deciding whether to write in third or first person. We chose the latter for the benefit of storytelling. But the truth is that both of us weren't there for everything, even though we write as if we were. Just so you know, stories from out on the water during excavations, on both the *QAR* site and other underwater locations throughout the state, were primarily witnessed by Mark. When our attention turns to analysis of *QAR* artifacts and activities taking place in the conservation laboratory at Greenville, it is most often from Linda's perspective.

So now that we have come clean and let you in on our little secret, we wish to tell you the story of *Queen Anne's Revenge*, its early history, its use, its capture, its abandonment, and finally, its re-emergence into this modern world. Along the way, we will share what we learned about the events leading up to the wrecking, and about the ship's construction, cargo, crew, and pirate captain. We have written this book to enlighten and engage your imagination as well as to educate those curious about eighteenth-century nautical life. It's been a rewarding journey for us, for we too have learned many things along the way. So now is the time for you to grab your favorite drink, perhaps a flagon of watery grog, find a comfortable, quiet corner below deck, and let us tell you an incredible shipwreck story.

Blackbeard's
SUNKEN PRIZE

CHAPTER ONE

Meeting a Pirate Captain

In the fall of 1996, one of the great mysteries of America's maritime history finally was solved. Intersal LLC, a treasure-salvage company, had been searching for eighteenth-century ships that according to historical records had gone down in the vicinity of North Carolina's Beaufort Inlet. Seasoned shipwreck researcher Mike Daniel joined the Intersal effort that year to direct search operations. He brought with him a strategy that used remote sensing instruments to detect potential sunken vessels, followed by a relatively quick site inspection using professional divers. They located numerous targets; some turned out to be shipwrecks, but none were of the age they sought. There was one target, however, that particularly interested Captain Daniel because of its strong, wide, and long magnetic reading. The first dive inspection was inconclusive, since the water visibility was nearly zero. Daniel was intent on giving the site another look, which he was able to fit in on the day before they were to leave the area. His persistence paid off.

Intersal's primary quest was finding the sunken remains and cargo of the Spanish merchantman *El Salvador*, which foundered and was lost in 1750 on its way home in a fierce hurricane. The company's ongoing research and survey activities had been in the works for over a decade without suc-

cess. By the time Captain Daniel had come aboard, Intersal also held permits from the state of North Carolina to search for two other vessels. These were pirate ships that, according to eyewitness accounts, ran aground and were abandoned by their crews in early June 1718. The larger vessel was a three-masted ship, a former French privateer, which had been captured by pirates who later heavily armed it with upward of 40 iron cannons. Of the three wrecked vessels he sought, Daniel knew that with tons of iron from cannons and anchors, the larger pirate ship would produce a significant magnetometer signal, much like the one they had not been able to identify on their first dive inspection.

When the team returned, Captain Daniel sent his two professional divers in, one at a time. The first diver, using a metal detector, reported lots of metal, what appeared to be a cannon and an anchor, and what turned out to be a lead cannon touchhole cover. The second diver confirmed three cannons and brought up a ship's bell and the barrel of a blunderbuss. Daniel then donned his wet suit and scuba gear and entered the water to see for himself; he was able to identify a large cluster of cannons, maybe a dozen or so. He also brought up a lead sounding weight. Collectively, they had gathered a small but exciting trove of artifacts that

Intersal's *Pelican III*. (Courtesy of the North Carolina Department of Natural and Cultural Resources)

Bell and assorted artifacts recovered on the day of discovery. (Courtesy of the North Carolina Department of Natural and Cultural Resources)

provided critical evidence of the time period and ship's mission, enough to make Daniel believe he had indeed found a long-lost pirate ship.

But this was no ordinary vessel. Captain Daniel and his team knew it was likely the site of *Queen Anne's Revenge* (*QAR*), once known as the flagship commanded by Edward Thache, better known as Blackbeard.

Thache (pronounced Teach, but also spelled Thach, Tach, Thatch, or Teach),[1] arguably the most famous pirate of the Atlantic coast, built his reputation during two years of pure pirate action—and not so much for the number of vessels he stole or the value of his plunder, but more for the way he went about business. Today we would call it his "brand," which was especially on display when he confronted his adversaries. Nathaniel Mist, a contemporary of Blackbeard, described his fearsome presence in detail.[2]

> Captain Teach, assumed the cognomen of Blackbeard from that large quantity of hair which, like a frightful meteor, covered his whole face and frightened America more than any comet that has appeared there a long time. This beard was black, which he suffered to grow of an extravagant length, as to breadth it came up to his eyes. He was accustomed to twist it with ribbons, in small tails, after the manner of our ramillies wigs, and turn it about his ears. In time of action, he wore a sling over his shoulders with three brace of pistols hanging in holsters like bandoliers, and stuck lighted matches under his hat, which appearing on each side of his face, his eyes naturally looking fierce and wild, made him altogether such a figure, that imagination cannot form an idea of a fury, from hell, to look more frightful.[3]

Captain Thache's bravado extended to his naval tactics. Most pirates of the day used small

Meeting a Pirate Captain

fast sloops or canoes, from which they struck with stealth and speed and then, just as quickly, dispersed and disappeared over the horizon to remote coastal hideaways. Not so with Blackbeard. After capturing the French slave ship and former privateer *Concorde*, he decided to keep it as his flagship and augmented its armament to meet any challenges the authorities could muster at the time. Instead of "hit and run" tactics, he preferred strength and intimidation, surrounding his battleship, now renamed *Queen Anne's Revenge*, with three smaller ships. His fleet was a match for any naval force he was likely to meet at that time.

After a six-month spree using his armada to pillage, plunder, and seriously threaten the American colonies, Captain Thache and his company unceremoniously wrecked and abandoned their flagship just off the North Carolina coastline. Five months later, Blackbeard was dead after a fierce fight to the finish on Ocracoke Island, again described by Mist: "They were now closely and warmly engaged, the lieutenant and twelve men, against Blackbeard and fourteen, 'till the sea was tinctured with blood round the vessel. Blackbeard received a shot into his body from the pistol that Lieutenant Maynard discharged, yet he stood his ground and fought with great fury, 'till he received five-and-twenty wounds, five of them by shot. At length, as he was cocking another pistol, having fired several before, he fell down dead."[4]

With his outrageous exploits and violent death, Blackbeard, and the stories that surround him, has fascinated and terrified his contemporaries, the same being true for current readers and fans of the *Pirates of the Caribbean* franchise. As matter of fact, it seems that since the time Blackbeard roamed the high seas, his notoriety has continued to expand in leaps and bounds thanks to deeply rooted and persistent local lore, three centuries of popular print matter, and the recent attention from Hollywood.

Therefore, when Captain Daniel found the Beaufort Inlet shipwreck, he set in motion one of the

"Blackbeard Approaching: Blackbeard and His Crew Approach in their Longboats," by Frank E. Schoonover (1922), in Ralph Delahaye Paine, *Blackbeard: Buccaneer* (Philadelphia: Penn Publishing, 1922), 309.

most significant underwater archaeology projects in the history of the United States, bringing extraordinary expertise and effort to the waters off the North Carolina coast. We were among the government officials, managers, researchers, and instructors who came on board the *Queen Anne's Revenge* Shipwreck Project, beginning a voyage of discovery that commenced in 1997 and continues to this day. What we learned has allowed us to uncover astonishing details of life aboard an eighteenth-century pirate ship. Coinciding with the 300th anniversary of the sinking of this iconic vessel, we hope this book will provide our readers the same sense of discovery and excitement that marked our work on the project, immersing us in the fascinating world of Blackbeard and his sunken flagship.

A Discovery Decades in the Making

To fully appreciate how exploration of *Queen Anne's Revenge* played out, we should understand the origins and nature of historical research conducted below the surface of North Carolina's oceans, sounds, and rivers. During the 1960s and 1970s, the staff of the Underwater Archaeology Branch (UAB), a specialized unit within the N.C. Department of Natural and Cultural Resources, formerly the Department of Cultural Resources, worked primarily in the Cape Fear River and focused on Civil War shipwrecks. Only occasionally did they pay attention to research into other time periods, such as a search for the Spanish privateer *Fortuna* (1748) off the banks of colonial Brunswick Town and the discovery of an Indian log canoe in Lake Waccamaw. No pirates or their shipwrecks, for the most part, were on the radar of the UAB in these early days. By the late 1970s, however, archaeology and pirate lore began to intersect as underwater archaeologists ventured into other areas of the state and were faced with submerged sites other than those from the Civil War period.

In 1979, state archaeologists in cooperation with the Maritime Studies Program at East Carolina University held the first of four summer field schools in underwater archaeology. Participants conducted fieldwork to locate and register shipwrecks, landing locations, and a variety of inundated structures. Researchers believed that adding to their database of submerged sites would help identify discernible patterns in what they discovered and enhance the protection of the state's cultural heritage—made possible thanks to newly enacted state and federal environmental laws.[5] The logical place to begin searching was the small harbor of Bath, which served as North Carolina's economic center during the colony's early development in the first quarter of the eighteenth century. Adding to the intrigue, however, was the possibility of discoveries related to Blackbeard. The pirate was known to have stayed in Bath and the surrounding

North Carolina Underwater Archaeology Branch staff conducting 1979 field school survey of Bath harbor. (Courtesy of the North Carolina Department of Natural and Cultural Resources)

waters; UAB staff and students arrived that summer with the expectation that their thorough combing of the dark waters of Bath Creek would produce tangible evidence of the famous pirate captain. We were disappointed not to discover any sunken ships, cannons, buried treasure, or any other artifacts that could be tied to the pirate's brief stay in Bath during the summer and fall of 1718. But as it turned out, we did come close.

On June 21, 1979, we pushed our survey vessel carrying a magnetometer and bow-mounted sensor through shallow water along the western shore of Bath Creek. Just as the "mag's" needle began to move, indicating that something of interest may lie below, we suddenly met with a low wall of smooth, round stones in the shallow water, some as large as boulders. Cobbles such as these do not naturally occur on North Carolina's coastal plain and must have been imported by humans. Further examination determined that they formed a causeway or wharf made of ballast stones. These transportable cobbles had been extracted from the bilges of visiting sailing ships when they docked at Bath and subsequently replaced with the area's exports of heavy raw materials, primarily naval stores—turpentine, lumber, tar, pitch, and other products derived from processing pine trees and their sap from nearby forests. With an abundance of ballast, wharves were extended from the eighteenth-century shoreline to deeper water, where vessels could be loaded and unloaded.

Using historical research and local folklore, we were able to piece together a reason for the wharf's existence.[6] Early maps and land deeds revealed that the stone wharf we found was associated with a 400-acre land tract first purchased and occupied by Governor Charles Eden in 1714. Close to the town of Bath the governor built his brick residence, where he reportedly often conducted official business. His appointed deputy, Tobias Knight, lived on the plantation next door. And who was an associate of both? None other than Blackbeard. Legend has it that a subterranean passage ran from the cellar under the governor's mansion to the steep bank adjacent to Bath Creek from which pirates could come and go without being seen. It is very likely that Blackbeard once walked down the very stone wharf that we had, quite literally, stumbled upon.

Another thread of local lore comes from the town of Oriental, which lies on the lower Neuse River as it opens out into Pamlico Sound. Some years after the Bath field school of 1979, UAB staff were examining the mouth of a creek across from the town's small harbor where a marina and channel dredging were proposed. In such instances, we would typically take a firsthand look at areas slated for construction to make sure unknown archaeological sites (e.g., sunken ships and other forgotten artifacts) were not disturbed or destroyed. Using the magnetometer, we detected a magnetic disturbance within the project area that called for additional investigation. Not being equipped to dive, we probed from the survey boat with a pole and detected a solid structure within the creek's soft bottom. This prompted us to wade out in our shorts and, while holding our breath, grope down in the mud to feel for clues. The effort revealed a line of rotten wooden ribs from a rather large vessel, its width being 23 ft. across. Based on the ship's pro-

"Teach's Oak, Oriental, N.C." (North Carolina Postcard Collection (P052), North Carolina Collection, University of North Carolina, Chapel Hill, ca. 1905–15, http://dc.lib.unc .edu/cdm/location/collection/nc_post/)

jected size and its location near a major shipping channel, we surmised that the remains were from a merchant sailing ship that for unknown reasons had been abandoned in this creek where it could be later salvaged and would not hinder navigation. Among the pieces collected to help identify the vessel was a heavily corroded rudder hinge that had a reflective glint. A couple of the locals who saw it joked that it might be made of silver, since nearby a venerable tree had once stood, known to locals as Teach's Oak. According to legend, it was here that Blackbeard set up camp and from high up in the tree kept watch on local shipping activities.[7]

In the months that followed, scuttlebutt surrounding the old ship began to circulate within the community. It seemed that it was only a matter of time before relic hunters might visit the site and dig for its phantom treasure. As a cautionary measure, we returned to the site and collected additional artifacts manufactured in the late eighteenth century, thus clearly placing the ship many decades after Blackbeard's day. The rudder hinge also was definitely not made of silver, as the locals had wished, but rather of wrought iron, a strong material made to support the rudder and the stresses put on it. These details were provided to a newspaper reporter to quell treasure seekers. The article, written by a United Press International (UPI) reporter,

A Dive to Remember

RICHARD W. LAWRENCE

The day was November 22, 1996. It was not a day you would normally choose to go diving. The skies were overcast, with winds from the northwest at over 20 miles per hour, and the air temperature hovered in the upper 40s. Yet the state's underwater archaeological conservator, Leslie Bright, and I found ourselves on the deck of Intersal's research vessel *Pelican III* anchored a mile off the beach in Beaufort Inlet preparing to explore a newly discovered shipwreck. Mike Daniel and his crew had found the site the day before and immediately called our office to report their find. Mike's words over the phone—"Richard, I think we've found *Queen Anne's Revenge*"—initiated a flurry of activity. Leslie and I gathered our dive gear and made plans to drive the 100 miles to Beaufort early the next morning. Somehow, Phil Masters made it down from New York overnight to join us for the dive.

Entering the chilly water, Leslie and I made our way down the buoy line marking the site. The rising tide brought in relatively clear ocean water with a noticeable green tint. About 10 ft. from the bottom an unforgettable sight came into view. A school of spadefish slowly circled an encrusted mound of oddly shaped objects rising several feet above the flat sandy bottom. The unmistakable shape of two large anchors and several elongated objects we recognized as cannons came into focus. Although the details of cannons were obscured by a thick layer of concretion, with closer inspection we could tell from their general shape that they pre-dated 1750. We spent about 30 minutes examining the mound, counting 10 cannons with the possibility that others were obscured or buried in the extensive pile of ballast stones. On one side of the mound, in a shallow depression, we noted several wooden frames, the inner surface of the ship's hull.

Back on shore, Mike brought out the sample artifacts that they had recovered the day before and kept stored in a tank of fresh water. Of immediate interest was a bronze bell and a brass blunderbuss barrel, both covered with a thin

began, "The sunken hull of an old wooden vessel found in Blackbeard's hideaway is that of a massive two-masted ship that was apparently abandoned," before moving on to evidence that dispelled any possible connection between pirate lore and the Oriental shipwreck. As it moved across the UPI wire, the story was picked up by the *Washington Post* and then circulated widely to an eager public who did not seem to care that the ship was not Blackbeard's. This was confirmed a few days later when we found ourselves conducting a radio interview with a Canadian station out of Vancouver, over 3,000 miles away. It was but a glimpse of what was to come our way.

As matter of fact, while we were wrestling with the Oriental shipwreck, local pirate lore, and the brief but widespread media frenzy, events that would lead to the finding of an actual pirate ship were just beginning. It started as an offhand comment from UAB director Richard Lawrence alerting Phil Masters, the president of the commercial salvage company Intersal, that within their search area they might find two other eighteenth-century shipwrecks—*Queen Anne's Revenge* and *Adventure*.

layer of corrosion. While no maker's marks were readily visible, they held the promise of further identifying the wreck. After an afternoon of excited conversation with Phil and Mike about the implications of discovering Blackbeard's flagship, Leslie and I loaded the artifacts into our truck and returned to Wilmington.

After much anticipation over the weekend, on Monday morning I was peering over Leslie's shoulder in the state's artifact preservation lab as he used an air-scribe to carefully remove the corrosion from the bell's surface. The number 1 was soon visible, cast into the bell's surface. Moving slightly to the right Leslie uncovered a second number, a 7. We knew that if this was a date, the next numerals would be crucial: a date after 1718 would all but rule out the shipwreck as *Queen Anne's Revenge*. As Leslie continued, the casting became clear. It was the year 1705. Our multidecades' pursuit to explore, protect, and ultimately recover the flagship of history's most infamous pirate had thus begun.

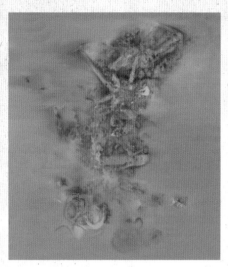

1997 photo-mosaic of the *QAR* site. Photographs by Richard Lawrence. (Courtesy of the North Carolina Department of Natural and Cultural Resources)

After completing additional historical research, in 1988 Masters requested and received a permit from the state of North Carolina to search for the sunken pirate vessels. Eight years later, using historical accounts and maps provided by Masters, Captain Daniel narrowed his attention to the inlet's

Divers investigating the newly discovered shipwreck in Beaufort Inlet. Bernie Case, illustrator (1999). (Courtesy of the North Carolina Department of Natural and Cultural Resources)

eighteenth-century entrance channel and the sandbars where ships of that period were likely to have grounded. As soon as he identified what he knew was significant wreckage, Captain Daniel immediately called UAB. The next day Lawrence and archaeological conservator Leslie Bright confirmed the discovery.[8]

The Historical Record

Not only are archaeologists called out to investigate sites and sometimes stumble upon others, but our active mission is to seek these physical remains from the past to answer a multitude of research questions. If the time period we are researching is within the past 500 years or so, in tandem with written documents, we call it historical archaeology. The existence of both sets of data, archaeological evidence and archival records, allows us to utilize mutual types of records, first to develop questions and hypotheses from one data set and then to see if our suppositions prove true based on evidence from the other. This is not a simple task. Often it is hard to comb through the remnants left centuries after a battle took place or a ship went down and try to make sense of it all knowing some pieces are missing or not retrievable. We encounter the same difficulty with written records, which may also be incomplete or missing parts but more often are also biased by the author's perspective and knowledge. This is particularly true when we investigate pirates and the 300-year-old physical evidence they have left behind, which in our case is found in the sunken remains of a prize ship Blackbeard named *Queen Anne's Revenge*.

As we sift through the ship's heavily weathered debris field in search of clues that will help uncover *QAR*'s history and meaning, we tend to construct scenarios of what happened before, during, and after the ship sank. We draw on our knowledge based on what we've read or heard about pirates, and in our case, it's a fair amount due to the notoriety of *QAR*'s commander, Blackbeard. We have this impression that he was authoritarian, audacious, driven, bold, cunning, and cruel, characteristics that we suspect were witnessed during the events that took place at Beaufort Inlet. Pulling bits and pieces from eyewitness accounts, newspaper articles, and books written after these events and drawing upon our experiences camping on these same undeveloped North Carolina beaches, we offer this glimpse of what we suspect happened that fateful day the ship went down.

Marooned, June 13, 1718. A hard push in the back propelled Ignatius Pell roughly over the boat's gunnel, across an extended oar, and into the shallow water, where he struggled to get his footing. It was the second week of June 1718 when he, along with the others, waded onto this foreign shore. The sandy stretch of beach with low dunes supported only sparse, scruffy vegetation and few animals, which meant no shelter from the blazing sun or food to survive on. Pell and his company consisted of two dozen hardened, seafaring men who were being forced ashore at the hands of Captain Edward Thache, an aloof and unpredictable man. It began when Thache had come aboard their sloop with five of his henchmen, weapons drawn, and ordered everyone up on deck. Once there, Pell and the others were roughly shaken down for anything of value and then crowded into boats and rowed several miles to the spot where they now found themselves. The men were left with no more than the clothes on their backs. They were helpless, angry, and now marooned.

As the afternoon passed, dark clouds of a squall appeared, and soon large, heavy drops of chilly rain were drenching everyone and thoroughly soaking their clothes. As this passed, the wind dropped out, and in the damp stillness there came a vicious attack from the tiniest of flies, biting midges (Ceratopogonidae), or "no-see-ums" as some called them. The insects attacked relentlessly in untold numbers, sinking their sharp snouts into any exposed flesh. In better circumstances, the stranded party might have used the plentiful driftwood along the beach

The Marooning of Ignatius Pell and Other Crewmen by Blackbeard, oil painting by
Virginia Wright-Frierson (2017), Mark Wilde-Ramsing and Linda Carnes-McNaughton
private collection. (Used by permission)

to make a smoldering fire and smoke the pests away, but there was neither steel nor strike-a-light to start a blaze. Even the ruddiest of seafaring men in Pell's company were brought to their knees in tears. When darkness came, the castaways spent the night in sleepless discomfort.

Wetness and insects from the evening before only aggravated a worsening situation for the group. What rankled Pell's beach mates was the notion that they were the ones who had been marooned on a deserted island instead of Captain Thache, since it was he who had taken it all, including the riches made during the Charleston raid. Understanding

that marooning was the accepted punishment for all brethren caught taking more than their share, this act by Thache was like adding salt to their wounds. Without food, shelter, drink, or any means to survive, though, the castaways soon returned their thoughts to the situation at hand and the bleak prospect of perishing under the blazing sun in the days to come.

As they suffered through their second night, the gloom of defeat overwhelmed the men, and they began to fear for the worst. Hope was fading that their captain and the others, who had taken a wherry up Core Sound to receive the king's pardon

"Major Stede Bonnet," engraving in Captain Charles Johnson [Nathaniel Mist], *A General History of the Robberies and Murders of the Most Notorious Pyrates* (1725), 38.

in Bath, would arrive in time to save them. After another restless night, daybreak offered nothing more than isolation, misery, and despair.

While we may never know exactly what happened on that remote island, government documents in the form of court records provide a basis to interpret how Ignatius Pell and his cohorts felt over those several days. We can assume they were not only miserable but also angry at how they had been treated and cheated by North Carolina's infamous pirate captain. "[Pell] Says, he heard by the Pirate Crew aboard Thatch, that Thatch took out of the Vessels that were taken off of the Bar of South Carolina, in Gold and Silver, to the Value of one thousand Pounds Sterling Money; and by

others of them, to the Value of fifteen hundred Pounds Sterling Money: But that when Thatch broke up the Company, and before they came to any Share of what was taken by Thatch, Thatch took all away with him."[9]

This testimony revealed much more about life aboard *Queen Anne's Revenge* under the command of Blackbeard from the statements of Pell's 29 other shipmates, including their captain, Stede Bonnet. When these men were put on trial for piracy in Charleston, South Carolina, within a few months after *Queen Anne's Revenge* was lost, they recounted the sinking event in detail. It seems that once Bonnet returned after seeking a pardon from Governor Eden in Bath and rescued his marooned crew, they set back out to sea in their vessel *Royal James* and once again took to attacking and looting merchant ships along the mid-Atlantic seaboard for six weeks. Bonnet, known as the Gentleman Pirate for his refined tastes, was a rarity in the world of piracy. He was an educated and wealthy sugar plantation owner from the island of Barbados who decided, perhaps on a whim, to take up piracy. He bought and armed a 10-gun sloop and then hired and paid a 70-member crew specifically to go out a-pirating. His tactical training was not geared to the sea, although he did hold the rank of major in the Barbadian militia. Thus Gentleman Bonnet was forced to rely on the skills of his quartermaster and crew; but after a while he linked up with Blackbeard, who convinced him to give up the command of his sloop and sail along for the ride in his cabin—that is, until everything came crashing to an end at Beaufort. Once they were reunited, Captain Bonnet and his crew left the scene and enjoyed a relatively successful pirating spree until they were apprehended in the lower reaches of the Cape Fear River and put on trial.

Presiding over their trial, Nicholas Trott, Esq, Judge of the Vice-Admiralty and Chief-Justice of the said Province of South-Carolina, described the charge of piracy to Bonnet and his men. "Thus the Nature of the Offence is sufficiently set forth in the Definition of it. As to the Heinousness or Wickedness of the Offence, it needs no Aggravation, it being evident to the Reason of all Men. Therefore a Pirate is called (r) *Hostis Humani Generis*, with whom neither Faith nor Oath is to be kept. And in our Law they are termed (s) *Brutes*, and (f) *Beasts of Prey*; and that it is lawful for any one that takes them, if they cannot with safety to themselves bring them under some Government to be tried, to put them to Death."[10] Put simply, government officials in colonial America were dead set to stamp out rampant piracy during the first quarter of the eighteenth century. Their view of pirates as outlaws, however, wasn't shared by everyone in the colonies. On the contrary, there was a wave of popular opinion that more or less romanticized the pirates as Robin Hoods of their day, which some pirates claimed outright, such as those who sailed with Captain Black Sam Bellamy of the *Whydah*.[11] This sentiment survives even today, as we generally view pirates of that period rather lightly, as characters with peg legs, eye patches, and gold teeth and earrings, performing daring antics and speaking the everlasting talk-like-a-pirate banter. We tend not to view them as the serious and menacing threat they posed to maritime commerce and the people it involved.

The truth is that pirates and their behavior during the early eighteenth century are mostly misunderstood because of a lack of primary archival materials. Pirates were not apt to record their version of events through diaries or log entries or to write home detailing their exploits or to pen memoirs later in life, mainly for fear of recrimination. But more to the point, many were illiterate. Available documentary evidence comes from the perspective of others whose accounts of piracy have tended to exaggerate, cloud, or even ignore what may have truly occurred.

English and colonial newspapers of the day reporting on piratical activities would often reprint a single article, sometimes adding inaccuracies and embellishments of their own. What really brought

Treasure Island **cover illustration by N. C. Wyeth (1911).**

pirate activity under the public's eye, however, was a publication by Nathaniel Mist (aka Captain Charles Johnson) titled *A General History of the Robberies and Murders of the Most Notorious Pyrates*. Released in May 1724, the book was an overnight success, so much so that a second edition was published a few months later. A third and an expanded fourth edition were released in 1725 and 1726. Even in the eighteenth century, people simply could not get enough of pirate lore, same as today! Although he used newspaper articles, Mist, a former sailor, printer, and journalist in London, had access to trial records and other government documents, as well as firsthand personal contact with retired pirates. From these primary sources, he created his biographical sketches of the most prominent characters, including Thache (Teach, aka Blackbeard),

The hero of whom we are writing was thoroughly accomplished this way, and some of his frolics of wickedness, were so extravagant, as if he aimed at making his men believe he was a devil incarnate; for being one day at sea, and a little flushed with drink, "Come," says he, "let us make a hell of our own, and try how long we can bear it." Accordingly he, with two or three others, went down into the hold and, closing up all the hatches, filled several pots full of brimstone and other combustible matter, and set it on fire, and so continued till they were almost suffocated, when some of the men cried out for air; at length he opened the hatches, not a little pleased that he held out the longest.[13]

At the end of his chapter on Blackbeard, Mist invited his readers to view the pirate captain with a degree of sympathy: "Here was an end of that courageous brute, who might have passed the world for a hero had he been employed in a good cause."[14] Anyone directly affected by pirates of the day, from government officials and shipowners to the merchant ship captains and conscripted sailors, may well have vehemently disagreed. The public, on the other hand, far removed from the atrocities being committed on the high seas, were more apt to assume a more romantic view of piracy as being a struggle between the common man and authority.

Until recently the truth regarding Blackbeard was sparse. Little was known about him, including the origin of his birth name. We have now learned that Blackbeard was born Edward Thache Jr. in or about 1683 in Gloucestershire, England, which lies up the Severn River from the port of Bristol. As a

Bonnet, and Bellamy. Through the years, Mist's books provided inspiration for plays such as J. M. Barrie's *Peter Pan*, numerous books (most notably Robert Louis Stevenson's *Treasure Island*), and various Hollywood productions from *Captain Blood* (1935) to the *Pirates of the Caribbean* series popular today. Among nearly all these accounts, the pirate Blackbeard looms large, fierce, and lasting.

Nathaniel Mist described the pirate captain as a man with an enormous amount of black, bristly hair who "frightened America more than any comet that has appeared there in a long time."[12] Mist reported his deeds as outrageous and scary. Some were real and documented, like the blockading of the British port of Charleston. Others are less substantiated, such as this account demonstrating Blackbeard's ferocity:

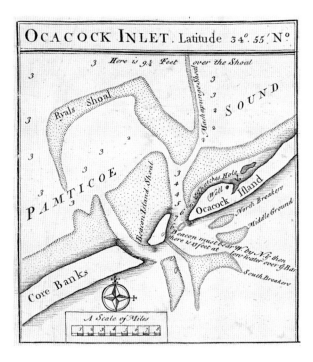

child, he moved with his parents, Edward Sr. and Elizabeth, and his sister Elizabeth to St. Jago de la Vega (Spanish Town), Jamaica. His father was a mariner and became a respected plantation owner on the island. In his early twenties, the same year that his father died, Edward Jr. was serving on the HMS *Windsor* in 1706. Thache, it appears, moved into privateering under the English flag near the end of Queen Anne's War (1702–13), a conflict that was known to breed those who took up piracy later. The first mention of Thache was as a pirate commander of an eight-gun sloop out of Jamaica in late 1716 sailing alongside another key pirate, Captain Benjamin Hornigold. Their early focus was "fishing" for treasure on the Spanish ships lost off the coast of Florida in 1715, before they turned to all-out robbery of ships sailing on the high seas.[15]

Thache's exploits over the 18 months that followed, including the capture of *Concorde*, which became his flagship *Queen Anne's Revenge*, propelled him to become the most recognized pirate of his era, a distinction that remains true to this day. After the loss of two of his four vessels at Beaufort Inlet in early June 1718, Thache spent the final

five months of his life mostly in and around North Carolina. During that time, he moved about the rivers and sounds of the state, using Ocracoke Island as his base to prey on merchant vessels. The remote barrier island provided an advantageous location from which to monitor oceangoing commerce as it funneled through Ocracoke Inlet. Even more fortuitous, major shipping lanes of the Atlantic seaboard were not far offshore. While some in the colony welcomed his presence for the money and goods he brought in, others did not. William Bell, a planter living on the banks of the Pamlico River near Bath, charged Thache with petty thievery and harassment.[16] Other government records, however, show that the pirate captain was often absent from home. On August 11, 1718, for example, Pennsylvania governor William Keith issued a warrant for the arrest of Edward Thache in Philadelphia.[17] Toward the end of August, the pirate captain was cruising the waters of Bermuda, where he captured the French merchant ship *Rose Emelye*; he brought the vessel into Bath and claimed he found it abandoned at sea.[18] In October, Governor Keith was so perturbed that he sent out an expedition to the nearby capes to pursue him.[19] Despite Thache's relatively brief time in North Carolina, his name, or variations such as Teach or Thatch, dominate popular history along the Tar Heel coastline even today.

Blackbeard lore is strongest in Bath, which was the young colony's first established town, incorporated on March 8, 1705. The pirate captain is said to have been in cahoots with the governor, whose residence was nearby. According to local hearsay, Thache was said to have married a young woman there and sired numerous little Eddies and Edwinas. Moreover, he and his cohorts provided the fledgling town with a flow of cash, black market goods, and manpower for protection from roving

Indians. To the southeast, Ocracoke, accessible only by ferry today, provided a secured base of operation. The island's protected anchorage, known as Thatches Hole, was the perfect pirate hideout. It was here in late November 1718 that Thache and nine members of his crew were caught and killed by Lieutenant Robert Maynard of Virginia. Despite all this, any real and tangible evidence of the man or his activities at either place has remained elusive. His house is said to have been on Plum Point, near Bath Town; his encampment, at Springer's Point on Ocracoke Island. Not unexpectedly, both areas have been extensively dug and re-dug for pirate treasure, beginning the moment he was killed. No one has openly claimed success at either place.

North Carolina is full of pirate lore, more specifically Blackbeard lore. Even the remotest chance of discovering pirate treasure raises hopes and keeps tradition alive. But what of this we hear and read about can we trust to be true? With the discovery of a known pirate ship such as *Queen Anne's Revenge*, historical research and archaeology can help us bridge fantasy and reality and better understand the people from the past.

Historical Archaeology: Unlocking Secrets

For several years, a small plastic container sat on the shelf in the *QAR* conservation lab, somewhat isolated from the ongoing action. The container, the kind whipped topping comes in, held an artifact that was in rough shape: a crooked, corroded piece of iron, wrapped with cordage and looking like a woolly worm. Its identification was uncertain. Our best guess was a small cargo hook missing both its eye and pointed end. Perhaps it was part of gun carriage tackle, since it had been found next to the English 4-pounder cannon. The cord wrapping was thought to keep the hook from damaging whatever it was lifting or holding in place when in use on *Queen Anne's Revenge*. The bottom line was that

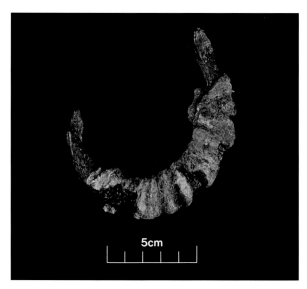

The *QAR* mystery artifact. (Courtesy of the North Carolina Department of Natural and Cultural Resources)

we were not quite sure what to do with it. A complex, time-intensive regimen would be required to clean, dry, and stabilize the item, since it consisted of two materials, fiber and iron, both of which were quite fragile from centuries of inundation in salt water. Since the object was relatively stable in a bath of distilled water, attention was given to the many other pressing conservation needs and more glamorous objects, like iron cannons, pewter plates, and brass instruments—the types of artifacts museums were clamoring to put on display.

A few years later we learned there was more to be gleaned about this oddly shaped artifact, specifically who used it and for what purpose. As historical archaeologists, we search the archives for documentary evidence as well as artifact inventories of previously excavated ships to identify and maximize the information that can be learned from specific artifacts within the context of the sites in which they are found. In this case, a breakthrough came when a *National Geographic* magazine photograph featured an artifact recovered from the slave ship *Henrietta Marie*.[20] As soon as project archaeologists saw it, we realized the "cargo hook" was not that at all but, rather, a leg iron used to restrain the ankle of an enslaved African. Suddenly this seemingly insignificant old hook took on a new cultural meaning. Rather than an ordinary piece of equipment for loading ships, it was an object that personalized the cruelty and pain inflicted on generations of innocent people who were ripped from their homelands and shipped thousands of miles away to foreign soil.

Artifacts, when properly identified, can enlighten our understanding of the past, its people, and how they lived and worked. Archaeology gives voice to poorly documented cultures and peoples who are not part of oral and written histories passed down through time. They are sometimes called the silent population. These many generations of men and women, some our direct ancestors, form the very core of society as they lived and died. Their voices, when they can speak through archaeology, may provide us with knowledge of the past and even a sense of who we are today.

As archaeologists, we also consider the disenfranchised people that exist on the outskirts of main society. These groups are often inaccurately represented by contemporary records and oral accounts. One such group is the men and women who chose piracy as a way of life. Their stories have been told often, but what is truth and what is fiction? This question excites us, especially when we are given the opportunity to study sites such as the physical wreckage of Blackbeard's notorious flagship. For us this site provides a large, open window through which to focus our spyglass on piracy during the early eighteenth century.

Over the years, underwater archaeologists and the many individuals who support them have recovered tens of thousands of artifacts from the wreck site of *Queen Anne's Revenge*. Assigned to each object is a number, which identifies its context and location on the site, as well as its association with other items. As analysis is completed on the overall artifact assemblage, we can begin to see patterns

Queen Anne's Revenge approaching Beaufort Inlet. Bernie Case, illustrator, 1999. (Courtesy of the North Carolina Department of Natural and Cultural Resources)

that confirm the popular version of pirates seen in Hollywood productions or, conversely, reflect the normal seafarer. As investigators, we also know that not all the questions we ask of the artifacts can be so easily answered. We liken ourselves to detectives looking for clues to piece together a crime scene. We are sometimes drawn in various directions in search of the truth and sometimes into dead ends. That is the nature of the scientific process.

Researchers like us are intrigued by the unknowns surrounding a pirate ship and the suspense of never knowing what to expect. At any moment, a startling artifact from the ocean floor might make the archaeological recovery team jump with surprise as it emerges into daylight above the water. The same goes for conservators in the laboratory, who might be amazed as they use x-radiography to peer inside an encrusted object. Would any of these artifacts represent lost treasure? More likely many mundane things of seemingly little value would be recovered and routinely processed in the lab, until suddenly and unexpectedly something special

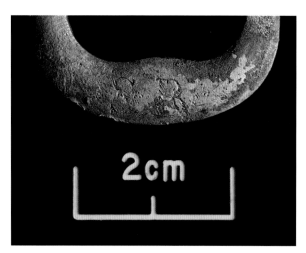

"SB" incised shoe buckle. (Courtesy of the North Carolina Department of Natural and Cultural Resources)

astounds us—something like a shoe buckle that, as it was being cleaned, revealed the incised initials "S B," which led us to wonder, "Are we holding a piece of finery worn by Stede Bonnet himself?"

A myriad of such remarkable discoveries along with many, many more ordinary artifacts, like tons of ballast stone and hundreds of thousands of tiny lead shot, have come to light in the years since *Queen Anne's Revenge* was discovered. Of all the artifacts, the most visible to the public are individual cannons and anchors, which are recovered under the watchful eyes and cameras from media and guest boats surrounding the recovery vessel. Once the behemoth artifact, weighing a ton or more, is successfully lifted from the seabed and transported to land, the public is treated to a viewing of the "fresh catch" of the day. It gives them a quick glimpse of history, before the crusty, smelly object heads off to the lab for years of cleaning and treatment. With each successful large artifact recovery comes a phenomenal level of interest from a worldwide audience that likely parallels what Nathaniel Mist experienced nearly 300 years ago in England when he wrote *A General History of the Robberies and Murders of the Most Notorious Pyrates*. What follows in this book is our story, *Blackbeard's Sunken Prize: The 300-Year Voyage of* Queen Anne's Revenge, providing an archaeological view of the fascinating world of eighteenth-century piracy.

CHAPTER TWO

A Wild and Crazy Ride

The map "Ghost Fleet of the Outer Banks" appeared tucked into the pages of the September 1970 edition of *National Geographic* magazine. This foldout encompassed the nearshore waters of North Carolina and featured the locations of "over 500 ill-fated ships that lie forever anchored on the Atlantic coastal sea floor." The collection of sunken vessels spanned four centuries, from the foundering of the British *Tiger* near Ocracoke Inlet in 1585 to the sinking of the trawler *Oriental* near Bodie Island in 1969. North Carolina's offshore waters remain treacherous even today, exemplified by the tragic sinking on October 29, 2012, of the replica HMS *Bounty* roughly 90 miles southeast of the Outer Banks as it attempted to sail through Superstorm Sandy.

Yet one historic vessel, *Queen Anne's Revenge,* was not included in the "Ghost Fleet" map. Nor was it listed among the many shipwreck losses identified on the *Oceanographic Atlas of the Carolina Continental Margin* that came out a year later.[1] How could this be? How could the wrecked flagship of the infamous pirate Blackbeard not occupy a hugely prominent place in Tar Heel shipwreck lore? How could it not be included on the state's shipwreck registry? One would think with all the searching for pirate treasure wherever Blackbeard

was reported to have roamed, the shallow waters where *Queen Anne's Revenge* and *Adventure* sank would have been a prime place to look. Oddly enough, the wrecking event in early June 1718 was not a big secret, nor was it surrounded by conspiracy but, rather, openly reported in trial records, reports by British naval officers, and newspapers of the day.[2] In fact, the event was clearly described and documented in Nathaniel Mist's *General History of the Robberies and Murders of the Most Notorious Pyrates* in 1724, based on court testimony given by Ignatius Pell and the other pirates during their trials, the proceedings of which were published in 1719. Prominent historians writing about Blackbeard have echoed the account of how *Queen Anne's Revenge* was lost.[3] Surprisingly though, not a whisper of the sunken vessel was passed down through local lore, despite the fact that within its hold is the one place where someone might realistically expect to find physical evidence tied directly to the pirate captain. Through this book we now offer a glimpse of the actual artifacts, which have eluded North Carolinians for so many years.

It wasn't until staff historians from the Department of Natural and Cultural Resources's Research Branch conducted a routine background check for shipwrecks prior to the 1982 summer field school

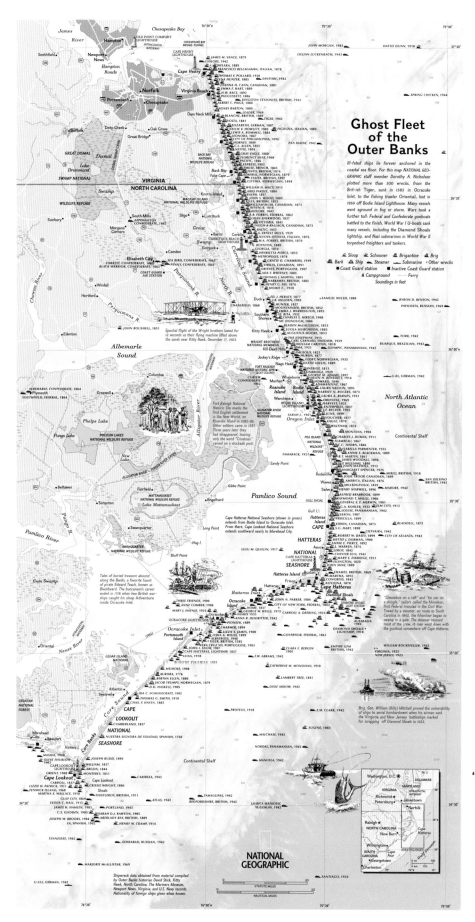

"Ghost Fleet of the
Outer Banks,"
National Geographic,
September 1970.
(Used by permission)

Queen Anne Appears aboard QAR

DR. LINDA F. CARNES-McNAUGHTON

Though small in size, weighing 7.7 grams and not much more than a half-inch in diameter, the Queen Anne coin weight was monumental, if not regal, in importance. It was so named because it featured the profiled portrait of the popular monarch Queen Anne, who ruled England, Scotland, and Ireland from 1702 until her death in 1714. The embossed lettering was "ANNA DEI GRATIA," translated Latin for "Anne by the Grace of God." English monarchs were often shown on coinage in profile, left face or right face, in alternate directions; so William III (Anne's predecessor) was depicted by his right profile, Anne was shown by her left profile, her successor George I was shown in right profile, and so on. It was also common for monarchs to be depicted in classical Roman attire (to imitate emperors), so Anne appeared with a draped bust and a garland head wreath.

On the other side was embossed a crown, the word GUINEA, the letter W, and the number 1. Rather than functioning as a coin, the copper alloy disk was used by an assayer to measure the exact weight of a true coin made of gold (in this case the measurement was one guinea). Typically, this coin weight was part of a boxed set that included a hanging balance scale in which a coin was placed in one tray (or pan) and the weight in the opposite tray to measure any differences. Gold guineas were first made in 1663 and, of course, were very popular among pirates. It was also important for the freebooters to have proper weighing accouterments to divide their plunder equitably among their brotherhood. In 1717 Blackbeard named his stolen French ship

Queen Anne's Revenge, apparently to champion her approval of privateering and/or conversely as a gesture of political satire aimed at her successor and reigning king, George I. The Queen Anne coin weight is a relatively rare piece today, and its discovery provided a tantalizing link between the ship and its namesake.

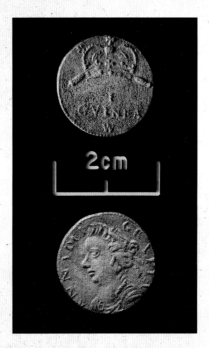

Queen Anne coin weight. (Courtesy of the North Carolina Department of Natural and Cultural Resources)

with East Carolina University that we became fully aware that *Queen Anne's Revenge* was lost in the Cape Lookout area.[4] While survey efforts during that summer's investigation did not locate any potential pirate ships, our interest was now piqued. More about *QAR*'s goings and comings were fleshed out from historical records, and within a few years Intersal, under permit from the state, began to search the waters of Beaufort Inlet, which ultimately led to the ship's discovery ten years later.

The discovery of the Beaufort Inlet shipwreck brought a flurry of further research in Caribbean and French archives that quickly revealed key elements of the pirate ship's prior history. It was learned that before becoming *Queen Anne's Revenge*, the ship was first identified in the historical records in 1710 as *Concorde de Nantes*, a privateer sailing during the latter part of Queen Anne's War (1702–13). Soon after the war ended, the French vessel was put into service carrying enslaved Africans to the New World during voyages in 1713, 1715, and 1717. On the last trip, in late November 1717, the ship was captured by Anglo-American pirates under the command of Blackbeard near the island of Martinique. For the next six months, the pirate captain sailed around the Caribbean in the newly named *Queen Anne's Revenge* before heading up the Atlantic coast and eventually arriving at North Carolina, where the ship wrecked in June 1718.

Despite two decades of archival research since the discovery of *Queen Anne's Revenge*, important gaps still exist. Most importantly, the place where *Concorde* was built has not been identified. The time of the ship's construction may correspond with the casting date of 1705 on the bell recovered from the wreckage, but this also has not been confirmed.[5] Also scarce are written records from when the vessel served as Blackbeard's flagship. One reason may be that keeping shipboard logs, manifests, and other official paperwork was not a prerequisite for pirate captains, for obvious reasons. In lieu of specific documents, historians have relied on bits of information gleaned from trends in early

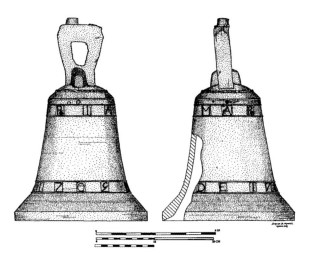

QAR ship's bell. David D. Moore, illustrator. (Courtesy of the North Carolina Department of Natural and Cultural Resources)

eighteenth-century French warfare, shipbuilding, and trade,[6] as well as contemporary accounts from Blackbeard's victims and eyewitness testimonies, to better understand the sailing career of *Queen Anne's Revenge* (ex. *Concorde*).

Another rich repository of information is available through archaeological investigation of the vessel's wreckage and contents. The ship's bell is only one of tens of thousands of eighteenth-century artifacts that offer tantalizing clues as to what happened aboard *Queen Anne's Revenge*. Although fragmented and scattered, their physical characteristics and relative distribution reveal what was on the ship and how these items may have been used by Blackbeard and his men. Using twenty-first-century tools and analyses provided by a host of physical scientists, archaeologists now focus their spyglasses on a bona fide pirate prize.

Thirsting to learn more, are ye? Have patience, lads and lasses, and go slow, for your own sake. Ye must first listen to what historians have discovered about Queen Anne's Revenge *before attempting to gaze upon its archaeological treasures!*

A Wild and Crazy Ride

Privateering for Louis XIV during Queen Anne's War

Nathaniel Mist wrote in 1724 that the vessel Blackbeard captured was "a large French Guinea-man" (i.e., a slave ship). It was not until the 1998 discovery of an official deposition given to Charles Mesnier, the acting intendant of Martinique, however, that the ship's identity was confirmed. In that document, Captain Pierre Dosset reported an English pirate known as "Edouard Titche" took his vessel, *La Concorde de Nantes*, in late November 1717.[7] The ship, owned by the prominent business-man René Montaudoin, was on its third voyage transporting enslaved Africans to the New World. Prior to its service as a slave ship, the wealthy Frenchman had outfitted *Concorde* for privateering in 1710. The ship most likely was built sometime prior at a commercial shipyard in or around Nantes, France, since records reveal that René Montaudoin had contracted with local shipyards to build several vessels for privateering. *Concorde* was within a class of French frigates that measured less than 100 ft. in length. A comparable although slightly smaller vessel, *Jules César*, weighed 280 tons and was built by the master carpenter of La Fosse, Rialland, in 1706. The vessel was 70 ft. on keel with a breadth of 24 ft. and a draft of 9 ft. The depth of the hold below the main deck beams was 9 ft. The ship accommodated 24 guns with 20 ports along the main deck and the remainder in the bow or stern. The stern castle had a height of 5½ ft.[8]

On July 21, 1710, the French frigate *Concorde* of 300 tons, armed with 26 cannons and under the command of Captain Jean Le Roux, sailed out of the Nantes harbor carrying a letter of marque from Louis XIV permitting Le Roux to intercept and plunder merchant ships hailing from England and its allies. Difficult winds made the voyage slow, but eventually *Concorde* arrived on Africa's west coast, where soon a small Portuguese slave ship was de-tained and not released until its human cargo was transferred to the privateer. After months of cruis-

"Frigate (1670–80), Chabert Junior," in Jean Boudriot and Hubert Bertia, *The History of the French Frigate, 1650–1850* (East Essex, England: Jean Boudriot Publications, 1993).

ing, Captain Le Roux stopped a Dutch slave trader and added to the number of stolen Africans impris-oned in his ship's hold. Leaking badly and in need of major repair, the privateer was sailed across the Atlantic to the French colonial port of Martinique, arriving in February 1711. There, Captain Le Roux was able to cash in, quite literally, by selling the slaves he had confiscated. After repairs, *Concorde* cruised the Caribbean for most of the spring and summer months, capturing several English coasting vessels before leaving Havana in late August and re-turning to Nantes in November 1711. The privateer had been out to sea for nearly 15 months.[9]

Change in Mission: Sailing into a Dark Business

On April 13, 1713, just two days after France signed the Treaty of Utrecht with England to end Queen Anne's War, *Concorde* was again leaving Nantes, this time to trade in slaves for shipowner René Montaudoin. During this slaving voyage and a second one in 1715, *Concorde* carried 418 and 331 enslaved Africans with a French crew of 62 and 65 men, respectively.[10] For both voyages, the vessel was listed as 250 tons, a typical size for slave ships

Sugar and Slavery

DR. LYNN WOOD MOLLENAUER

How did Blackbeard come to captain a flagship that was once a French slaver? The answer lies in the demands of the sugar economy and the history of the French Atlantic slave trade. Between the fifteenth and nineteenth centuries, European ships made over 40,000 voyages to Africa, bringing more than 11 million captives across the Atlantic Ocean and into slavery. The demand for slave labor during this 400-year period was driven primarily by Europe's voracious hunger for sugar.

A rare and expensive indulgence during the Middle Ages, sugar became an affordable and sought-after commodity in Europe by the beginning of the 1700s. Its affordability was made possible by a "sugar revolution," a rapid increase in production in the colonies established in the tropical zones of the New World. The Portuguese started sugar plantations in Brazil; the Spanish, English, and French did so throughout the Caribbean. By 1700, New World sugar plantations exported tons of sugar to meet European demand. By the middle of the century, the French colony of Saint-Domingue (present-day Haiti), at the time the wealthiest colony in the New World, sent 61 tons of raw and refined sugar back to France each year.

Europeans believed that the economic viability of their sugar plantations, and their rich profits, depended upon slave labor. Sugar required slaves, yet the sugar plantations consumed them. If African captives survived the Middle Passage, their life expectancy in the New World was relatively short. On France's colony of Sainte-Domingue, for example, between 5 and 10 percent of its slaves died each year.

The various European states therefore competed for shares of the lucrative slave trade that supplied the labor for sugar production. Although its involvement was relatively low at first, by 1700 France had become the third largest participant after England and Portugal. In the eighteenth century alone, French ships brought 1 million enslaved Africans to the New World, and of those, 90 percent were disembarked in its Caribbean colonies.

The port of Nantes, located in the province of Brittany, was the hub of France's slave trade. It was known as the "city of slavers," and 70 percent of all French slave ships left from its docks. Building and equipping a ship that could sail to Africa was an expensive undertaking that only a few shipbuilders could manage. René Montaudoin, the wealthiest shipbuilder in Nantes, sent more slavers than anyone else.

The ships of Montaudoin's slaving fleet, including *Concorde*, followed the same triangular pattern. They sailed south from Nantes on the first passage through the Atlantic to West African ports such as Whydah (or Juida) to buy slaves—as many as 700 might be forced into a ship's hold—then headed northeast on the Middle Passage to the French colonies of Martinique, Grenada, or Saint-Domingue to sell their human cargo. Once emptied of their captives, the slavers traveled to the Antilles to buy sugar, cotton,

"Slave Trade," engraving by John Raphael Smith after the painting by
George Morland (1791). (Courtesy of the Rijks Museum)

cocoa, and other goods and then departed eastward for markets in France, completing the final passage. Following the same routes, season after season, made ships vulnerable to pirates, as *Concorde*'s capture demonstrated. That particular incident provided Captain Thache a large armed ship, a party of skilled Frenchmen, and Africans to sell or serve as menial laborers. Captain Pierre Dosset, representing shipowner Montaudoin, on the other hand, cut his losses, thankful to have been permitted to retain and sell a majority of his cargo of slaves, who were passed through the slave markets and on to the sugar fields of Martinique.

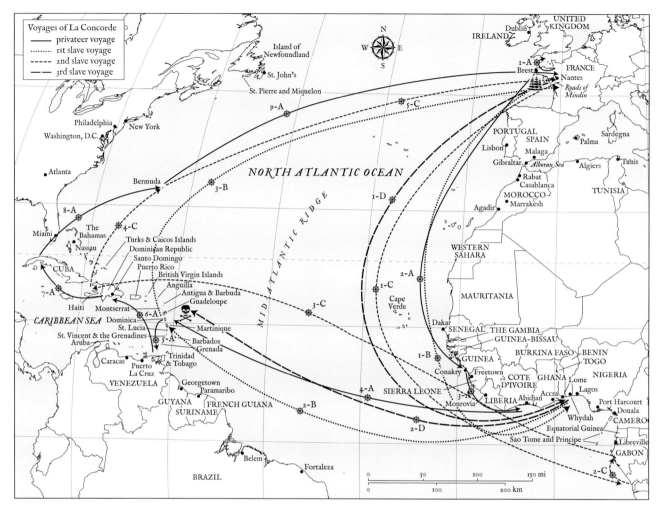

Travels of *Concorde*.
(Courtesy of the North Carolina Department of Natural and Cultural Resources; original created by Allison Suggs)

Sources: Richard W. Lawrence and Mark Wilde-Ramsing, "In Search of Blackbeard: Historical and Archaeological Research at Shipwreck Site 0003BUI," *Southeastern Geology* 40, no. (February 2001): 1–9; Jacques Ducoin, *Compte Rendu de Recherches dans les Archives Francaises sur le Navire Nantais La Concorde Capturé par des Pirates en 1717* (Raleigh: North Carolina Division of Archives and History, 2001)

(Mindin)

Queen Anne's Revenge began its life as *Concorde*, a French frigate of 250 to 300 tons, armed as a privateer with 26 guns by French merchant and entrepreneur René Montaudoin during the War of Spanish Succession (Queen Anne's War).

⚙ **(1-A)**

July 1710 Departs the Roads of Mindin, located in France on the River Loire, with 14 other ships.

August 1710 In Brest, France.

⚙ **(2-A)**

September 1710 Captures a small Portuguese vessel near the anchorage of Sestre along the coast of Guinea.

⚙ **(3-A)**

November 1710 Captures a Dutch slave trader and seizes its prisoners at Cape Lahou, now known as the Ivory Coast.

⚙ **(4-A)**

February 1711 Arrives at Martinique for repairs.

⚙ **(5-A)**

March 1711 In Tobago.

⚙ **(6-A)**

April 1711 Captures a small English ship off the southern coast of Santo Domingo in the Dominican Republic.

⚙ **(7-A)**

Summer 1711 To Havana, Cuba.

⚙ **(8-A)**

August 1711 Departs Havana for France.

September 1711 Captures and ransoms a small ship of Boston off Bermuda.

⚙ **(9-A)**

November 1711 Returns to Nantes, France.

⚓ (1-B)

Spring 1713 *Concorde* becomes a slave trader for owner René Montaudoin with the resumption of normal maritime trade at the end of the War of Spanish Succession and begins its first slave trading expedition leaving Nantes and arriving in Benin.

⚓ (2-B)

December 1713 Sails to Martinique to sell its 465 slaves.

⚓ (3-B)

July 1714 Returns to Nantes.

⚓ (1-C)

Spring 1715 *Concorde* leaves Nantes bound for the west coast of Africa on its second slave trading expedition and arrives in Loango Buali (just north of the mouth of the Congo [Zaire] River).

⚓ (2-C)

June 1715 Heads north to Gambingue (Gabon).

⚓ (3-C)

November 1715 Sails for Leogane (Haiti) with a cargo of slaves.

⚓ (4-C)

February 1716 Heads back to France, stopping by Bermuda, where 5 sailors desert the ship.

⚓ (5-C)

Summer 1716 Sails home to Nantes.

⚓ (1-D)

March 24, 1717 *Concorde* leaves Nantes on its third and final voyage for René Montaudoin.

July 8, 1717 Arrives at the port of Judas (Whydah) in modern-day Benin, Africa.

⚓ (2-D)

September 1717 Leaves Africa bound for Martinique with a cargo of 516 African captives.

November 28, 1717 Encounters Blackbeard's ships approximately 100 miles from Martinique. With his crew reduced to 21 functional sailors, due to scurvy and dysentery, Captain Pierre Dosset surrenders without a fight to the overwhelming pirate force of two sloops and 150 men.

The fact that *Concorde* was a frigate corsair during the War of Spanish Succession is likely significant in its capture and confiscation by Edward Thache, aka Blackbeard. Thache fought in the English ranks during the conflict and probably faced French frigates like *Concorde*. He therefore knew the qualities of the design, which no doubt factored in his decision to turn the slave trader of René Montaudoin into his flagship.

sailing out of Nantes during the eighteenth century. Despite the international truce following Queen Anne's War, ships engaged in the profitable slave-trade business remained armed due to the rise of piracy. It was therefore common practice to convert former privateers, such as *Concorde*, for this purpose. In doing so, however, shipowners were faced with balancing the expense of large crews necessary to tend the ship's guns against any pirate attacks. In the case of *Concorde*, by the third slaving voyage of its original 26 cannons, only 14 or 16 were mounted, the discrepancy coming from respective depositions by the ship's captain and lieutenant.[11]

On March 22, 1717, *Concorde* left Nantes destined for the West African trading center of Whydah under the command of Captain Pierre Dosset on its third slaving voyage. This was about the same time that Edward Thache is mentioned commanding a six-gun sloop and 70 men among a large contingency of pirates operating out of New Providence in the Bahamas.[12] The French slave ship arrived at Whydah in early July and, after three months, departed for the Americas. The English pirates meanwhile were operating along the sea lanes of the Caribbean until their paths crossed in late November, when *Concorde* was approximately 60 miles short of its destination, the French trading port of Martinique. In packed conditions, the human cargo of 455 Africans had suffered; worse yet, 61 others had already succumbed during the transatlantic crossing. The French crew had also fared poorly, losing 17 of 75 men due to illness or accident.[13] With an additional 36 sailors restricted to sick bay, *Concorde* was in a crippled state and offered little resistance when approached by two sloops and teams of able-bodied English pirates.

After capture, *Concorde* was escorted a short distance to the small island of Bequia, where negotiations took place. The pirates opted to take command of the French ship, sailing away with 157 Africans and 14 members of the French crew, 4 of whom came aboard of their own volition. The newly acquired prize was named *Queen Anne's Revenge* in what was likely intended as a snub to the English queen's successor King George I.[14] The French crew, on the other hand, were left with one of the two pirate sloops, which they despairingly called *Mauvaise Rencontre* (Unfortunate Encounter). The crew received the short end of the deal, but the trade allowed them to safely transport themselves and the remaining Africans to Martinique, where the latter were subsequently sold.

A Pirate's Life for Me:
Flagship of the Fleet

Under Blackbeard's command, the newly christened ship once again became a predator prowling the sea lanes in search of floating prizes. Over the next six months, *Queen Anne's Revenge* served as the flagship while one or more fast sloops in its company ventured out to locate and run down merchant shipping. The pirates sailed up past the Leeward Islands, then traveled deep into the Caribbean Sea, and ultimately made their way to the Carolinas. From the onset, a number of merchant ships were seized and plundered. Their treatment, revealed through firsthand depositions by the merchant captains or eyewitnesses, varied according to the pirates' needs and Blackbeard's whim. Some, such as Richard Joy's *New Division* and Benjamin Hobhouse's *Monserrat Merchant*, both island trading sloops, were detained and then released, although one of Joy's men was retained, apparently against his will.[15]

A much more dramatic encounter involved the ship *Great Allen* from Boston, commanded by Christopher Taylor, whom "they put 24 hours in Irons, and Whipt him, in order to make him confess what Money he had on board, burnt his Ship, put his Men on Shore at Martinico."[16] They went on to burn Captain Robert McGill's sloop out of Antigua. Soon after, Captain Henry Bostock was held captive while his sloop *Margaret* was thoroughly ransacked

and several of his skilled sailors, including the cooper Edward Salter, were forced to join the pirates.[17]

After this flurry of heavy-handed dealings, *Queen Anne's Revenge* sailed into the western Caribbean and on to the Bay of Honduras, where the pirates kept a low profile for several months.[18] No incidents were reported regarding Blackbeard and his men until late March 1718, when a new rampage began. It all started when *Protestant Caesar*, a large Boston-owned merchantman under the command of William Wyer, successfully repulsed an attack by a pirate sloop off Roatan. The sloop was *Revenge*, Stede Bonnet's ship, which at the time of the capture of *Concorde* was sailing with Blackbeard but now was on its own.[19] When Thache received news of Bonnet's failure, he was determined to retaliate so other merchant captains would not be emboldened to resist future pirate advances.

To increase his chances against Wyer, Blackbeard detained several sloops trading in the area, including Thomas Newton's *Land of Promise*, and added them to his fleet. Merchant sailors were encouraged to become pirates, and when one captain refused to let his crewmen join, his ship was burned. At the time, the pirates also captured David Harriot's sloop *Adventure*, and Blackbeard appointed his confidant Israel Hands as its captain. Another trusted friend, Lieutenant Richards, was at the helm of Bonnet's *Revenge*. With odds squarely in their favor, the pirate fleet confronted *Protestant Caesar* while it was anchored close to shore taking on a cargo of logwood. Recognizing they were no match, Wyer and his crew abandoned ship and hid in the Honduran jungle, where they watched the pirates ransack and burn their ship. Blackbeard later allowed Wyer and his men to board one of the detained sloops and sail back to Boston, where he hoped they would report to authorities and citizens alike that pirates meant business! Harriot, his boatswain Ignatius Pell, and their Jamaican crew were not so fortunate as to be let go. Blackbeard informed them that *Adventure* was to stay with him

Travels of *Queen Anne's Revenge* through the Caribbean

View of Charles-Town, by Thomas Leitch (ca. 1774), oil on canvas, Museum of Early Southern Decorative Arts, Winston Salem, N.C. (acc. 2024.30). (Used by permission)

and be sacrificed as a fireship should they be confronted by a naval force.[20]

Sailing east from the Bay of Honduras, pirates aboard *Queen Anne's Revenge*, *Revenge*, and *Adventure* passed near to the Cayman Islands, where they stopped a turtler[21] engaged in hunting for sea turtles and ended up keeping the small sloop.[22] This gave Blackbeard an armed fleet of four vessels and the boldness to fear nothing. Nathaniel Mist writes,

> We shall add here a few particulars (not mentioned in our first volume) of the famous Blackbeard, relating to his taking the South Carolina ships and insulting that Colony. This was at the time that the Pirates had obtained such an acquisition of strength that they were in no concern about preserving themselves from the justice of the laws, but of advancing their power, and maintaining their sovereignty, not over the seas only, but to stretch their dominions to the plantations themselves, and the Governors thereof; insomuch, that when their prisoners came aboard their captors' ships, the Pirates freely owned their acquaintance with them, and never endeavored to conceal their names, or habitations; as if they had been inhabitants of a legal commonwealth, and were resolved to treat with all the world on the foot of a free state. And all judicial acts went in the name of Teach [aka Thache], under the title of Commodore.[23]

The fleet headed north through the Straits of Florida and then along the Atlantic seaboard, descending upon Charleston, South Carolina (formerly Charles Town), near the end of May 1718. The relatively isolated British port was susceptible to pirate attack, and Blackbeard took advantage. Governor Robert Johnson of South Carolina gave this report (provided here in the original, uncorrected version) of the ensuing events:

> Four sail of them appeared in sight of the Town took our pilot boat and afterwards 8 or 9 sail wth. several of the best inhabitants of this place on board and then sent me word if I did not imediately send them a chest of medicines they would put every prisoner to death which for there sakes being complied with after plundering them all they had were sent ashore almost naked. This company is commanded by one Teach alias Blackbeard has a ship of 40 od guns under him and 3 sloopes tenders besides and are in all above 400 men. I don't perceive H.M. gracious proclamacon of pardon works any good

A Wild and Crazy Ride

efect upon them, some few indeed surrender and take a certificate of there so doing and then severall of them return to the sport again.[24]

Having received ransom from town officials in the form of a chest of medicine, the pirates had a "general consultation" and afterward hastily released their captives and ships before heading north. Within a week they rendezvoused at Beaufort. *Queen Anne's Revenge*, as it lay off the coast of North Carolina, was a three-masted, ship-rigged, floating war machine. It was constructed of sawn planking held together with fasteners of iron or wood sealed with coatings of pitch and tar. Propelled by the natural forces of water and wind, the ship had yards of sailcloth that were manipulated through a matrix of ropes, pulleys, and cleats. Its sailing ability and particular tendencies were intimately known by its officers and crew. Some of these men, such as the French pilot Charles Duval, had been aboard since the ship left Nantes over a year before. As a means of transport, the French vessel was a vital component of the social, political, and economic systems that the Old World was imposing on the Americas through conquest and exploitation. The quasi-military ship had imparted political force when serving the French government and expressed social unrest when controlled by pirates. At its core, however, regardless of who was at the helm, *Queen Anne's Revenge*, ex. *Concorde*, was a servant of the slave trade, transporting enslaved Africans from one continent to another along common trade routes. In that business, the only difference when the ship changed hands was who benefited financially. When *Concorde* was a French privateer, King Louis XIV, owner René Montaudoin, and the hired crew reaped the rewards of removing slaves from enemy ships off the coast of Africa and delivering them to Caribbean ports. Later, as an armed merchant engaging in legal commerce, Montaudoin alone profited. After the ship became *Queen Anne's Revenge*, the trading of human cargo did not stop, but this time it was on

the black market for benefit of the pirates—*one for all, and all for one*!

While reflecting nautical cultural purposes and trends, ships as an enterprise are self-contained, floating systems comprised of a captain, crew, equipment, passengers, and cargo. Based on historical accounts, a closer look at Blackbeard's ship as it prepared to enter Beaufort harbor helps us to interpret what archaeologists have found 300 years later.

In terms of armament, *Concorde*'s 14 cannons were supplemented soon after its capture, presumably by the crew taking on 8 from the sloop they left to the Frenchmen. The re-arming of *Queen Anne's Revenge* continued. Once the ship's original gun ports were filled, small carriage guns were placed on the upper decks and yoke-mounted swivel guns lined the vessel's railings. The pirates, at this point, were feeling quite bold, given what Captain Taylor of the *Great Allen* told authorities: "They hoped to find a ship of war, as they were strong enough to make themselves masters of one as the ship they captured from Dosset had 300 men and 32 cannons. In addition, they had the help of an associate whose vessel was armed with 12 cannons and crewed by more than a hundred men."[25] By the time Blackbeard's flagship arrived at Charleston, it bristled with 40 cannons. *Queen Anne's Revenge* was a formidable presence with firepower equivalent to a fifth-rate royal navy ship, of which only a few were on station in the Americas at the time.[26]

Historical accounts mentioning the number of pirates under Blackbeard's command vary widely, but the total number on the four ships, including Africans, appears to have been between 300 and 400 men, with at least half serving aboard *Queen Anne's Revenge*. Sailors were not assigned to individual vessels and were shifted from ship to ship. Most importantly, it was not their number but collective skills that were crucial in terms of maneuvering the vessel and firing its guns when needed, as reflected in the crew roster, or quarter bill, for a 24-gun British privateer from the eighteenth century.

Infestation of Pirates in the New World

DR. LINDLEY S. BUTLER

For decades preceding the early eighteenth-century Golden Age of Piracy, Europe had been embroiled in a series of wars largely instigated by France and opposed by English-led coalitions. To supplement their fleets, the maritime powers—England, France, Spain, and the Netherlands—unleashed a horde of privateers authorized to seize enemy shipping for profit. At the conclusion of Queen Anne's War (1702–13), thousands of sailors and privateers, suddenly unemployed, faced a bleak future unless they turned to piracy.

From homeland or overseas ports, out-of-work mariners headed for the West Indies. Gradually a loose international outlaw community formed, basing their organization on the egalitarian and democratic buccaneers of the previous century who elected their captains and divided their spoils equally. Scattered among the islands, they finally gathered in the free-wheeling port of Nassau in the Bahamas, where a compliant proprietary government welcomed any economic activity. Fortuitously, the Bahama Islands lay on the eastern flank of the Florida Straits, through which the Gulf Stream funneled Caribbean trade to North America and Europe.

From Nassau the pirates launched forays to the mainland coast from South Carolina to New England and throughout the West Indies. In seedy taverns, gambling dens, and brothels, partnerships were sealed, plans were laid for the next voyage, and loot was brought back to be sold to the thriving waterfront businesses. Easy targets were the lightly armed merchant-men carrying the region's products of sugar, molasses, hides, provisions, and slaves. The flexible pirates became commodities dealers, offering low-priced merchandise to colonial merchants who asked no questions. African slaves were readily sold in the colonies, but some enslaved men joined the crews as free and equal pirates.

Pirates' notoriety and threat to shipping alarmed colonial governors, whose pleas for aid finally elicited a response from the Crown. The Bahamas became a royal colony, with Woodes Rogers, a former privateer, named as their governor. Rogers brought soldiers and armed vessels that reinforced the meager royal naval forces stationed from Barbados to Boston. Pirates were offered a blanket royal pardon, the Act of Grace, for past crimes if they retired; those who refused were to be hunted down and executed. When Rogers arrived in July 1718, most pirates accepted the pardon, some becoming pirate hunters. Charles Vane escaped, while Blackbeard and

Securing men to fill these and other skilled positions was a constant struggle, and they often had to be forcibly taken from captured merchant ships to fully staff a pirate ship. When taking *Concorde*, Thache conscripted the pilot, the chief surgeon and two assistants, two carpenters, two cooks, a gunsmith, and a trumpeter from the French crew. He later forced the cooper, Edward Salter, from the merchant ship *Margaret* to join him.

If they could be accommodated and fed, an excess of nonskilled labor was desirable because pirates in sheer numbers could overwhelm merchant

Stede Bonnet were at sea in a powerful flotilla crewed by 300 to 400 men.

After scouring the Caribbean for prizes, Blackbeard and Bonnet sailed north to the mainland. There behind dangerous barrier islands lay North Carolina, where a destructive Indian war had left burned-out farms, a depleted militia, many widows and orphans, and hard-pressed merchants who had difficulty securing goods. Strategically located mid-continent between wealthy Virginia and South Carolina, this isolated colony became an ideal pirate haven.

Following the audacious blockade of Charles Town in May 1718, Blackbeard's cruise ended in disaster at Beaufort with two vessels lost and hundreds of pirates stranded. All of them took the pardon, but Bonnet quickly returned to piracy, and Blackbeard established a base at Ocracoke Island. For a weakly defended colony still facing Indian unrest, nearly 200 armed, unmarried men with cash would be welcome if they kept the pardon and settled down. Farms owned by widows with children added luster to the pardon for any pirate ready to retire. The majority blended into the tidewater, acquiring families and building a life trading, farming, or fishing, becoming ancestors of many coastal Carolinians.

"The Buccaneer Was a Picturesque Fellow," by Howard Pyle (1905), illustration from "The Fate of a Treasure Town," originally published in *Harper's Monthly Magazine*, December 1905.

crews. Each member of this force of heavily armed men would have carried some form of personal weapon(s) such as knives, small swords, hatchets, pistols, and axes. Famously, Blackbeard is depicted as having a complement of six pistols strapped to his chest.[27] There is little doubt that the flagship carried enough personal weapons and ammunition to arm a large number of men.

Sailors often joined pirates when given the opportunity to lead a life free from the hardships of merchant service, which were especially bleak for crews serving on slave ships. The young were

Table 2.1 A Quarter Bill for a Privateer of Twenty 9-Pounders and Four 3-Pounders for the Quarter Deck and Forecastle

Position	Number of Crew Members
Captain	1
Master	1
Midshipman	1
Quartermaster	2
1st marine and musketeers	25
Gun crew two 3-pounder cannons	4
Gun officers and gunner	3
Master mates	2
Boatswain's mate	3
Carpenter and crew	4
Gun crew twenty 9-pounder cannons	70
Boatswain and crew	3
Gun crew two 3-pounder cannons	4
2nd marine and musketeers	10
3rd marine and musketeers	9
Maintop: Midshipman and men with small arms and to repair rigging (mainmast)	6
Fore-top: Men with small arms and to repair rigging	5
Mizzen-top: Men with small arms and to repair rigging	3
Gunner's mate and assistant	2
Doctor and mate	2
Total	**160**

Source: William Hutchinson, *A Treatise on Naval Architecture founded upon Philosophical and Principles, towards Established Fixed Rules for the Best Form and Proportional Dimensions in Length, Breadth and Depth, of Merchants Ships in General, and also the Management of them to the Greatest Advantage, by Practical Seamanship; with Important Hints and Remarks relating thereto, especially both for Defense and Attacks in War at Sea, from Long Approved Experience* (1794; reprint, Annapolis: United States Naval Institute, 1969), 225–26.

particularly affected by the lure of the freebooter's life. Two of those jumping ship from *Concorde* were teenaged cabin boys, Julian Joseph Moisant, nicknamed La Mornyax, and Louis Arot.[28] The duties of the unskilled involved menial shipboard tasks, as well as chores to procure water and firewood when near shore.

African slaves must have garnered some hope that they might also be freed to serve the pirate company, regardless of how hard the labor. There were even some examples of freedom aboard *Concorde*, as was the case with Joseph Alabard, a "Negro from Juda," listed on the muster roll as a seaman (and paid more or less equal to others). Another "Negro," whose name was unknown but reportedly had been married in St. Malo, was forced to sail with the pirates; his fate is unknown.[29] Historical accounts regarding Africans aboard *Queen Anne's Revenge* reveal that most were not elevated in status but, instead, were traded on the black market as the opportunity arose. Of the 157 Africans retained at the taking of *Concorde*, Thache reportedly sold at least half before leaving the French Caribbean. Another 5 Africans were given to 4 officers from *Great Allen* as a reward for joining the pirates and securing the ship's valuables.[30] Near the end of his final cruise, the pirate captain was still interested in acquiring Africans; he confiscated 14 individuals from the slave vessel *Princess* just days before reaching Beaufort. According to Ignatius Pell, Blackbeard flippantly referred to them as a "baker's dozen."[31] Given the presence of Africans aboard *Queen Anne's Revenge* throughout its career, iron shackles, also known as bilbaos, would have been plentiful. The same was probably true of items referred to as reward incentives, such as strings of glass beads for adornment and clay tobacco pipes, which were provided as forms of incentives aboard slave ships.[32]

Some Africans sailing on pirate ships, however, appear to have been freed members of the crew, particularly those with useful skills in terms of combat and sailing, coupled with a loyalty to the

"The Buccaneers," by F. J. Waugh (ca. 1912). (Courtesy of the Library of Congress)

freebooters' cause. The testimony of Jonathan Clarke, a white man on trial during the Bonnet trials in Charleston, suggested some Africans moved about the ship freely, with "freedom of tongue" despite their skin color. "Pell, don't you remember that I was abaft, and one of the Negroes came and damned me, and asked me what I did there? Why I did not go and work amongst the rest? And told me I should be used as a Negroe."[33]

Captain Ellis Brand, HMS *Lyme*, reported that the men under Blackbeard's command, as he lay off the Carolina coast, consisted of 320 whites and Africans. Of those, David Harriot witnessed Blackbeard leaving the Beaufort area after the loss

of *Queen Anne's Revenge* with 40 whites and 60 Africans. Six months later, 5 men of African descent were among the pirate captain's crew of 14 fighting with him during the epic battle at Ocracoke.

With hundreds of men under his command, the business of provisioning must have been a constant concern for Captain Thache. Since pirates were not afforded the luxury of stopping at major ports to purchase food and supplies, they relied on what could be confiscated at sea. Seldom did prize vessels carry large sums of money; however, they often held provisions, equipment, and cargo that could help meet their basic needs. Newspaper accounts from July 1715 to January 1719 demonstrate

Table 2.2 Goods Taken by Pirates, from the *Boston News-Letter*

Type of Goods Taken	Number of Times Mentioned
Alcohol	8
Provisions	6
Ship's supplies (sails, rigging, anchors, etc.)	6
Clothing	5
Sundries	5
Money	4
Slaves	4
Arms and armament	2
Medicinal	1

what pirates in general were removing from ships along the Atlantic seaboard and eastern Caribbean Ocean.[34]

True to the pirate image, while feeding the pirate crew was a primary concern, the procurement of alcohol appears to have been of equal or perhaps greater concern. Seamen were traditionally hard drinkers, and many pirates stayed perpetually drunk to relieve stress and boredom. Spirituous beverage was the most common item taken by pirates, and the balance of authority aboard their ships may very well have depended upon the captain's ability to obtain it.

One would think these things should induce them to reform their lives; but so many reprobates together encouraged and spirited one another up in their wickedness, to which a continual course of drinking did not a little contribute. For in Black-beard's journal which was taken, there were several memorandums of the following nature, found writ with his own hand: *Such a day, rum all out:—Our company somewhat sober:—A damn'd confusion amongst us!— Rogues a-plotting:—Great talk of separation—so I looked sharp for a prize:—Such a day took one, with a great deal of liquor on board, so kept the company hot, damned hot; then all things went well again.*[35]

To meet other needs, an array of items was taken by the crew of *Queen Anne's Revenge* when they detained captured ships. For example, when Blackbeard stopped the sloop *Margaret*, its captain, Henry Bostock, reported that the pirates removed "four beeves and 35 hogs, two-thirds barrel of gunpowder, five small arms, two cutlasses, his books and instruments, and some linen."[36] Pirates also took advantage to enhance their wardrobes, for they took clothes from *Concorde*'s officers and crew and, later, from the ships detained at Charleston. The main focus in South Carolina, however, was receiving a "chest of medicine," highlighting the difficulty pirates faced in securing critical supplies needed by the surgeons.[37]

The pirates under Blackbeard's command also succeeded in gaining financial plunder, the highlights of which began when 20 lbs. of gold dust were taken from *Concorde*'s officers. In another capture, a large amount of "plate" and a ceremonial drinking cup, likely all of it silver, were taken from the *Great Allen*. The largest haul, however, came from captured ships and their passengers during the Charleston blockade, when the pirates plundered "about fifteen hundred Pounds Sterling, in Gold and Pieces of Eight."[38] All that monetary booty, about a quarter-million in today's dollars, passed across the decks of *Queen Anne's Revenge* and was, no doubt, kept in a guarded place in Captain Thache's cabin. As is known from testimony by Bonnet's men, most never received their share of the loot!

Carolina, Here We Come: Crashing into the Coast

After a successful vessel capture or raid on a town, pirates often sought sanctuary from government authorities, a safe haven where they could assess and divvy up the takings, make repairs, and revel in their success. Harbors such as the then-lawless town of New Providence, Bahamas, offered such a retreat for Blackbeard and others. After his 1718 raid on Charleston, however, the pirate captain was aware that the recently appointed governor of the Bahamas, Woodes Rogers, was soon to arrive. He was to administer the king's pardon for pirates willing to quit the freebooting business; those who didn't would be hunted down and hanged in a co-ordinated effort to rid the seas of rampant piracy. Thus Blackbeard and his men headed north from Charleston.

Today, as it was in colonial times, the coast of North Carolina is rimmed with a long string of islands known as the Outer Banks. They are laced with shallow waterways and tricky inlets, which, in the "days of sail," hampered legitimate waterborne commerce but also provided secluded harbors and hideouts. A few years before Blackbeard's flotilla arrived, the British Board of Trade noted the geo-graphical limitations of North Carolina, stating that "the situation renders it forever uncapable of being a place of considerable trade by reason of a great sound near sixty miles over, that lyes between this Coast and the Sea, barr'd by a vast chain of sand banks so very shallow and shifting that sloops drawing only five foot of water run great risk of crossing them."[39] The report also provides refer-ence to the fledgling colony's attraction for pirates. "The Government of this Province having for many years been a very disorderly one this becomes a place of Refuge for all the Vagabonds."[40] As an added bonus for pirates, not far offshore were well-traveled shipping lanes full of targets. Because of its relatively deep, natural harbor, Beaufort must have seemed appealing as a potential base of operation for Thache. Indeed, just a few years later, privateers used it for that purpose during the War of Jenkins' Ear (1739–48) and King George's War (1744–48).

To access the protected harbor at Beaufort, ships had to thread a needle, the eye being Topsail Inlet (now called Beaufort Inlet) that ran between the two sea islands of Bogue and Shackleford. Narrow-

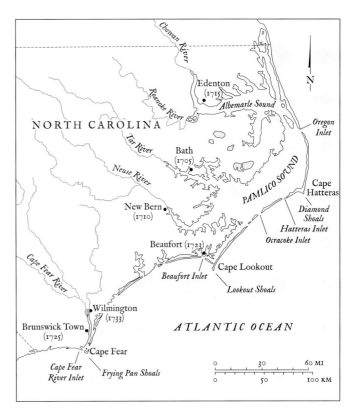

North Carolina's colonial settlement

ing to only 100 ft. in places, the channel's depth at its entrance provided ships only 12 ft. at low tide and 16 ft. at high. Bringing sailing ships through an ocean inlet was never an easy task. Captains and pilots had to balance the forces of wind, tides, and ocean currents, all of which influenced a ship's movement. In restricted channels, a square-rigged vessel such as *Queen Anne's Revenge* was particu-larly difficult to maneuver, and extreme caution was urged, even in well-traveled or known areas, such as those guarding Liverpool. Sailors were warned that "where the dangers are so many and great, as to require not only a proper time of tide, but clear weather and day-light, to proceed with a common chance for safety. Yet such has been the imprudence and folly of pilots and commanders of ships, as to run for our dangerous crooked bar channels, when no guides could be seen, and no compass course nor the lead could be relied on; by which they have lost their ships and lives."[41] In a much more remote

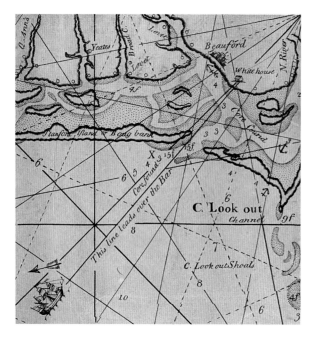

Thatch's ship *Queen Anne's Revenge* run a-ground off of the bar of Topsail-Inlet, the said Thatch sent his Quarter-Master [William Howard] to command this Deponent's Sloop to come to his assistance; but she run a-ground likewise about gun-shot from the said Thatch, before his said sloop could come to their assistance, and both the said Thatch's ship and this Deponent's Sloop were wreck'd; and the said Thatch and all the other Sloop's companies went on board the *Revenge*, afterwards called the *Royal James*, and on board the other sloop they found empty off the Havana.[43]

part of the world, the town of Beaufort, founded in 1713, remained a small fishing village throughout the eighteenth century, and commerce through the inlet was shouldered almost exclusively by small sloops trading up and down the coast with ports in New England.[42]

Captain Thache may have believed he could bring his ship through the inlet, but he also must have recognized that *Queen Anne's Revenge* was handicapped by the extra armament on its deck, making it top-heavy, unstable, and difficult to handle, especially if the guns were being carried "run out" in a battle-ready position. Maneuverability and control were further hampered by the leaky and fouled condition of its hull, having been at sea for more than a year. Thache took some precaution by waiting until daylight and presumably high tide to attempt passage. He also had the benefit of watching *Revenge, Adventure,* and the small Spanish sloop thread their way through the inlet channel successfully. The flagship, however, didn't make it, as reported by David Harriot.

That the next morning after they had all got safe into Topsail-Inlet, except Thatch, the said

Three months after the wrecking event, Stede Bonnet and his followers were captured and charged with piracy. Collectively, they testified during their trial proceedings in South Carolina that Blackbeard had intentionally grounded the flagship at Beaufort in order to remove "moneys and effects" before departing the scene without sharing it with the entire crew, counter to the fair sharing they expected according to the "pirate's consent." It seems, however, that Blackbeard didn't strictly enforce this, for Henry Virgin testified, "But I never gave my Consent, for Capt. Thatch never asked any of us."[44] The loss of a second ship, the marooning of some men, and his sailing away from the scene in the Spanish sloop with a small number of handpicked crew members lends credence to their claim that the whole incident was a preconceived plot favoring Blackbeard and his allies. When he reached Bath, Captain Thache officially registered the previously unnamed sloop *Adventure*, presumably using the papers taken from David Harriot's sunken sloop, *Adventure*. It was on the "new" *Adventure* that Blackbeard was later killed at Ocracoke. Perhaps, though, the pirate

"Colonel Rhett and the Pirate," by Howard Pyle (1901), in *Howard Pyle's Book of Pirates*, ed. Merle De Vore Johnson (New York: Harper and Brothers, 1921), 162–63; originally published in Woodrow Wilson, "Colonies and Nation," *Harper's Monthly Magazine*, May 1901.

captain simply took advantage of a deteriorating situation at Beaufort toward his best interest. Regardless of intention, the truth is the flagship would never have served the pirates well in the shallow coastal waters of North Carolina, given its size, weight, and condition.

In retrospect, the low-impact nature of the wrecking and availability of the remaining two sloops prevented injury or loss of life and afforded some time for men to remove items from *Queen Anne's Revenge*. Offshore winds and tidal currents would have restricted efforts to free the flagship located on the outer edge of the inlet shoals, though it is unclear if any were made. As the tide rushed out, the vessel heeled over on its port side, making rescue difficult. A premium would have been put on grabbing clothing, personal possessions, small

arms, and hand tools, all of which were light and manageable but also held value to their owners as they faced life in their new surroundings. Beyond what the pirates took, there is no mention of salvage by others. In 1718, Beaufort was a "poor little village" with only a few resident families. Their capabilities for offshore salvage in terms of boats and equipment were limited, but they no doubt took advantage of goods and materials that broke free from the derelict flagship and sloop and washed up on local beaches in the days, weeks, and months after their wrecking. It is less of a surprise that there is no mention of commercial salvage at the time because such activities required expensive ships, equipment, provisions, and labor to make the effort financially successful. Although the ships' cannons and anchors carried value, investors were generally reluctant to commit to salvage operations unless silver and gold were involved. Eyewitness accounts made it certain that Blackbeard had removed those items prior to leaving the wrecks.

So it was that Captain Thache's flagship, the battleship that had served him well for six months, was abandoned on a sandbar in Beaufort Inlet, along with the smaller sloop. Despite Blackbeard's notoriety at the time, local memories of the existence of the ships, as well as their physical remains, were simply lost in time. It is odd that the residents of Beaufort never embraced and bragged about those ships, commanded by the notorious pirate captain, who left them on their doorstep. Or perhaps, like the pirates themselves, they chose to keep their secrets deeply buried beneath the sands of time.

North Carolina Invaded by Virginia

DR. LINDLEY S. BUTLER

In 1718, an alarming crescendo of piracy terrorized North America from the Carolinas to New England. Shipping had been seized off Virginia throughout the year, and by that summer Governor Alexander Spotswood faced a nightmare: the infamous Blackbeard had created "a nest of pyrates" on Ocracoke Island, North Carolina. Born in Tangier, then a British possession, Spotswood had had a distinguished army career in the European wars, rising to the rank of colonel and serving as a line officer and quartermaster general.

After Blackbeard lost half his fleet at Beaufort, he and his men took the king's pardon from Governor Charles Eden. Since Eden's militia had been decimated by the recent Tuscarora War, he risked giving the former pirates a second chance. Blackbeard, alias Edward Thache, settled in Bath and married. Unsuited to domesticity, he soon became restless and went to sea. In August he returned to Bath with an "abandoned" French vessel laden with sugar and cocoa, which the vice admiralty court declared salvage.

Eden's political opponents, Edward Moseley and Maurice Moore, who considered the pirates a blot on the colony's reputation, quietly urged Spotswood to intervene, although he had no legal authority to do so without permission. Suspecting Eden of collusion with Blackbeard, Spotswood set in motion an illegal, secret preemptive invasion of North Carolina without informing Eden.

Unlike North Carolina, Virginia had a large, well-trained militia, complemented by two royal navy guard ships. Advised by captains Ellis Brand of HMS *Lyme* and George Gordon of HMS *Pearl* and Brand's executive officer Lieutenant Robert Maynard, Spotswood devised a land-and-sea invasion of North Carolina. Since the warships were too large for the shallow inlets and the sound, he sent two small sloops, *Jane* and *Ranger*, commanded by Maynard. North Carolina pilots were hired, and the sloops were manned by volunteer sailors, militia, and marines. In overall command, Captain Brand would lead the overland force to occupy Bath. Incentive bounties were set, ranging from £100 for Blackbeard to £10 for seamen.

By November 21, 1718, Maynard's sloops arrived at Ocracoke, and the next morning they engaged Blackbeard in a bloody battle that killed or wounded all of the pirates. Blackbeard's head was taken to Virginia as a trophy. Guided by Moseley and Moore, Brand's column occupied Bath on November 23, confiscating sugar that had been collected as either court fees or gifts to Governor Eden and Secretary Tobias Knight. Sugar and cocoa from the Ocracoke camp, combined with that found in Bath, were sold at auction in Virginia for £2,250, to be divided among the invaders. The surviving pirates were tried and executed in Williamsburg.

Governor Eden complained to London officials about the illegal invasion and confiscation of

personal and government property. Spotswood
was plagued by the controversy for the next
year. Accused of colluding with the pirates or
accepting bribes, Secretary Knight was subjected
to a court hearing that completely exonerated
him only a short time before his death. Seeking evidence on Eden and Knight, Moseley and
Moore broke into the secretary's office but found
nothing incriminating. They were convicted
of sedition and fined. The heroes' welcome for
Maynard and Brand turned sour over prolonged
squabbling about the prize money. As the
Golden Age ended, most of the pirates took the
pardon, while a series of trials and mass execu-
tions disposed of the unrepentant.

Portrait of Alexander Spotswood, attributed to Charles
Bridges, Spotsylvania County, Virginia (1736), oil on
canvas, Colonial Williamsburg Foundation, museum
purchase (accession #1940-359, A, image #DS1993-0257).
(Used by permission)

[CHAPTER THREE]

The Prize Is Lost

The Journey through Time

On September 19, 1998, divers making the initial inspection of that year's archaeological expedition to the *QAR* site were elated to find the bright yellow orb still in place. It had withstood the turbulence of Hurricane Bonnie, looking only a bit worse for wear with a smattering of barnacles attached to its surface and thin strands of algae waving in the current. This good news meant the InterOcean S-4A electromagnetic current meter had survived the category 2 hurricane and its 24-hour pounding.

The instrument, the size of a basketball and resembling Sputnik 1, was the central piece of a scientific experiment taking place 40 years after the Russian satellite's historic mission, not in the realm of outer space but under the waters of Beaufort Inlet. Rather than circling the earth in low orbit, S-4A was mounted to a rigid stand 50 ft. from the *QAR* wreckage. Located just above the seabed, sensors collected critical measurements for nearly a year, including the day Hurricane Bonnie visited. Dr. John Wells, a marine geologist and, at the time, director of the Institute for Marine Sciences at the University of North Carolina (UNC), and his colleagues needed this information to better understand the physical forces that had affected the ship's remains over the past three centuries. This was not the first time that we relied on colleagues in marine

geology to help interpret underwater finds. Remember the shipwreck described in Chapter 1 that we found in the vicinity of Teach's Oak, near Oriental, North Carolina? Wells was also contacted then. In that situation, the central question was whether the buildup of creek bottom sediments layered over the sunken remains could be used to determine how long the ship had been there, and thus confirm or refute local claims that this vessel dated to the days of Blackbeard. As it turned out, Wells knew from prior research that, in this area, soft mud accumulated on the creek bottom at a rate of one foot per century. For the Oriental shipwreck analysis, a fancy instrument was not required. It only took an aluminum coring tube shoved down by hand to determine that an 18-in. buildup of homogenous muck lay over the timbers, which translated to approximately 150 years. Having sought the assistance of marine geologists familiar with the area, we were soon assured that the ship's demise occurred well after Blackbeard's time in North Carolina, a finding that was corroborated by datable construction details and artifacts from the wreck.

The *QAR* wreckage within Beaufort Inlet lay in a drastically different physical environment, one made up of highly mobile sands rather than the silty muds of a slow-moving creek. The primary question posed to marine geologists was also different. Why is the wreckage lying 23 ft. below today's water surface when the ship would have grounded in about 10 ft.? What would cause it to settle so far down through the sediments? To answer this and related questions about how the environment affected the ship's remains for 300 years, Wells, along with marine geologists Dr. Jesse McNinch of the U.S. Army Corps of Engineers Field Research Center, Dr. Chris Martens of the University of North Carolina at Chapel Hill, Chris Freeman, now president of Geodynamics LLC, and others have over the years unleashed a barrage of tests and equipment. All told, over the first several years they conducted two cartographic studies, five bathymetric surveys, one year-long current meter survey, two sediment coring studies, two side-scan sonar surveys, one sub-bottom sonar survey, and numerous multibeam sonar surveys, collectively. That is a lot of data to process, but before we find out what was learned, it is important to understand where, exactly, *Queen Anne's Revenge* ended up.

The *QAR* site is situated along the Atlantic coast of central North Carolina within the influence of Beaufort Inlet. Today its wreckage lies 1.3 miles off Fort Macon and 1,500 ft. west of the present shipping channel. Because the shipwreck is located southwest of the Cape Lookout shoreline, it is somewhat protected from the predominant wind patterns that originate from the north during winter months, including storms called nor'easters. Despite this protection, the site is subjected to significant wave energy during hurricanes and prominent southwesterlies that arrive with force from the Atlantic Ocean. Winds are variable during the day, particularly in the summer, when they typically blow seaward in the morning and then shift around and stiffen by afternoon as the land surface warms from solar radiation.

North Carolina barrier islands, including Bogue Banks and Shackleford Banks that flank Beaufort Inlet, are linear features paralleling the shoreline. The primary coastal processes affecting their for-

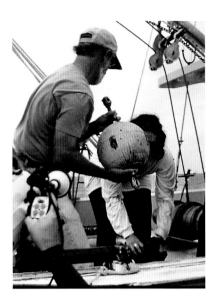

Dr. John Wells brings the S-4A current meter aboard R/V *Capricorn*. (Courtesy of the North Carolina Department of Natural and Cultural Resources)

Marine geologists aboard Virginia Institute of Marine Science vessel taking sediment cores. (Courtesy of the North Carolina Department of Natural and Cultural Resources)

mation are waves and tides, which influence how sediment is dispersed and reworked. Waves at high tide, particularly during storms, can inundate low-lying barrier islands, and their action continuously stirs up sediment, putting it into suspension and moving it around. This mechanism, known as littoral drift, is important for the redistribution of sand along the beach and nearshore zones. Sediment movement, at times, is interrupted and altered by breaks, called inlets, in the barrier islands.[1]

Along North Carolina's coast, there are 17 active barrier island inlets that have been known since European contact. Beaufort Inlet (formerly Topsail

Pola Palekh grounded in Beaufort Inlet, November 2016.
(Courtesy of Mark Wilde-Ramsing)

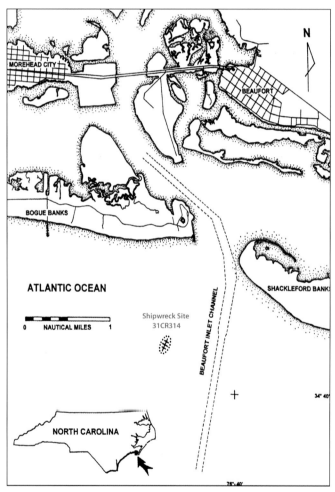

Queen Anne's Revenge site location map.
(Courtesy of the North Carolina Department of
Natural and Cultural Resources)

Inlet) has been one of the largest and most stable of them.[2] Ocean water flowing through barrier inlets is bidirectional, consisting of outgoing (ebb) and incoming (flood) tides. The strongest currents, which occur during the outgoing tidal cycle, create a delta at the inlet's offshore entrance. These ebb tidal deltas are similar to those found at river mouths but are in a constant state of flux, always losing as well as gaining sediments. Littoral drift and wave action constantly rework deposits to form a matrix of channels and shoals. At the terminal end of the inlet's ocean channel looms a relatively steep, seaward-sloping deposit of sand, known as the bar.

Crossing over this impediment when returning from the ocean was a challenge to mariners as they sought anchorage inside the barrier islands. It demanded setting a proper alignment and easing over the bar while maintaining a steady course within the confines of shallow shoulders until safety was reached. Coastal inlets provided critical routes through which ships had to pass; however, navigating them was extremely hazardous. Historically, 110 shipwrecks have come to grief in or near Beaufort Inlet, the oldest being the grounding of *Queen Anne's Revenge* "on the bar" in 1718.[3] Many other ships from all ages experienced close calls, including the 590-ft. cargo ship *Pola Palekh*, which the *Wilmington Star News* reported had run aground in the channel on November 18, 2016, with its cargo

The Journey through Time

of 35,800 metric tons of fertilizer. It was freed after several hours, and locals were relieved that no injuries, spillage, or damage to the vessel or cargo were reported.

What Maps Tell Us: Hundreds of Years in Beaufort Inlet

Over the years since the day Blackbeard's flagship sank, there have been significant changes to the inlet. Understanding how the forces of nature reduced this magnificent sailing ship to the debris field it is today is critical to us. During three centuries of degradation, many items floated away or disintegrated, while the remainder were twisted, eaten, encrusted, and often displaced. Recognizing how a site has formed, or its site formation process, enables us to better interpret the presence and context of artifacts and, in turn, reveal aspects of life aboard *Queen Anne's Revenge*.

Again we turn to marine geologists to help interpret shipwrecks because the very nature of their research focuses on physical changes that occur along the coast that in turn impact site condition. Since marine geologists most often work from research vessels out on the water and employ an array of highly sophisticated instrumentation, we were a bit surprised when Wells's first course of action was to examine old maps and charts, a method used in cartography. It makes sense, though, for changes to the Beaufort area landscape over time reflect environmental forces, then just as they do now, that would have impacted the shipwreck.

First and foremost, we hoped Wells would uncover a map from 1718 showing the exact inlet configuration that Captain Thache faced when *Queen Anne's Revenge* was lost. Unfortunately, no renderings from his time were found. The first reasonably accurate charts of the area were drawn 15 to 20 years later by Edward Moseley in 1733 and James Wimble in 1738. From then until the late twentieth century, geologists found 40 different

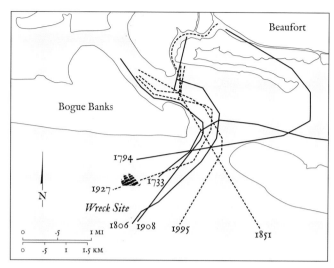

Beaufort Inlet channel orientations through three centuries. (Courtesy of John T. Wells and Jesse E. McNinch)

renditions, 22 of which they selected for further study.[4] With few prominent reference points in the barren, sandy landscape, the charts, especially the earliest ones, lacked accuracy and could only be used to estimate channel depths. All the maps showed outer sandbars, with a key feature being the one that extended out from Shackleford Banks. This fingerlike projection was subject to constant change, and when it grew, the inlet channel was forced in an east/west orientation. Consequently, this restricted channel flow caused shallow areas to form that created havoc for mariners. In time, everything changed when major hurricanes passed through the area and violently forced ocean water into nearby estuaries and their inland tributaries. Upon receding during an outgoing tide, water flow moved with such great force that a more direct path was cut through the inlet shoals, once again restoring a relatively deep channel to a more direct, north/south alignment.

The cartographic study showed that the orientation of the outer channel wagged back and forth at least nine times over the past three centuries. This meant the inlet passed over the *QAR* wreckage at least twice during the nineteenth century and again

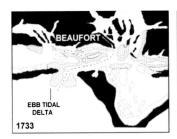

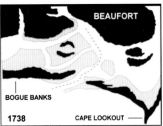

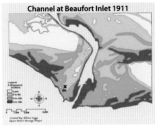

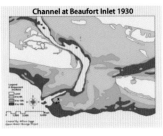

Composite of eighteenth- and twentieth-century maps showing relative inlet alignments. (Courtesy of John T. Wells and Jesse E. McNinch and the North Carolina Department of Natural and Cultural Resources)

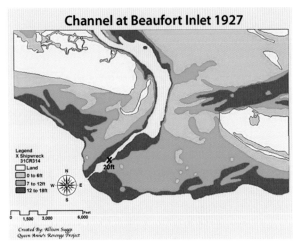

Coast & Geodetic Survey chart with *Queen Anne's Revenge* site location (1927). (Courtesy of the North Carolina Department of Natural and Cultural Resources)

in the late 1920s. During these periods, the wreck site was exposed to intense currents. Mostly, however, the shipwreck lay buried, sometimes covered by as much as 17 ft. of sand!

Interestingly, the Moseley and Wimble charts, recorded only a few years apart, exhibit very different channel alignments. These two historic charts were remarkably similar to two highly accurate hydrographic maps recorded in 1911 and 1930. The paired maps exemplify the inlet's volatile and unpredictable nature over a relatively short period of time, at least in geological terms. In both sets, one from the eighteenth century and the other from the twentieth century, the throat of the inlet remained stable while the channel moved farther west over time. When superimposed onto either alignment, however, the loss of *Queen Anne's Revenge* appears to have occurred in the immediate vicinity of the bar at the seaward entrance to historic Beaufort Inlet.

When the inlet's tidal currents flowed directly across the wreck site, especially during storms, any exposed artifacts were subjected to intense, sand-laced water pressure. This likely accelerated degradation and may have rearranged or displaced lighter artifacts from their original locations on the ship. The good news is that direct impact from the migrating inlet channel appears to have been relatively short in duration, measured in months, even weeks, rather than years. This finding is based on the last time the inlet naturally impacted the site around 1927. At that time, water depths were 22 ft. or more, with seabed currents washing over exposed wreckage. As the inlet migrated away, water depths decreased while a sandy overburden accumulated. In 1928 the water was 15 ft. with 8 ft. of sand covering, and by 1930, the *QAR* site had the water-to-sand strata flipped with only 6 ft. of water over it and 17 ft. of sand atop it. This sequence revealed that when wreckage was exposed by inlet currents, in very short order it was likely to quickly become reburied. Man-made changes aimed at

The Journey through Time

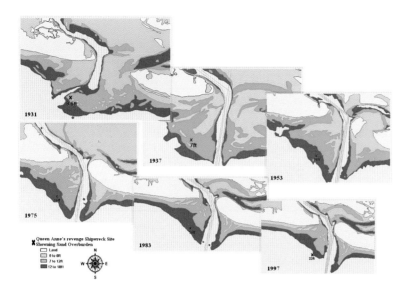

Physical changes at Beaufort Inlet during the twentieth century. (Courtesy of the North Carolina Department of Natural and Cultural Resources)

improving navigation through Beaufort Inlet, however, would alter this protective cover.

The U.S. Army Corps of Engineers began mechanical dredging at Beaufort Inlet in 1904. By following the inlet's natural course, they attempted to maintain a navigation channel 20 ft. deep and 300 ft. wide. Dredging continued for three years before being suspended. Less than two years later, shoals were again making navigation difficult. In 1911, maintenance dredging resumed off and on for the next 20 years as the channel continued to migrate slowly westward. When the inlet flowed directly over the shipwreck in 1927, it is possible that dredge activities may have damaged the shipwreck site. We suspect that only a large mechanical force could have dislodged the ship's massive sternpost assembly from where it was originally attached to where we found it more than 30 ft. away.

Even as shipping demands increased and vessels grew ever larger, the Corps of Engineers continued to be plagued by the lack of maintenance funds to keep the passage through Beaufort Inlet safe. Federal funds were eventually allocated to establish a fixed channel that ran straight out from the inlet throat. By 1936, the stabilized inlet was being maintained at a width of 400 ft. and depth to 30 ft.

nearly 1,000 ft. east of the *QAR* site. In 1975 and again in 1994, the dredging project dimensions were increased to arrive at today's navigation channel width of 450 ft. and depth of 47 ft. as it passes between Bogue Banks and Shackleford Banks.[5]

A series of nautical charts covering the past 60 years shows the narrowing of the inlet throat and the shrinking of the ebb tidal delta, which correlate to inlet dredging.[6] Keeping the artificially enlarged shipping channel open has removed large volumes of sediment from the historic ebb tidal delta at the wreckage site and placed it in offshore disposal areas. Consequently, cartographic evidence shows that the thick sand layer covering the shipwreck in the early 1930s was depleted by the early 1980s. Site exposure at this time was substantiated by age-dating the largest living specimens of temperate coral colonies (*Oculina arbuscula*) collected from the shipwreck in 1998, which were determined to be 16 years old.[7] The deflation of Beaufort Inlet's ebb tidal delta, as a direct consequence of human efforts to tame Beaufort Inlet, leaves the historic remains of *Queen Anne's Revenge* today more exposed than ever, with no prospect that the sands of yesteryear will ever again provide the protection they deserve.

Scour-Burial Mechanism: Undercut, Then Cover Up!

The wreckage of *Queen Anne's Revenge* lies in 23 ft. of water today, although it likely grounded in 10 ft. of water, based on the ship's estimated draft. Under the lead of Dr. Jesse McNinch, geologists addressed this discrepancy by examining how energetic forces of the nearshore coastal environment impacted a ship's deterioration. Using analogous studies of submerged military mines and how they settle once deployed, geologists identified a similar process as ship remains settle onto unconsolidated seabed sediments and become buried.[8] When water flowing along the bottom is strong enough, the "scour-burial" process begins. As heightened currents encounter wreckage on the seabed, sediment is scoured from around it. When flow is strong enough over a long enough period, these scour areas will become large and deep enough for the ship remains to slip down into the depression. This is the same process that beachgoers experience when standing at the edge of the surf as waves work their feet down into the soft sand. As wreckage becomes level with the seabed and no longer restricts current flow, scouring and downward migration slow and then stop. After the storm dies out or the inlet channel passes on, sediments fall out of suspension and fill the scour pit to complete the burial cycle. The scour-burial sequence is reactivated whenever current flow is strong enough to mobilize sediments and expose elements of the shipwreck so that they become obstructions again.

In order to develop a predictive scour-burial model specific to the *QAR* site, McNinch and Wells used data from the InterOcean S-4A electromagnetic current meter anchored near the wreckage. The yellow orb continuously recorded current velocity and direction, as well as wave height and duration, for 12 minutes every hour from May 1998 through April 1999. Over the course of its deployment, S-4A captured the full range of data

Divers Jim Dugan and Julep Gillman-Bryan prepare to deploy the S-4A current meter. (Courtesy of the North Carolina Department of Natural and Cultural Resources)

from calm periods to storm conditions, including nor'easters, southwesterlies, and the direct impact from Hurricane Bonnie. This provided the basis for an empirical model geologists developed specifically for the *QAR* site.[9]

To get an understanding of how various parts of wreckage were impacted, the *QAR* scour-burial model was applied to three hypothetical objects of varying diameters: a cannonball (6 in.), a cannon (10 in.), and a portion of the ballast mound (6.5 ft.), representing the entire shipwreck. Computer modeling predicted that wave-generated flow during hurricanes would be sufficient to scour and bury all objects, including the ballast mound. Of a lesser impact were southwesterlies that dominate summer weather. Relatively strong after crossing a large expanse of ocean, their wind-generated wave energy was sufficient to completely bury the hypothetical cannonball and cannon. The ballast mound, however, was only partially scoured at 30 percent and thus remained mostly exposed. Because the *QAR* wreckage has been sheltered by Cape Lookout, nor'easters appeared to have had even less impact. During those times, energy was sufficient to completely scour the cannonball but only partially uncover the cannon and leave all but 2 percent of the ballast mound exposed. Periods of calm weather provided negligible scour and thus promoted in-fill and burial following storms.

How does this relate to our understanding of the early deterioration of *Queen Anne's Revenge* after it was lost in June 1718? Well, since the vessel sank at the beginning of the summer, it was initially exposed to predominant winds from the southwest. Objects that rolled off the vessel, such as cannon-balls and cannons, would have quickly been buried. The hull itself, however, remained mostly exposed and subject to constant battering from waves and currents, which worked to loosen and wash away masts, sails, and rigging. The majority of vessel structure likely remained mostly exposed to the elements for months, if not years. Historical accounts do not record any tropical storms impacting the Beaufort area for at least four years after the wrecking event, and no major hurricanes hit the North Carolina coast for at least a decade.[10]

Diver observations and sediment corings from around and under the wreckage were noted, since the scour-burial model assumed the consistency of the seabed sand to be uniform. They found that, for the most part, surrounding sediments were typical coastal sands.[11] However, what lay directly below the wreckage was different. That layer consisted of very fine-grained sand that likely was a relic river bottom from many millennia ago. Its tightly packed nature prevented further downward movement of objects that normally occur through the scour-burial process, regardless of current strength. This finding was alarming because an underlying, scour-resistant strata coupled with the disappearance of protective sand during the twentieth century meant that artifacts would be prone to scatter during periods of seabed turbulence and would lose their provenience. Furthermore, continuous exposure in seawater is devastating for 300-year-old artifacts.

Shipworms and Electro-Chemical Processes: Can There Be Anything Left?

The worms crawl in
The worms crawl out
The worms they crawl
all about.

The worms crawl in
The worms crawl out
They play pinochle
on your snout!
From the Hearse Song[12]

Seawater exposure subjects the vestiges of a once vibrant pirate ship to chemical and biological factors that hasten deterioration and, quite literally, return it to nature. Besides constant water flow and grating sands, there is more, much more, that eats away at the original structure and affects the archaeological remains. Organic materials, including wood, rope, leather, and cloth, of which the vast majority of the shipwreck and its contents are made, suffer the most when exposed to the elements. A host of ocean organisms causes rapid deterioration, starting with marine fungi, which attack almost immediately and lead the way for an invasion of other biological agents, including fish and a variety of marine borers. Particularly menacing are the latter, which include members of the *Teredinidae* family, appropriately called shipworms. These critters have been the bane of all mariners who sailed in tropical waters. Shipworms attack and devour the bottom of a wooden ship while afloat, and when it sinks, they continue to weaken the hull structure to the point that seabed currents end up washing it away in pieces. What little wood remains on the *QAR* site shows evidence of extensive shipworm damage, providing testament to the voracious appetite of these tiny animals.

When buried underneath a couple of feet or more of protective sediment, however, artifacts

Sand and Sonar Provide Unique Protection

DAVID J. BERNSTEIN

For a brief few years after its discovery, the wreckage of *Queen Anne's Revenge* lay lightly protected beneath the shifting sands of Beaufort Inlet. The dynamic, energetic, and ephemeral coastal processes that had revealed the shipwreck in 1996 left it in danger, exposed to the undersea elements that would quickly threaten artifacts and important archaeological information. An experimental sand berm project, designed to protect the wreckage while recovery of artifacts still occurred, was set in motion in 2006 by taking advantage of a nearby dredging project. Load after load of sand was placed in a pile on the seabed just updrift of the wreckage. Would the mound provide enough barrier so storm waves wouldn't continue to damage the wreckage? Would it slow down the scouring around the site?

We would only learn the fate and effectiveness of the sand berm by studying three-dimensional maps of the seafloor produced from high-resolution hydrographic surveys. Once the ship's remains were located, a variety of research activities and scientific instruments were used to study the wreck site. Diver observations, photographs, current measurements, sonar imagery, and single-beam sonar soundings were among the early techniques used to better understand the environment in which the wreckage lies. Most recently, high-resolution multibeam sonar surveys provided impressive accuracy and precision in a colorful three-dimensional seafloor map. More than 20 times in a second, pulses of acoustic energy were pinged to the seabed and received back at the survey vessel. Ping after ping produced thousands of soundings in a wide swath along the seabed. Swath after swath, like mowing the lawn, millions of soundings were stitched together to reveal the shape of the seabed.

Over five years, data from six multibeam surveys were composed, showing a vivid sequence of changes to the seabed.[1] The mound of sand, piled high at the start, slowly began flattening out across the seabed toward the wreckage. Filling the scours and covering the site, the sand berm was protecting the site, if only for a while, as archaeologists worked to remove all artifacts from harm's way.

1. David J. Bernstein, Mark Wilde-Ramsing, Christopher W. Freeman, and Benjamin W. Sumners, "2015 Shallow Water Hydrographic Surveys in Support of Archaeological Site Preservation: *Queen Anne's Revenge* Wreck Site, North Carolina," *Proceedings of U.S. Hydrographic Conference 2015*.

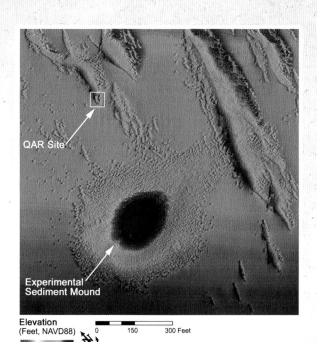

QAR Site

Experimental
Sediment Mound

Elevation
(Feet, NAVD88) 0   150   300 Feet

-20   -27

**Geodynamics team of hydrographers and
multibeam sonar instrumentation provide
a vivid view of the seabed at the *QAR* site.
(Courtesy of Geodynamics LLC)**

**_QAR_ wooden hull frames exposed on the seabed.
Photograph by Julep Gillman-Bryan. (Courtesy of the
North Carolina Department of Natural and Cultural
Resources)**

made of organic materials can last for centuries.
They also survive within concretions. Concretions,
which consist of deposits of calcium carbonate,
shells, sand, and corrosion, are electrochemical
products that form when metallic artifacts, principally iron, come in contact with seawater. During
this process, smaller artifacts in close proximity
can become enveloped and encased in a concretion.
Through careful cleaning, the many crusty concretions found on a shipwreck provide a wealth of
fragmentary clues, some made of wood, bone, and
fiber, that normally would have decomposed and
been lost.

As one can imagine, there is a wide range of
materials that comprise the *QAR* artifact assemblage. These items are listed in Table 3.1 and are
organized by material or composition type, from
the most durable to the least likely to survive. In
the pages to come, you will learn much more about
each of these artifacts and their link to the past.

Many artifacts recovered from the *QAR* site
show signs of stress, abrasion, and alteration that
occurred at some time during their submersion.
Cannons and the large iron rings holding the ship's
rigging were coated with more than an inch of con-

Table 3.1 *Queen Anne's Revenge* Artifact Material Types

Material Type	Noninclusive List of Artifacts for Each Type
Gold	Gold grains, nuggets, clipped jewelry
Mercury	Residue from medical syringe
Stone (lithic)	Ballast, grinding stones, whetstones, paint muller, gunflints
Lead	Ammunition, sounding weights, bilge strainers, numerals, aprons, toilet liner, lantern rivets, cloth seal
Pewter	Plates, porringer, spoons, clyster, syringe, gaming pieces
Ceramic	Vessel forms, bricks, tobacco pipes
Glass	Bottles, stemware, trade beads, window panes
Silver	Coins, sewing needle, ladle and spoons, ornamental spangle, musket worm, buckles (silver plated)
Copper alloy	Bells, lamp finial, navigational and surveying instruments, weights (nested and coin), powder scoop, mortar and pestle, straight pins, buttons, buckles, beads, clothing hook, parts from copper kettles, fishing leader, chain, pickler, stopcock
Iron, cast	Cannon, cannonballs, hand grenades, musket barrels, cooking pots, cauterizing iron, scissors
Iron, wrought	Nails, spikes, barrel hoops, hooks, bars, lifting jacks, hand tools, rigging elements, shackles
Coal	Clinkers (possibly intrusive)
Chemical compound	Gunpowder residue from grenade
Modern synthetic	Intrusive items—plastic bottles, tin can and food tray, golf ball, wooden cigar tip, galvanized nails, plywood, fishing line, net, and lures
Bone	Food remains (mostly pig or cattle)
Hair	Caulking
Horn and shell	Lantern pane, sword handle, pearl
Wood	Hull planks, frames, sheathing, cannon tampions, grenade fuses, sternpost, dirk handle, cask heads and staves, button core
Other forest products	Tar, resin
Plant fiber	Rope, cannon wadding, sailcloth, paper from cannon powder charge

cretion. Lead patches from the ship's lower hull and pewter plates from the dining table were twisted and distorted. Glass and ceramic containers from that same table were mostly broken and widely dispersed. A good example is a large ceramic container (an oil jar), once located in the stern of the sinking ship, whose pieces have been found scattered throughout the debris field. It is imperative for us to determine the physical ability of artifacts to withstand post-sinking conditions and survive, as well as what might have been lost from the record, as we conduct our archaeological investigations seeking to learn more about the life of pirates.

Despite the ravages of time, we have been recovering hundreds of thousands of individual artifacts from the *QAR* site for study and with them a trove of information, intrigue, and mystery. Now let us move on and find out how underwater archaeologists and their colleagues continue the business of collecting evidence left aboard Blackbeard's abandoned flagship.

Concretion buildup on iron ring straps that held deadeyes and ship's rigging. Photograph by Julep Gillman-Bryan. (Courtesy of the North Carolina Department of Natural and Cultural Resources)

CHAPTER FOUR

Opening the Pirate's Chest

Archaeological Investigations

The helmsman's arms and shoulders ached for days after bringing the vessel through the fickle ocean inlet. As he reached the seaward entrance channel, the offshore winds had unexpectedly stiffened, coinciding with the start of ebb tide. This unwelcome occurrence brought a clash of opposing forces to the water's surface, which danced in agitation. As the vessel sank into the trough, angry waves crested above the cabin roof and threatened to crash onto the frightened crew. They huddled behind the helmsman as he labored to keep the surging craft moving forward into the oncoming swell and fight its natural tendency to turn sideways to the waves. If that happened, he knew no further corrective action would be possible. Doom loomed large.

After 20 minutes of battling through Beaufort Inlet, in an instant the helmsman's effort was rewarded by calmness. The waters flattened out as the vessel cruised into the inlet throat and out of the wind. The relieved crew began to unwind and offer a hearty hurrah; their thoughts turned to setting foot on land and filling their hungry bellies. Then with a jolt, the vessel slammed to a complete stop. In the haze and without experience navigating the web of channels, the helmsman had inadvertently allowed the craft to stray. The impact of running hard onto the sandbar had not only sent the crew

sprawling but also sheared off the vessel's steering mechanism, rendering it helpless. Meanwhile the rapidly retreating tide threatened to leave the vessel high and dry on the shoal, like a beached whale. The crew worked fervently to free themselves.

This scenario may resemble the situation that occurred in early June 1718 as Blackbeard attempted to bring his flagship through the unmarked inlet; however, this was an account of our first dive on the *QAR* wreck site on December 17, 1996, just a few weeks after its initial discovery. Earlier in the day, we deployed a buoy using a set of land ranges provided by UAB archaeological conservator Leslie Bright, who recorded them on his visit to the site the day after discovery. This was a tried-and-true mapping method used along the coast since the eighteenth century to navigate Beaufort Inlet according to the 1738 Wimble map. As soon as we anchored near the marker buoy, things began to deteriorate. Our first diver suffered leg cramps as he kicked hard against a strong current in the cool December water. By the time he reached the anchor line to start his descent, the pain was too much, and he clung to the bowline trying to get the attention of the boat crew, who meanwhile were at the stern helping a second diver into a dry suit, which is specially designed to protect divers from frigid water.

Unfortunately, we seldom used them in our work, and to make matters worse, the one onboard was a bit too small. After much struggling by the diver to squeeze into the suit, he immediately aborted his dive because the suit restricted his movement and caused unacceptable discomfort. Both divers were then fished back into the boat.

As this was going on, a shift in tide brought inlet water flowing back out against the wind. With the turbulent seas demanding immediate departure, there was no time to recover the deployed buoy. This was the beginning of the scary scene navigating the inlet we described above, which ended in the grounding of UAB's *Snap Dragon II*. Eventually, we worked our vessel off the sandbar and continued on. With a broken steering cable and dusk becoming night, the boat was guided manually at idle speed back to the public boat ramp, where the first crewman to jump ashore lost his footing on the slippery dock and fell hard on his back. With all that happened that day, several of us thought that the ghost of Blackbeard must still be guarding his vessel. Needless to say, we gained a healthy dose of respect for the conditions we would face in the future. After the initial dives of 1996, however, the earliest stage of the *QAR* project did not take place in the waters of Beaufort Inlet but on dry land, where we began planning how best to proceed with exploring and understanding the shipwreck.

Archaeological Investigations: Planning to Engage

No one involved with the *QAR* Shipwreck Project, including us, anticipated the extreme excitement from the public at the discovery of *Queen Anne's Revenge*. While the media attention and public scrutiny were a bit much at times, they pushed us to provide detailed research, site recovery, and artifact conservation procedures prior to expeditions to the *QAR* site. Planning is certainly a good thing when working on a high-profile site out on the ocean.

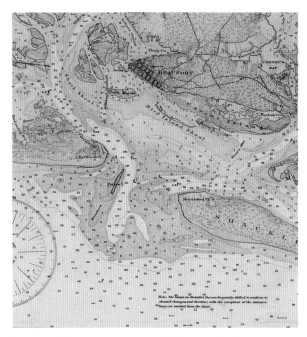

Beaufort Inlet prior to the establishment of a fixed channel shown on Coast & Geodetic Survey chart #420 (1900). (Historical Chart and Map Collection, Office of Coast Survey, NOAA)

R/V *Snap Dragon II* battles rough sea conditions in Beaufort Inlet. (Courtesy of the North Carolina Department of Natural and Cultural Resources)

Tribute to the Late Phil Masters

DR. MARK U. WILDE-RAMSING

The late Philip D. Masters's persistence and enthusiasm not only led to the discovery of *Queen Anne's Revenge* but helped sustain archaeological investigations and public outreach ever since. Phil lobbied North Carolina legislators, promoted the *QAR* shipwreck project beyond the borders of the Tar Heel state, and provided his company's equipment, time, and research to advance better understanding of the eighteenth-century wreck site with its trove of artifacts.

Phil's unwavering dedication was best illustrated by his commitment to discover every shipwreck lying on the ocean floor within Beaufort Inlet. From 1997 until 2005, he surveyed the entire area with increasing sophistication and intensity. His aim was to identify any outlying remains associated with Blackbeard's flagship, as well as search for *Adventure*, which was reportedly lost at the same time within "gunshot" range of *Queen Anne's Revenge*. Phil's primary target, however, continued to be the Spanish ship *El Salvador*, which foundered in the area in 1750 on its return voyage to Europe carrying a shipment of silver. Phil's ability to detect signals that might lead to the discovery of historic shipwrecks was enhanced by his purchase of the survey vessel *Anomaly*, which he outfitted with a high-tech cesium magnetometer, a differential GPS navigational system, and sophisticated computer equipment. By dividing the search area into dozens of survey blocks, he meticulously covered the entire area surrounding Beaufort Inlet. Spacing survey runs 30 ft. apart enabled him to detect very small disturbances in the earth's magnetic field, some caused by objects as small as a cast-iron kettle, which divers found as they investigated promising areas.

In the end, Phil piloted *Anomaly* nearly 2,000 miles while recording hundreds of targets of interest. Areas where he detected nothing were equally important. Such was the case for the area immediately surrounding *Queen Anne's Revenge*, which provided evidence that Blackbeard's flagship did not break up in a storm but, rather, ran aground and deteriorated in place, as reported by eyewitnesses. A single eighteenth-century anchor lying 420 ft. offshore, however, probably was associated with the pirate ship.

That is not to say there wasn't precedent for similar situations, for indeed today's North Carolina Underwater Archaeology Branch began and developed during the Civil War centennial with the highly visible 1962–63 exploration and salvage of the British blockade-runner *Modern Greece*. UAB offices are still located on the grounds of Fort Fisher State Historic Site and within a half-mile of the wreck site. Ten years later, UAB was involved in the discovery and early exploration of the USS *Monitor*.

In the years that followed, however, attention was directed toward implementing a management program designed to identify, assess, and protect the broader spectrum of submerged sites within North Carolina waters. The state's historical shipwreck database includes data for over 5,000 sinkings spanning 400 years.[1]

By the time the suspected *QAR* wreckage was discovered, the North Carolina Department of Natural and Cultural Resources boasted one of

With its shaft and ring in a set position and aligned toward *Queen Anne's Revenge*, the anchor may have been used by the pirates to kedge the stranded vessel during rescue operations immediately after sinking.

Under Phil's direction, his divers investigated hundreds of magnetometer targets and, in doing so, found most were caused by iron dredge pipes, steel cable, and other modern debris. A few sites, however, dated to the eighteenth century. Of note was a widely scattered debris field on the western edge of the inlet that included cannons, anchors, a wagon axle, and other artifacts and has yet to be fully explored. It is also very likely that one of his promising targets lying near *Queen Anne's Revenge*, let's say "about Gunshot" away, that has yet to be investigated due to thick sand cover will someday be identified as *Adventure*. When that happens, Phil Masters's dedication and pioneering spirit will once again rise to the surface and be recognized by an international audience.

Phil Masters aboard *Pelican III*. (Courtesy of the North Carolina Department of Natural and Cultural Resources)

the strongest underwater archaeology programs in the nation with five full-time staff members, its research boat *Snap Dragon II*, a modest conservation laboratory, and various tools for finding, positioning, and exploring submerged sites. "State waters" include all navigable interior bays, rivers, and creeks and ocean waters out to the three-mile limit. Within that area, any shipwrecks and artifacts lost for more than ten years become state property.[2] In our role as custodians of this rich vestige of maritime history, we would more often be found wading in the shallows of a muddy creek exploring a discarded derelict vessel stripped of anything valuable than diving in open ocean water on actual shipwrecks. On November 21, 1996, however, everyone's attention was drawn to the shipwreck found in Beaufort Inlet.

Conversations between UAB staff, officials in Raleigh, and Intersal personnel in Florida were held in secret over the next three months, since our leading

U.S. Navy divers assist the state in salvaging artifacts from the *Modern Greece* shipwreck site in 1962 and 1963. (Courtesy of the North Carolina Department of Natural and Cultural Resources)

UAB archaeological conservator Leslie Bright with the *Modern Greece* artifact collection. (Courtesy of the North Carolina Department of Natural and Cultural Resources)

concern was how to protect the site from looting once word spread that Blackbeard's flagship may have been found. The site's relatively accessible location gave rise to the fear that relic hunters would quickly pick apart the remnants of the shipwreck. Various protective measures were considered, and by the time field operations began in the fall of 1997, a 30-ft. tower with a radar detection system had been erected at Fort Macon State Park, the nearest point of land to the shipwreck. Unfortunately, the sensitive radar was often tripped by severe weather or seabirds, which became an irritant to staff, especially when we were awakened in the

dead of night by the automated phone message, "Radar alert! Radar alert!" With advancements in security technology, the radar was replaced by a motion-activated, high-definition camera tied to a computer station housed in the storage building at the base of the tower. The system was designed to activate when a boat lingered in the zone around the shipwreck site. From the office or at home we could evaluate "incidents" captured by the camera. The only difficulty with this system came from a very persistent grackle, who for a time was determined to nest in the camera housing. As for real threats, over the years no serious cases of looting were detected by site security systems or observed during inspection dives.

In hindsight, our most effective security system at the *QAR* site was one that cost us no money but, rather, came in response to a simple invitation. The Cape Lookout region, with its many World War II shipwrecks, provides some of the best dive opportunities along the east coast. During the 1998 *QAR* expedition, local shop owners, charter boat captains, and scuba instructors were invited to come visit us at the *QAR* site. The local crew eagerly jumped at the chance to see the pirate ship up close. Fortunately, clear water on the day they dove provided an unobstructed view of the small pile of cannons and anchors that protruded a few feet above the seabed. Around and around the divers circled, like riders on a merry-go-round they went, carefully inspecting every aspect of the mounded ruins. The experience brought them a deep sense of pride as they were among the first to explore the wreckage from the days of pirates. From that day on, the local dive community remained watchful stewards of the site.

Another much-debated security issue was whether to deploy a marker buoy near the shipwreck. Some argued that the buoy would give unauthorized divers a head start on finding the site, which would lead to artifact theft. Others suggested that it wasn't reasonable to expect boaters to stay out of the restricted area, which encompassed a 300-ft. diameter around *Queen Anne's Revenge*, if they didn't know where it was.[3] Ultimately, they argued, a buoy would provide an important reference for the security camera, which tipped the scale. In the fall of 1998, the same year the community divers were invited to visit the shipwreck, a buoy was deployed within close proximity to the shipwreck. It remained in place until March 2001, when a fierce nor'easter lashed the Cape Lookout coast. Its fury was strong enough to wear down and then break the mooring chain. The buoy drifted through the night and was found the next day on nearby Atlantic Beach. After being cleaned, the wayward marker was redeployed with heavier mooring chain and remained on the site until the fall of 2006, when it broke loose again. This time it drifted all the way inside Beaufort Inlet to Bird Shoal, more than two miles away! It was recovered with difficulty, but by then it was in no condition to be redeployed. By that time, we deemed a replacement buoy was unnecessary because accurate Global Positioning System (GPS) units were available to the boating public, which provided them the knowledge to avoid the restricted area. Likewise, the security camera had become obsolete, having been replaced by the watchful eyes of the local community.

Otherwise, our planning in the pilot stages focused on how best to investigate the newly discovered site in Beaufort Inlet. Underwater archaeological operations can be complex and require a high degree of preparation to determine the overall goals, strategies, and methods to be used dependent on available vessels, equipment, and personnel. We took a phased approach aimed at determining what the site represented, what condition it was in, its historical and archaeological significance, and how best to share the exciting discovery with an eager public. Most importantly, we sought to protect its remains.[4]

A paramount concern was what money would be available to support the necessary fieldwork and associated studies. The announcement of the discovery by Governor James Hunt on March 3, 1997, was greeted with great fanfare. That, no doubt,

View from the security camera mounted on a 30-ft. tower at Fort Macon State Park showing the *QAR* wreck site in the distance. (Courtesy of the North Carolina Department of Natural and Cultural Resources)

Local dive boat visits the *QAR* site. (Courtesy of the North Carolina Department of Natural and Cultural Resources)

QAR marker buoy ashore on Atlantic Beach, March 21, 2001. (Courtesy of the North Carolina Department of Natural and Cultural Resources)

Fleet of *QAR* research vessels, from left to right: R/V *Sea Hawk*, R/V *Snap Dragon II*, and Intersal's *Pelican III*. Photo taken from R/V *Capricorn*. (Courtesy of the North Carolina Department of Natural and Cultural Resources)

led North Carolina legislators to look favorably on the funds we requested to explore and evaluate the *QAR* site. Annual state appropriations supported three years of funding, which gave us the chance to gather information upon which to produce a site management plan. Based on those findings, our overall recommendation was to move forward with full recovery of the shipwreck because of its historical significance and vulnerable nature, but not before a comprehensive recovery plan was developed, conservation facilities were in place, and permanent staff was hired. Once these prerequisites were met, we estimated that field recovery would take 5 years and conservation another 20 years, with a total price tag of an estimated $4.5 million.[5]

State funding on an annual basis was forthcoming for the project over the next few years in varying amounts, but other factors were in play. The one-two punch packed by Hurricanes Dennis and Floyd in August and September 1999 had a detrimental impact through scouring at the *QAR* site, which required us to focus on salvaging portions of the shipwreck. The eventual loss of state allocations for the *QAR* recovery project because of costly hurricane cleanup and reparation was equally devastating. What state funds were available went toward developing the *QAR* conservation facility on the West

Research Campus of East Carolina University and provided time to develop a comprehensive recovery plan. Additional funding for lab development and limited field projects came from federal and corporate grants and private donations. Beginning in the fall of 2006, state funds once again began flowing to the *QAR* project and were used to create a permanent *QAR* staff for artifact recovery and, most importantly, conservation. With state aid coupled with major corporate support, we began a decade of full-scale recovery efforts. During this period, approximately 60 percent of the projected site area was excavated, and all artifacts were taken to the conservation laboratory. In the summer of 2015, a onetime state appropriation of $1.5 million accelerated the conservation of recovered materials and supported expansion of museum exhibits in preparation for June 2018 and the 300th anniversary of the sinking of *Queen Anne's Revenge*.

From the inception of *QAR* fieldwork, *Snap Dragon II*, the UAB's 24-ft. dive boat, with Captain Julep Gillman-Bryan at the helm, has been a mainstay during recovery efforts. Additionally, other larger research vessels provided support roles, notably UNC-Wilmington's R/V *Sea Hawk* (Captain Jerry Compeau), Intersal's *Pelican III* (Captain Mike Daniel), and UNC–Chapel Hill's R/V *Capricorn* (Captain Joe Purifoy). The N.C. Marine Fisheries Division's motorized barge R/V *Shell Point* (Captain Tom Piner), however, was by far the best suited for major dive and recovery operations at the site and became the *QAR* project's primary work platform beginning in the fall of 2000. Used to transport and deploy oyster shells for reef construction projects in the state's inland waters, the vessel featured a spacious open deck from which to conduct dive and recovery operations. Its diesel pump drove hydraulic dredges used by divers to move large volumes of sand and bring sediments to the surface, where they were sifted for artifacts. Captain Piner could navigate R/V *Shell Point* to the shipwreck within minutes of leaving the dock and, once there, maneuver quickly to a position directly over the shipwreck. In the last few years of full recovery operations, R/V *Jones Bay*, a similar but smaller motorized barge also provided by the N.C. Marine Fisheries Division, enabled archaeological work to continue when its sister ship was needed elsewhere.

Finding a place from which to stage and conduct field expeditions in a resort town was a challenge. Eventually, an ideal situation for accommodating both vessels and crew was achieved not much more than a mile from the shipwreck site. Beginning in 2005, the U.S. Coast Guard Station Fort Macon provided dock space and secure shore storage for recovered objects, and within walking distance were the barracks at Fort Macon State Park where the field crew was housed. Those of us working on-site varied from a handful of archaeologists and boat crew to more than two dozen members of a recovery team, which also included nondiving conservators, temporary staff, students and professors, and volunteer divers. Due to the nature of the work and the excitement surrounding exploration of Blackbeard's ship, there was never any shortage of offers to help when it came to working at the *QAR* site.

In terms of equipment, standard scuba gear was used during archaeological investigations. Because expeditions took place in the late spring or fall before water temperatures dipped below 70°F, divers donned wet suits of varying thicknesses to keep warm and protect their skin from crustaceans and critters. A tank of air provided about an hour on the bottom, which gave divers a good working period before they fatigued. Divers generally made 3 to 4 dives daily; the highest total for all divers in a single day was 28 dives.

One of the most important technological developments during the project was the Interspiro Divator Mark II, a full-face mask with wireless communication known simply as an AGA mask. During the first dive expedition in 1997, *QAR* project divers could only communicate by writing notes to one another using pencils and slates and had no contact

N.C. Marine Fisheries R/V *Shell Point*. (Courtesy of the North Carolina Department of Natural and Cultural Resources)

Divers equipped with AGA masks preparing sandbags for deployment. Photograph by Julep Gillman-Bryan. (Courtesy of the North Carolina Department of Natural and Cultural Resources)

with operators on the research vessel above without coming to the surface. AGA masks, introduced during the second field season, were a transformational tool that greatly enhanced the efficiency of dive operations and overall safety. Divers could talk to one another, talk to a technician on the surface, or talk to the world during *QAR* Dive Live, as will be revealed later in our story. Although a bit cumbersome at first, AGA masks became a mainstay during the gradiometer survey of 1999, and we never worked without them afterward.

Having learned the general nature of field planning and operations, think back for a moment

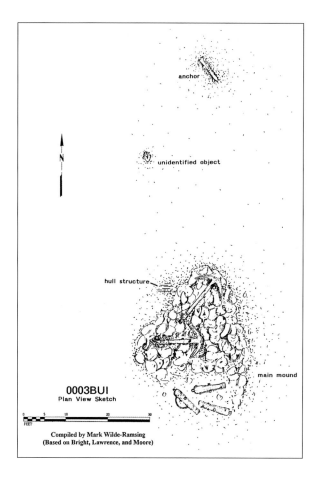

anchor

N

unidentified object

hull structure

main mound

0003BUI
Plan View Sketch

0   5   10   20   30
FEET

Compiled by Mark Wilde-Ramsing
(Based on Bright, Lawrence, and Moore)

We were not able to add much more to the initial report from the day after discovery that described the wreckage as a low mound of heavily encrusted objects. Water clarity, however, was about to dramatically change for the better.

Is It Really a Ship? The First Field Season

Returning in early October to begin the 1997 expedition, we marveled at the gin-clear waters that surrounded the *QAR* site. During the first week and again later in the expedition, water clarity allowed us to see, in its entirety, the room-size pile of cannons, anchors, and numerous unidentifiable concretions projecting from the seabed. Not far to the north, we sighted a large anchor with one fluke majestically stretching toward the water's surface.

The plan for the 1997 investigation was to retrieve the maximum amount of information using methods that created minimal disturbance to the shipwreck. Noninvasive techniques involved both still and video underwater photography, scale drawings, and artistic sketches. More direct procedures were manual probing, limited test excavations, wood and sediment sampling, and recovery of diagnostic and sample artifacts. Our overall goal was to determine the site's layout, components, and surrounding environmental conditions. We were particularly focused on key elements that could answer the most basic questions, the first being, did this site represent a shipwreck and not just a pile of ocean junk? The more difficult question after determining whether it was wreckage turned to figuring out which vessel it represented, specifically *Queen Anne's Revenge* (ex. *Concorde*) or not.

The first order of business was to set in place boat moorings made of large concrete blocks and

to the early days when we first visited the newly discovered shipwreck in Beaufort Inlet. After the ill-fated attempt in December, we again returned to the area on April 15, 1997, this time using a handheld GPS unit to relocate the site. As divers reached the bottom in the murky water, they found a small anchor within the wreckage; it was the very same one we had deployed during the December visit using only ranges. The find gave us a sense of pride in proving the value of doing things "the old way"! The April dive and the one that followed on July 11 increased our confidence that we would be able to find the wreck site on a daily basis in anticipation of the fall 1997 expedition. Water visibility and bottom conditions were poor both times, prompting divers to joke that they would have to practice up on their "braille" archaeology before returning in the fall.

Reference lines across the *QAR* site. (Courtesy of the North Carolina Department of Natural and Cultural Resources)

chain to which strong anchor lines and buoys were attached. We placed moorings at the cardinal ends of the site, 200 ft. from the central, exposed mound. Once the blocks settled into the seabed, they remained permanent and were able to hold research vessels directly above the shipwreck site. Our next task was to establish a reference system on the seafloor by placing two perpendicular lines over the *QAR* site. Yes, indeed, X marked the spot! Both the north/south baseline (150 ft.) and east/west transect line (100 ft.) were pinned down with metal stakes placed every 5 ft. that both secured the lines and provided points to tie measuring tapes. We used the method of triangulation, measuring distances from two baseline stakes or from one stake and recording the angle relative to the baseline to position excavation units and individual artifacts on the overall site plan.

As the expedition proceeded, other tasks were undertaken. The relative height of the wreckage was determined by stretching a thin line from a reference point on a vertical pole, holding it horizontal using an attached line level, and measuring down to an exposed object. This process revealed that the highest point atop the mound was the fluke of anchor A-1, which extended 4 ft. above the surrounding seabed. The rest of the exposed wreckage protruded 2 ft. or less above the sandy bottom. Divers

also conducted a thorough metal detector survey to investigate the extent of buried artifacts extending out from the center of the wreckage. We were surprised by the high number of targets within an area approximately 150 ft. by 90 ft.

Another technique used a metal rod to probe the seabed in an effort to detect the ship's wooden hull. It was difficult, however, to discern what the hard surfaces were; some may have been wood, but the rod could not be pushed down more than a foot or so in all the places we tried. Using a series of small test excavations, we determined that the rod encountered a layer of hard-packed sand. This was that zone of erosion-resistant sediment later identified by marine geologists during bottom coring studies. We were disappointed to realize that little or none of the ship's wooden hull had survived.

We placed a 3-ft.-by-6-ft. excavation unit, Test Unit 1, at the southern end of the site to record and systematically retrieve associated artifacts prior to the recovery of Cannon C-2. Divers used a small dredge to carefully excavate and peel back the layers of sand and shell. In profile, three separate sediment layers or zones were identified. The upper zone consisted of poorly sorted sand that constantly moved across the seabed. Below this was a 12-in. layer of sand and coarse shell that had been deposited during storm-generated scour events. This zone contained the vast majority of all artifacts dating to the eighteenth century, but it also included some nineteenth- and twentieth-century debris. The bottoms of large objects as well as smaller, heavier artifacts such as lead shot and gold grains sat at the interface between this layer and the underlying densely packed zone of fine sand and silt. No artifacts could migrate into this scour-resistant layer.

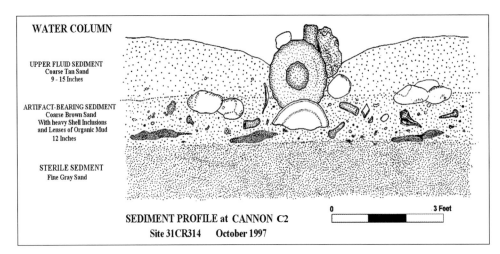

WATER COLUMN

UPPER FLUID SEDIMENT
Coarse Tan Sand
9 - 15 Inches

ARTIFACT-BEARING SEDIMENT
Coarse Brown Sand
With heavy Shell Inclusions
and Lenses of Organic Mud
12 Inches

STERILE SEDIMENT
Fine Gray Sand

SEDIMENT PROFILE at CANNON C2
Site 31CR314   October 1997

0   3 Feet

Stratigraphic profile of sediments and artifacts, Test Unit 1 sediment profile. Mark Wilde-Ramsing, illustrator. (Courtesy of the North Carolina Department of Natural and Cultural Resources)

Test Unit 1 produced 284 individual objects, including ceramics, glass, wood and bone fragments, and two pewter dishes, along with numerous lead shot and a large quantity of ballast stones and concretions, as well as Cannon C-2. Based on the number of items recovered from this relatively small excavation, we realized that the shipwreck had the potential to contain hundreds of thousands of individual artifacts, along with a wealth of archaeological information related to the ship's function, cultural affiliation, purpose, and place within society.[6]

At the end of the 1997 expedition, we were certain the debris represented the remains of a wrecked ship. And while we could not say for certain that *Queen Anne's Revenge* had been found, the site layout and types of artifacts fit the characteristics of only that one ship among those known through historical records to have been lost in the area. It was also apparent from excavations that recent scouring had deflated the shipwreck, leaving little overburden to protect its remains. Despite the success of the 1997 field season, we also realized that prior to developing a management plan, we needed a fuller understanding of the shipwreck's buried remains. Therefore, a major expedition was planned for the next year with a focus on further exploratory excavation.

Scattered Far and Wide: Continued Explorations

In the fall of 1998, as the sandy overburden was being sucked away from around buried artifacts, an amazing discovery was made. It was a speck of gold that caught the eye of *QAR* archaeological conservator Wayne Lusardi, who not only saw the tiny artifact but was able to gather it up in a plastic baggie and bring it to the surface. It was the first of many bits of gold dust that would be recovered. Its discovery fit neatly into the 1998 expedition goal to explore buried remains across the wreck site. To accomplish this, three exploratory trenches were placed to transect the site at its north, south, and middle portions. During excavation, once sediment was removed to the point where artifacts were partially exposed, archaeologists carefully mapped their relative locations and closely inspected them. Recognizable artifacts made of glass, ceramic, or metal were collected for analysis and eventual display rather than being left behind and potentially lost. In the fall of 2004, a fourth transect trench on the site's west side was excavated to complete the exploratory phase. All together an estimated 15 percent of the buried area was opened to allow examination, in situ mapping, and collection of diagnostic artifacts across the site.

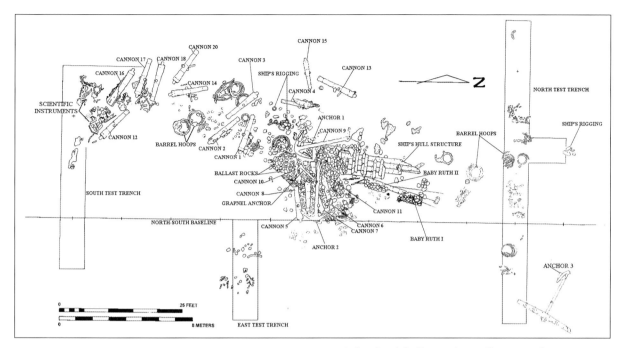

CANNON 20
CANNON 15
CANNON 17
CANNON 18
CANNON 3
CANNON 13
CANNON 16
CANNON 14
SHIP'S RIGGING
CANNON 4
NORTH TEST TRENCH
SCIENTIFIC
INSTRUMENTS
SHIP'S RIGGING
CANNON 12
ANCHOR 1
BARREL HOOPS
CANNON 2
CANNON 9
BARREL HOOPS
CANNON 1
SHIP'S HULL STRUCTURE
BALLAST ROCKS
BABY RUTH II
CANNON 10
SOUTH TEST TRENCH
CANNON 8
GRAPNEL ANCHOR
CANNON 11
NORTH-SOUTH BASELINE
CANNON 5
CANNON 6
BABY RUTH I
CANNON 7
ANCHOR 2
ANCHOR 3
0
25 FEET
0
8 METERS
EAST TEST TRENCH

1998 site plan labeling major artifacts. David D. Moore, illustrator. (Courtesy of the North Carolina Department of Natural and Cultural Resources)

To detect buried remains across the entire wreck site without digging and risking disturbance, we initiated a novel technique during expeditions in June and October 1999 and October 2001. Divers placed a gradiometer sensor at 2,064 separate locations on the seabed to collect readings across the entire site. Using this noninvasive instrument, our objective was to identify large, ferrous objects buried beneath bottom sediments, specifically cannons, and determine outer margins of artifact dispersal without further excavation of the site.[7]

The gradiometer, a Schonstadt Model GUA-30 Underwater Magnetic Locator provided by Rob Smith, president of Surface Interval Dive Company, is a type of magnetometer used to detect distortions in the earth's magnetic field, in our case caused primarily by ferrous material (iron) on the *QAR* site. The instrument receives signals from two separate sensors, approximately 2 ft. apart, contained in a single submersible casing. Because the instrument provides readings in terms of the difference, or gradient, between the two sensors, it registers only iron artifacts that affect one sensor

State archaeologist Steve Claggett examines gold grains recovered by *QAR* archaeological conservator Wayne Lusardi. (Courtesy of the North Carolina Department of Natural and Cultural Resources)

Diver placing the gradiometer sensor at a specified location prior to taking a reading. Photograph by Julep Gillman-Bryan. (Courtesy of the North Carolina Department of Natural and Cultural Resources)

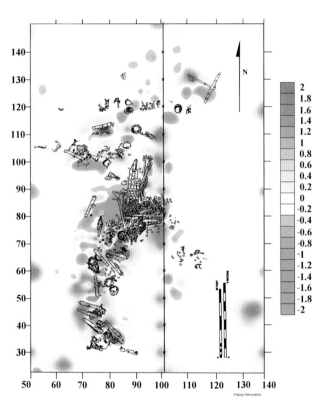

Gradiometer contour map, 1999. (Courtesy of the North Carolina Department of Natural and Cultural Resources)

more than the other. When the artifacts are located directly under the two sensors, the difference in readings allows us to make a projection as to their size and mass. "Noise" from the surroundings is eliminated because artifacts not directly under the two sensors will influence them equally, and since there is no difference, such artifacts do not register.

After recording and contouring the gradiometer data, we were able to produce a really cool, colorized map. This data was integrated with an existing site map, which helped to further delineate the debris field. It also became clear that magnetic disturbances matched well with previously recorded artifacts, such as cannons, anchors, and barrel hoops.

Some of the magnetic disturbances, however, were in places where artifacts remained buried and unknown. In one case, a large disturbance was suspected to represent a previously unknown cannon. And bingo! The presence of Cannon C-23 was confirmed a few years later. This technology allowed us to predict with accuracy what was buried beneath the seafloor without disturbing a grain of sand.

Emergency Recovery: Picking Up the Pieces, Preparing for the Worst

While portions of the ship's hull remained buried and undetected during the first year of archaeological investigations, the 1998 field season was preceded by Hurricane Bonnie, which exposed a portion of the ship's hull pinned under the exposed mound. These remains were mapped in detail

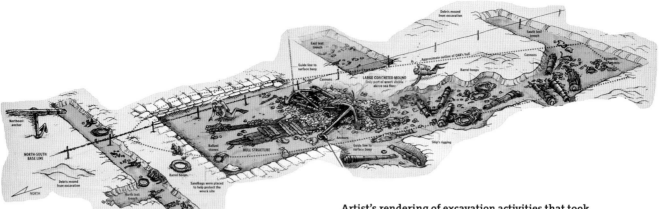

Artist's rendering of excavation activities that took place during the 1998 and 2000 *QAR* expeditions. (Courtesy of the *Charlotte Observer* and the North Carolina Department of Natural and Cultural Resources)

by underwater archaeologist David Moore from the North Carolina Maritime Museum. When we returned a year later, the structure was completely scoured out and exposed as a result of a 1999 hurricane trifecta: Dennis in August, Floyd in September, and Irene in October.

Suspecting this wooden section was all that remained of the ship, we launched an emergency expedition in May 2000 to remove hull timbers from the seafloor to the safety of the conservation lab. Unfortunately, the going was difficult. The first problem we encountered was that the scour hole had filled and completely reburied the structure, thus requiring extensive excavation we hadn't planned on. A bigger problem, though, was the weather; fierce winds out of the south and subsequent rough seas made work at the site impossible. Only during the last three days of the planned two-week expedition were we able to work effectively. On the other hand, once work commenced, water visibility was excellent, enabling us to quickly excavate the soft, sandy overburden and begin recovery. After the attached frame timbers had been gently pried away and brought to the surface, the hull planks were cut with a handsaw at the point where they disappeared under the main rubble mound. Padded ladders were used to support the delicate waterlogged artifacts as they were lifted to the surface. The final lift included thin pine boards

Divers placing hull plank timber on foam-covered ladder during emergency recovery operations. Photograph by Julep Gillman-Bryan. (Courtesy of the North Carolina Department of Natural and Cultural Resources)

that served as the outermost hull sheathing to deter hungry teredo worms from attacking the ship's oak hull planks. While recovery of the wooden section was a success, there was not time to excavate and recover small artifacts from under the hull structure. That was completed in the fall of 2000 when, for the first time, we used standardized 5-ft.-by-5-ft. excavation units delineated by metal grid frames.

Apothecary mortar recovered in September after Hurricane Ophelia passed near the *QAR* site. (Courtesy of the North Carolina Department of Natural and Cultural Resources)

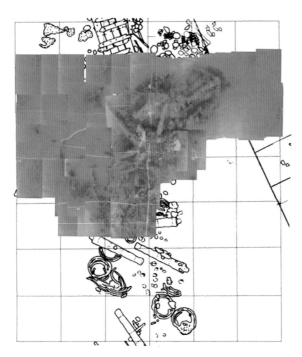

Individual photographs pieced together over *QAR* site map to create the 2004 photo-mosaic. (Courtesy of the North Carolina Department of Natural and Cultural Resources)

This method then became a mainstay for recovery operations. The overall density of artifacts under the hull section was considerably less than that found in Test Unit 1. We surmised that what we found had migrated to that location during episodes of scouring years after the ship was lost.

Hurricanes continued to blow across the site over the next few years, each time providing new evidence of the scour/burial process. After Hurricane Isabel's September 2003 visit, we recovered a lead bilge pump strainer from the scoured seabed. The poster child of our after-storm finds, however, appeared two years later when *QAR* archaeological field director Chris Southerly and his team found a brass apothecary mortar loose and rolling around on the bottom, dislodged by the forces of Hurricane Ophelia. The presence of only lead and brass artifacts in scour areas raised concerns for what "less robust" artifacts were being washed away and lost forever. With existing funding, we undertook two initiatives to counter the impacts from the seemingly endless barrage of tropical storms, including 15 hurricanes from 1996 through 2005.[8]

The first initiative was to record all exposed remains using photogrammetry and create a photo-mosaic. After several failed attempts due to weather, an expedition sponsored by *National Geographic* was launched in April 2004, during which divers successfully photo-documented exposed wreckage. During the five-day project, more than 300 digital images were taken across the wreckage, referenced by a 10-ft.-by-20-ft. metal grid set at a known height and tied into the site's baseline. *QAR* computer technician Karen Browning then pieced the images together like an intricate jigsaw puzzle to create a detailed, composite photograph revealing the extent of *QAR* artifact exposure existing at that time.[9]

We designed the second initiative to supplement the areas that had been fully excavated (meaning all artifacts in a unit are recovered), which over the course of the first ten years had totaled less than 2 percent of the projected site area. This would

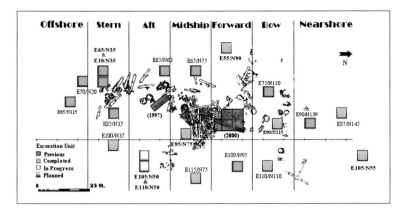

Plan showing units excavated during stratified sampling at *QAR* site. (Courtesy of the North Carolina Department of Natural and Cultural Resources)

provide a more comprehensive sampling of artifacts across the entire wreck site. These efforts were not the desired full recovery but a necessary interim step to ensure that should a catastrophic storm directly impact the *QAR* site, a representative portion would be saved. During expeditions in the spring of 2005 and spring of 2006, a stratified sampling regime was used to excavate an additional 9 percent of the shipwreck site. Based on our existing knowledge of site layout, seven zones (nearshore, bow, forward, midship, aft, stern, and offshore) were laid out across the site. Within each zone, three excavation units were placed to examine evidence related to port and starboard. Two units were placed at the nearshore and offshore ends to seek the extent of artifact distribution. In all, a total of 23 units were totally excavated, all bearing artifacts.[10]

During the sampling program, interesting individual artifacts came to the surface, and we made various observations regarding their overall distribution. One of the most exciting finds was a large portion of the lower sternpost. Dislodged, probably during an early twentieth-century channel dredging operation, it was found lying flat some distance from where it once had been attached. Sampling areas across the site also provided further insights related to activity areas and the ship's original layout. For instance, cask hoop parts and other classes of artifacts appeared to have been segregated, which would shed light on shipboard activities. Pleased with the success of the sampling program,

Sternpost recovery in 2007. (Courtesy of the North Carolina Department of Natural and Cultural Resources)

we were hopeful that full recovery would soon follow and bring many more surprises to expand our understanding of the ship once commanded by Blackbeard.

Total Recovery: Full Speed Ahead

On Tuesday, October 10, 2006, state archaeologists, conservators, and support crew rolled out of their bunks in the barracks at Fort Macon State Park, gathered gear for the week ahead, walked across the street, and entered the U.S. Coast Guard Station. Those who lived locally drove over the bridge to Atlantic Beach and up the strand highway to the north end of Bogue Banks. After passing through the guard gate, some stopped by the small dining

Pirate Archaeology and the Archaeology of Pirates

DR. CHARLES R. EWEN

Pirates and buried treasure: two images that in the popular imagination are inseparable. Curiously, only Captain Kidd is known to have cached some treasure that was later retrieved, but it doesn't seem to be stopping anybody, especially the professional treasure hunters, from looking. Archaeologists also look for treasure, but they are more interested in the story the treasure and other artifacts can tell. That is why working with treasure hunters is something that most archaeologists would only do under duress. Their different goals are not always compatible. Archaeologists take their time and record *all* the data from a wreck. That meticulousness cuts into the treasure hunters' bottom line. Treasure hunters want to find things, while archaeologists want to find things out.

Conducting archaeology on pirate sites is not the rollicking adventure one might think or see portrayed in movies. Finding pirate sites is difficult. Piracy, like any other illegal activity, was often hidden from the authorities of the time. It is well known to law enforcement that if crimes aren't solved in the first 48 hours after they are committed, then the likelihood of successfully cracking the case is greatly diminished. That makes efforts to verify the identity of the centuries-old wreckage in Beaufort Inlet one of history's ultimate cold cases!

So, how does one distinguish a pirate from an honest sailor? If Hollywood has conveyed anything, it is how to spot a pirate. Indeed, pirates may have actually sported hooks, peg legs, and eye patches, but then, so did many less nefarious seafaring men. It was a dangerous profession. Perhaps their ships were distinctive? Since pirates usually stole theirs from merchants, they would also have been similar, at least initially. Without the historical record, it is very difficult to identify a pirate ship based on archaeology alone. At least so far.

Archaeologists are working toward developing a "pirate pattern" in the archaeological record. For instance, are there different proportions of arms, cargo, navigation instruments, and personal items between pirate ships, merchant ships, and naval vessels? Are there different types of artifacts that characterize each type

facility for breakfast before meeting others at the staging area and wharf where R/V *Shell Point* was moored. In a short while the vessel was loaded with equipment and personnel, then it slowly made its way out the basin for the short run to the *QAR* site. In the morning fog, laughing gulls followed close behind crying for food, just as their progenitors had bothered Ignatius Pell and fellow pirates centuries ago after Blackbeard had marooned them on a nearby island. The birds slowly dropped away, one by one, as R/V *Shell Point* rounded the point and entered the throat of the inlet. Crew members were afforded their first chance to gauge site conditions. Occasionally during this expedition, Captain Piner, dive safety officer Gillman-Bryan, and archaeological field director Southerly concurred that the seas would not allow safe working conditions and returned to shore. That happened to be the situation the day before, when the crew spent their time carefully sifting through sediment collected earlier of vessel? So far, with only a couple of pirate ships excavated, the data are anecdotal. Pirates appear to have often sailed with their cannons preloaded, always ready to fight. There also seem to be expensive personal items in the forecastle on pirate ships, where the ordinary crew was lodged. Every pirate ship that can be carefully excavated for its data in context and not merely looted for its treasure can provide a better understanding of those who lived onboard.

One additional hurdle to conducting archaeology on pirate sites is the accompanying notoriety. On one hand, it is great to have the public clamoring for information on your work. On the other hand, it is a real hindrance to try to thoughtfully interpret a site with the public clamoring for information. Fortunately, archaeologists excavating *Queen Anne's Revenge* have accommodated public interest, while conducting first-class research. It hasn't always been easy, but the results have made the challenges worthwhile.

"Buried Treasure," by Howard Pyle (1921), in *Howard Pyle's Book of Pirates*, ed. Merle De Vore Johnson (New York: Harper and Brothers, 1921), 75–76.

in the expedition while others repaired broken equipment. Down-days were welcomed every so often to catch up, but not when they came day after day due to inclement weather. Occasionally tropical storms washed out several weeks, and crews were sent home.

Loading R/V *Shell Point* at U.S. Coast Guard Station Fort Macon basin. (Courtesy of the North Carolina Department of Natural and Cultural Resources)

N.C. Marine Fisheries R/V *Shell Point* taking up moorings at the *QAR* site. (Courtesy of the North Carolina Department of Natural and Cultural Resources)

Archaeologists Mark Wilde-Ramsing and Anne Corscadden use a 3-in. dredge hose to remove sediment within an excavation unit. Photograph by Steve Workman. (Courtesy of Steve Workman and the North Carolina Department of Natural and Cultural Resources)

QAR archaeologists Anne Corscadden and Steven Lambert work the dredge sluice between dives. (Courtesy of the North Carolina Department of Natural and Cultural Resources)

On this day, however, Captain Piner continued forward, opting to motor out through the main channel before heading west, a trip of nearly 40 minutes. In calmer weather, taking a shortcut through an unmarked channel just off the surf line of Bogue Banks would halve the travel time. Arriving at the *QAR* site, the captain navigated the field of buoys, each connected to a heavy block anchor, and directed his deckhands to pick up and attach lines to two or three moorings. Securing the lines kept R/V *Shell Point* precisely over the work area. As wind and tide shifted throughout the day, deck crew adjusted mooring lines as needed.

Once Captain Piner cut the engines off, divers went over the side to inspect the aluminum grid frames marking excavation units. They found that the frames had been partially buried during the long weekend and therefore called for the 6-in. dredge to remove the overburden, directing its outfall away from the work area. As they neared the artifacts, the divers switched to two 3-in. dredges, each assigned to an excavation unit. These smaller dredges allowed them to work carefully in and around artifacts while sucking up sediment, which was carried up the discharge hose to the deck of R/V *Shell Point*. There it spilled into a gold miner's gravity sluice, across baffles, and through a quarter-inch screen box. What was not captured, which was mostly seawater and fine sediment, flowed over the other side and back into the ocean.

At any time, up to three dredges in any combination of 6-in. and 3-in. systems might be in operation. They were supplied pressurized water from R/V *Shell Point*'s main pump, which ran continuously throughout the day. When their dive was nearing completion, excavators passed the intake end of their dredge to a replacement diver, who continued the work. No time was lost. When not underwater, crew members worked the sluices, picking out small artifacts and keeping screens from clogging with shell. Meanwhile, the captain and his mate oversaw pumping operations and kept the vessel situated over the work area, the dive safety officer and communications operator tended the divers, and the field conservator and assistant kept track of the flow of artifacts.

Before recovering exposed artifacts, a designated member of the dive team mapped them within the excavation unit. In concert, a second diver tagged each artifact; small concretions and ballast stone were grouped together within their respective unit. When documentation was complete, artifacts were brought to the surface, sometimes individually, other times together in recovery baskets, using a davit and electric winch. When the artifacts arrived on deck, project field conservator Wendy Welsh made sure the artifact data coordinated with the archaeologist's excavation unit drawing and tag numbers logged onto corresponding conservation forms. Once confirmed, all artifacts were placed in water-filled and foam-lined containers for transport to shore. At times during excavation there was little or no action, but then a great flurry of activity commenced as dozens of artifacts were brought up and processed in short order. By midafternoon, dredges were cut off, the pump was silenced, equipment was secured on deck, mooring lines were released, and Captain Piner pointed R/V *Shell Point* toward the

Diver watches as a basket of small artifacts is recovered using an electric winch and davit. (Courtesy of the North Carolina Department of Natural and Cultural Resources)

QAR archaeologists Franklin Price and Anne Corscadden catalog removed artifacts as they come aboard the recovery vessel. (Courtesy of the North Carolina Department of Natural and Cultural Resources)

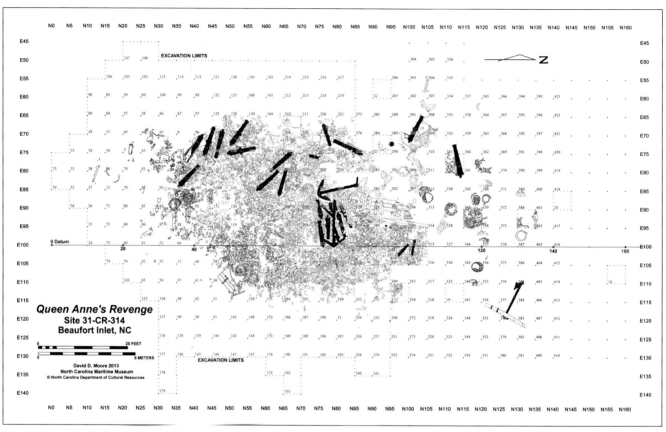

QAR site plan showing excavation units. Red are completed units and blue await excavation.
David D. Moore, illustrator. (Courtesy of the North Carolina Department of Natural and
Cultural Resources)

coast guard station for the short ride home. There was, however, still much to do before the workday ended.

As soon as the vessel was securely tied to its berth, the entire crew jumped into action with various tasks. Divers unloaded empty dive tanks in the back of a truck to haul away for air refills and then washed their gear; Captain Piner and his mate checked R/V *Shell Point*'s motor and pump and washed its deck; and conservator Welsh, with the help of almost everyone, made sure artifacts were carefully lifted onto shore and to an artifact processing area. Each artifact was then photographed and measured, and tags were double-checked before the items were placed in large, temporary hold-

ing tanks. Sluice sediments, stored in five-gallon buckets, were also recorded and secured for processing later, perhaps during a day when weather was too bad to dive or by technicians back at the conservation lab. The day had been a long one for the excavation crew, starting at 7:00 A.M. and not ending until just before 5:00 P.M. They were tired but satisfied that progress was being made and eagerly looked forward to the next day and what new discoveries might come to light.

This was the daily routine that continued over ten years. When the last diver ascended from the wreck site on November 5, 2015, state archaeologists and support crew had spent 242 days on the site in full recovery mode. A total of 3,176 dives had been made during which 2,926 hours and 45 minutes were spent on the ocean bottom. Now that is a lot of salt in divers' ears![11]

The effort resulted in full archaeological recovery of 285 excavation units or 1,725 sq. ft. of seabed or just over 60 percent of the estimated *QAR* site area. As a result, conservators assigned 2,682 artifact numbers to individual artifacts, artifact groups, or concretions, all of which were uncovered, mapped, tagged, brought to the surface, and then taken ashore to be documented and placed in a temporary storage tank. Then another voyage began. Every Friday, artifacts recovered during the week were packed in foam-filled containers and transported 80 miles up the road to the *QAR* conservation laboratory. There, the conservation team received the artifacts along with their trail of data to make sure everything was in order and placed safely in water-filled holding tanks, large and small, where they would await cleaning, conservation, and analysis.

If you wish to learn what all those artifacts can tell us about that long-forgotten ship, please read on. Almost every day secrets are unlocked in the conservation laboratory and their stories made known through subsequent scientific inquiry.

Archaeologists David Moore and Josh Daniel assist conservator Wendy Welsh to process artifacts brought to shore. (Courtesy of the North Carolina Department of Natural and Cultural Resources)

[C H A P T E R   F I V E]

Fragile Remains

The heavy metal door needed a strong jerk to get it started and then creaked and groaned as it begrudgingly opened. A strong smell of fish and the constant sound of running water greeted us as we made our way through the large metal building to the very back, where *QAR* artifacts were stored. Most of building no. 212 held operations and equipment related to Carteret Community College's Mariculture Program, a bubbling classroom aimed at promoting clam and oyster farming in the shallows of the surrounding waters. For many years prior to its current use, the building supported another sea-related business—catching and processing menhaden. The tiny fish, a common source of oil and fertilizers, had been the target of fishers for over a century. By all accounts Wallace Fisheries, which began in 1911, was one profitable and quite stinky business. When the plant ceased operation in the 1960s, its land, along with several of its buildings, became part of the local college campus. From 1999 until 2002, a portion of the mariculture building, once used to dry and repair the large seine nets used to scoop up menhaden, now also provided a conservation space for five cannons, large pieces of wooden hull, and many smaller, crusty artifacts recovered during early expeditions to the *QAR* shipwreck site. Here they were secured and kept wet in

storage tanks within a room-sized cage at the back of the building.

As we approached on this particular day, water on the floor signaled a problem. One of the large tanks had sprung a leak, leaving the upper surface of a 6-pounder cannon exposed to the air and drying out. This was not good at all because a concretion-laden, iron object fished from the ocean quickly deteriorates when exposed to air. If it is left to dry for any length of time, salts expand and place pressure on the metal, forcing it to crack. Eventually the untreated, drying cannon or cannonball or, for that matter, any encrusted artifact made of ferrous material disintegrates into a pile of worthless rusty, crusty iron chips. At that point, the once proud artifact from yesteryear becomes an unsolvable puzzle with little or no value.

The immediate solution was to simply add water, which would keep the cannon stable, but the tank would continue to leak. To further remedy the situation, the A-frame hoist was used to lift the one-ton cannon high enough into the air so a cheap blue tarp could be inserted underneath to serve as a temporary tank liner. There wasn't time or money to get the more durable pond-liner membrane, and anyway, we had no confidence it would last any longer under current conditions. Eventually, the

QAR archaeological conservator Wayne Lusardi works on a leaking cannon tank at the temporary QAR lab in Morehead City. (Courtesy of the North Carolina Department of Natural and Cultural Resources)

QAR cannon tank after fiberglass coating at Parker Boats of Beaufort. (Courtesy of the North Carolina Department of Natural and Cultural Resources)

cannon was set back down, the tank was refilled with water, and the surrounding floor was mopped. It was another morning wasted on maintenance rather than conservation and research, and we fully expected the tank to leak again soon. The problem lay in the fact that during routine inspecting and cleaning of the unwieldy cannon, a puncture or tear to the lining would be nearly impossible to avoid. It seemed that there must be a better solution.

One day help arrived unexpectedly. Some local boatbuilding executives were invited to visit the community college campus, specifically the Mariculture Program, in hopes they might provide corporate support. During the tour of the building, they noticed the chain-link fence cage in the back. They were invited into the QAR wet storage area, where they saw interesting artifacts. The boatbuilders also heard our lament concerning the leaky tanks and immediately proposed a remedy. If we could empty a tank of its contents, allow it to dry, and then transport it to their boatmaking factory in Beaufort, the interior could be coated with a permanent fiberglass and resin membrane. Their workers would fit it in around other jobs, using leftover materials. When the first tank rolled out, it was also festooned with large signs promoting their business. The company, from top to bottom,

was proud to be providing its donated expertise to ensure that QAR artifacts would no longer suffer further degradation from leaking tanks. We didn't mind the advertisement, for as it turned out, dozens of tanks were eventually retrofitted with fiberglass to seal them, and once filled with water and shipwreck materials, they have lost nary a drop since!

Conservation: Meeting the Challenge

The tale of the leaky tank is symbolic of those early days of conservation and one that might be forgotten on a tour of today's QAR state-of-the-science conservation facility. From the very beginning, the importance of conservation, which involves handling and caring for artifacts recovered from the shipwreck site, was paramount in all of our plans.[1] Why is conservation essential? The answer can be expressed in terms of time and money. While conducting underwater recovery operations is an expensive proposition, it has been estimated that nine-tenths of the overall expense of shipwreck archaeology is needed after excavations in order to analyze, clean, and stabilize recovered materials—conservation, that is.[2] For full recovery of the QAR remains, a specialized conservation laboratory dedicated solely to that project was im-

perative. Unfortunately, coming up with the money to support a project in its entirety was a sobering challenge. Millions of dollars would be needed to accomplish the recovery, lengthy conservation process, and permanent display or storage for a collection that was expected to include hundreds of thousands of individual artifacts and their accompanying records. Garnering that level of funding up front was, and still is, complicated by the fact that the public's interest in shipwrecks tends to focus mostly on underwater operations and especially on recovery of large artifacts, such as cannons. Afterward, excitement generally wanes, as most artifacts require years of treatment before they can be put on public display. We knew all this, so full recovery operations were delayed until long-term financial support, dedicated staff, and an adequate facility were in place. In the interim, we sought creative ways and means to handle, study, and conserve materials recovered during the initial forays to the site, as well as those pieces salvaged after storm events.

Before we began construction of the project's permanent conservation laboratory on the campus of East Carolina University in 2002, treatment of artifacts took place at several temporary locations. In the earliest years, archaeologists relied on the existing conservation facility located at the North Carolina Department of Cultural Resources Underwater Archaeology Branch in Kure Beach. There, space was limited and conservation was overseen by the UAB archaeological conservator Leslie Bright,

who had numerous other duties. He was aided by an assistant, Nathan Henry, who was hired and assigned to the *QAR* project. In those early days, the first three cannons were kept in a renovated cinder block building owned by the North Carolina Maritime Museum in Beaufort. Needless to say, responding to a cannon tank spill or other conservation duties when the staff was 100 miles away proved difficult.

By late 1999, archaeological offices and a conservation facility were established nearer to the *QAR* site. Laboratory and office space was provided at the Institute of Marine Sciences, a University of North Carolina satellite campus located in Morehead City. Large artifacts were housed nearby in the mariculture warehouse on the campus of Carteret Community College. This arrangement was again temporary; after two years of operation, *QAR* facilities were forced to close due to building renovations at both campuses (the mariculture warehouse was torn down). Artifacts were transported back to Kure Beach, where *QAR* conservators Wendy Welsh and Michael Tutwiler, under the direction of Henry, now the UAB's archaeological conservator, undertook the task of breaking down, cleaning, and treating 200 concretions and the artifacts held within, as well as five cannons. That early conservation work was enlightening because it gave us a better understanding of what difficulties and requirements these encrusted artifacts posed, thus offering vital insight as we planned the *QAR* conservation laboratory.

Meanwhile, Sarah Watkins-Kenney was hired as *QAR*'s chief conservator and stationed in Greenville at the East Carolina University campus. Here, she worked with university staff and faculty to develop a laboratory at the recently acquired property on the Western Campus formerly known as the Voice of America "Site C." With that move, an adequate and permanent conservation laboratory for the shipwreck collection was on the horizon and soon became a reality. This was an essential step toward enabling state archaeologists and conservators to undertake the full recovery of all remains from *Queen Anne's Revenge*.

The new conservation facility began receiving and processing artifacts recovered during the stratified sampling expeditions in 2005 and 2006. By the time full recovery began in the fall of 2006, the laboratory consisted of more than 4,000 sq. ft. of heated space and 4,000 sq. ft. of warehouse storage. Today the *QAR* Conservation Laboratory includes office and library space, treatment labs for both large and small artifacts, a documentation and record storage room, photography and illustration rooms, and x-radiography and processing rooms. At the facility four permanent conservators, a team of technicians, and several graduate students now spend their hours and days focused solely on *QAR* materials.

During the sampling program, 389 objects, most concreted and unidentifiable, were recovered and assigned *QAR* numbers. The conservation staff took nearly all of those concretions to the North Carolina Museum of Art in Raleigh for x-ray sessions funded by a National Geographic Expeditions Council grant titled Peering into a Pirate's Trove. X-radiography enabled researchers to identify lead shot, glass beads, nails and other iron fittings, and items of pewter, copper alloy, and gold flake hidden under concretion.[3] This process, along with visual inspection, added 8,230 identifiable artifacts to the *QAR* database.

With the 2006 full recovery operations, a significant influx of artifacts was sent to the *QAR* Conservation Laboratory. During that dive season, nearly 1,500 new artifact numbers were assigned, and by the end of the 2013 dive season, over 60 percent of the site had been excavated, resulting in a dramatic increase of 237,716 recognizable artifacts. By the end of 2014, nearly all of the 3,000 recovered con-

QAR conservators and technicians removing concretion using pneumatic air scribes in the lab processing area. (Courtesy of the North Carolina Department of Natural and Cultural Resources)

Nineteenth-century ginger beer bottle with cork stopper recovered from *QAR* site. (Courtesy of the North Carolina Department of Natural and Cultural Resources)

cretions had been x-rayed and inventoried and then prioritized, providing more than 400,000 artifacts for further analysis. With the exception of 39 relatively modern (nineteenth- and twentieth-century) objects, all others were contemporaneous with the sinking of *Queen Anne's Revenge*.

As expected, the *QAR* artifact assemblage represents a diversity of material types used to manufacture items during the early eighteenth century related to naval technology, shipboard life and provisioning, international trade, and pirating. Depending on their composition, those objects responded in various ways during the 300 years they were submersed in ocean waters prior to archaeological recovery. Some, such as those made of gold and lead, survived mostly intact, while those made of brass, bronze, glass, and ceramics remained unscathed to a lesser extent. For items made of iron, wood, and fabric, perhaps only a trace remains of their original composition. Artifacts, even those of the same material, survived in various states and thus needed specific treatments to stabilize them. Cleaning, reassembling, and restoring them to the closest semblance of what they were when Blackbeard's crew handled them continues to present challenges for conservators. It is a task that requires constant supervision, evaluation, and when necessary, procedural adjustments.

After 300 years in an undersea environment, artifacts are kept wet, or as noted above, they would quickly crack, shrivel up, or dissolve to a worthless state. With everything covered in wet rags or submerged in tanks of water, conservators work quickly to document each artifact's initial condition. They start by assigning a unique *QAR* number, which helps track an artifact through its lifetime in the conservation laboratory and, later, at the museum setting. Then the size, shape, weight, color, condition, and general description of each numbered object is recorded. Digital photographs are used to further document each piece. Various measurement systems are employed to describe whatever the item might have been. For example, lead shot is measured in millimeters, hole diameters from tobacco pipe stems are taken to the nearest 64th of an inch, and the diameters of pewter and ceramic plates are recorded in English inches. Weight is typically calculated in English ounces or in metric equivalents, again depending on the item being measured. Generally, information recorded by the conservator is the same as or

QAR archaeological illustrator Valerie Grussing documents a pewter plate. (Courtesy of the North Carolina Department of Natural and Cultural Resources)

compatible with that from the early eighteenth century. While taking detailed measurements on individual artifacts is tedious, the process can sometimes provide "eureka moments." These most often occur when researchers take into account the differences in French and English measurements of the eighteenth century, as will become evident in the coming pages.

Detailed recording and cataloging of each artifact provides the foundation for our archaeological analysis and that of other scientists from different disciplines. Collectively, we bring varied perspectives as a range of artifacts are closely inspected. Each artifact is carefully examined for maker's marks, evidence of manufacture, similarity with other known artifacts, broken pieces of the same artifact (like ceramics or glass containers) that can be cross-matched, function and use, and cultural identity. Part of the analysis step includes assigning classifications based on an artifact's intended function, time period, and cultural setting. It is often from this contextual information that we determine who may have used the item and for how long, and why it eventually ended up on the wreck site. These are the artifact stories that wait in Chapter 6, but none of this would be possible without artifacts first undergoing the rigors of conservation.

Stages of Conservation

Watkins-Kenney and her conservation staff are a crucial part of the *QAR* Shipwreck Project team, and their primary tasks are to preserve artifacts by sustaining their physical condition or, where that is not possible, in whole or in part, to record every detail they can. Entire books are written on the highly scientific conservation techniques used on artifacts from underwater archaeological sites such as that of *Queen Anne's Revenge*, but here and now we'd like to share with you the basic steps. The three-stage process, which involves many steps of different activities, traces each artifact's journey from the wet seafloor to the dry museum door. To make this journey possible, Courtney Page, *QAR* lab manager, carefully and painstakingly oversees the extensive digital database, the virtual project brain that keeps track of every artifact, registering incoming information as well as enabling access for conservation staff, archaeologists, and outside researchers.

The first stage in conservation involves the initial treatment of an artifact from the moment it is uncovered on the ocean floor, brought up to the recovery vessel, moved to a holding area onshore, and finally transported to the conservation laboratory. Referred to as Post-Recovery Processing, this stage involves the initial cataloging, documentation, and condition assessment and is critically important, since it is the foundation that supports what happens next to the items. This stage also includes artifact identification and x-radiography of concretions, placement of artifacts into stable storage (primarily in tanks or tubs of fresh water), and entering all recorded information into a computer database for easier access and tracking of the many, many thousands of artifacts recovered from *Queen Anne's Revenge*.

Next is the Treatment Stage, when the conservators get down to the nitty-gritty, quite literally, as they clean centuries of corrosion and concretion from the objects. Desalination, that ever-so-

X-ray images mounted on a light box to help conservators determine what is inside artifact concretions. (Courtesy of the North Carolina Department of Natural and Cultural Resources)

QAR conservators Erik Farrell and Kimberly Kenyon setting up electrolysis reduction equipment in large artifact warehouse. (Courtesy of the North Carolina Department of Natural and Cultural Resources)

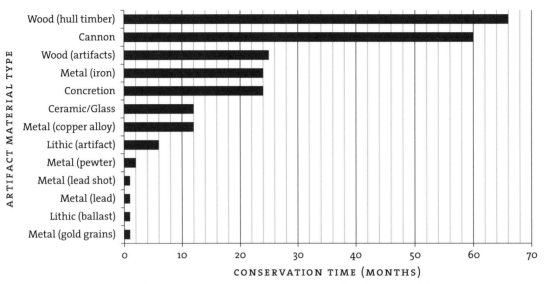

Estimated Minimum Time of Conservation (in Months) for Artifacts of Various Materials

important process of removing salts from the pores of most objects, takes months, even years, to complete. In the case of iron artifacts, of which there certainly is no shortage recovered from the *QAR* site, an electrolytic reduction process helps loosen concretion and draw out impurities from the metal. This is followed by consolidation (if required) and drying, which might also take considerable time, depending on the density of each object. Finally, once an artifact is stable, an application of some form of protective coating is applied to keep it that way and allow handling for analysis, transport, and public display. The vast majority of artifacts, however, are placed in long-term storage.

Throughout the conservation process, constant monitoring and testing of each artifact's condition is required. Adjustments and recalculations of their soaking solutions and treatment applications are sometimes necessary. The diversity of materials from which artifacts are made requires different treatment protocols, making the Treatment Stage by far the most complex, challenging, time consuming, and labor intensive of the three stages of conservation. Often Watkins-Kenney and her crew must adjust, show patience and perseverance, and

most importantly, be resourceful. Conservation times vary for artifacts according to the material they are composed of.[4] Those made of iron and wood often take years to complete the conservation process.

Last comes the Recording and Documentation Stage, which involves detailed scrutiny of each item to further confirm its identity, complete analysis recordation, and ensure that it is ready for museum exhibit or long-term storage. Often this involves specialists and researchers from outside the *QAR* Conservation Lab to ensure full documentation using comparative sources, which includes determining an item's origin, its function, and whether it had been subject to any modification (or recycling) or repairs. This step can often assist conservators in their efforts toward artifact reconstruction. Who are the other specialists, why are they interested in these crusty old pieces, and what in the world can they tell us? Let's have a look.

An International Crew Eyes the Evidence

Well, the truth be known, whenever we or any of the *QAR* staff have been seeking outside help for

QAR volunteer wood identification specialist Dr. Lee Newsom analyzes *QAR* timber samples. (Courtesy of the North Carolina Department of Natural and Cultural Resources).

analysis of a specific artifact or class of artifacts, our pitch has generally been met with interest but no commitment, mostly because we had little money to offer for services rendered. However, as details have been revealed about where these artifacts are from—a shipwreck, and not just any shipwreck, but a pirate shipwreck, and not just any pirate, but Blackbeard—well you guessed it, by the end most folks are paying close attention and eager to help. This has been true for the scientists and specialists from many parts of the United States and Europe who might examine some aspect of the *QAR* wreck site, its recovered artifacts, and associated residue samples. The manner in which these talented folks have been coming aboard the *QAR* analytical crew is a tale in itself. Sometimes they have been obvious choices, being known researchers in their field of study, but more likely word has passed from colleague to colleague until the right person surfaces. Invariably *QAR* researchers haven't been close by but often live in faraway locations and

sometimes speak a language other than English. But regardless, all are intrigued by the questions we are asking them. Whether it is the lure of pirates or simply having a unique, practical application on which to apply their specialty, an impressive group of experts have agreed to help *QAR* archaeologists in extracting every bit of information possible from the wreckage and its remains.

Nearly 50 outside researchers from a wide diversity of professional specialties in the physical and cultural sciences are inspecting every aspect of *Queen Anne's Revenge*, from its smallest artifacts (grains of gold) to cannons and anchors weighing over a ton. Their collective analyses are helping to solve the puzzle of this early eighteenth-century ship, its cargo, and the pirates who sailed it.

This brings to mind a story, a lesson of sorts. It involves the x-ray image of an amorphous, lumpy concretion that, when backlit in black and white, presented a ghostly mirage. A couple of years ago, during normal examination of this particular x-ray, a bright white U-shaped object of dense metal caught the attention of lab conservator Kim Kenyon. Seeking an identity, she emailed the x-ray image to various *QAR* staff members and museum curators. Excitement grew when it was tentatively identified as a manila, a type of metal (in this case probably brass) bracelet that had been previously found and documented on slave shipwrecks.[5] Usually made of brass or bronze, these unique bracelets were used as a type of currency in the African slave trade, so it would not be unusual to find one here, since *Concorde* was a slaver. Manilas were typically made of solid brass, generally U-shaped with open lozenge-shaped terminals, but came in different sizes for men, women, and children. Very distinct and symbolic, they were manufactured by the Spanish, Portuguese, French, and English to be used as exchange objects during slave trading.

If nestled in the *QAR* concretion was a real manila, it was exciting news indeed, for none had yet been found on *Queen Anne's Revenge*. A press announcement was subsequently released, and soon

Table 5.1 Specialists Who Have Contributed Analysis and Research to the *Queen Anne's Revenge* Shipwreck Project

Research Topic	Specialist	Affiliation	Region	Published
ARCHIVAL				
NC History	Lindley S. Butler	Rockingham Community College, Rockingham	NC-USA	2001
La Concorde	John De Bry	Center for Historical Archaeology, Melbourne Beach	FL-USA	1999
La Concorde	Jacques Ducoin	Independent researcher, Nantes	France	2001
La Concorde/QAR	Mike Daniel	Maritime Research Institute, Jupiter	FL-USA	2001
Queen Anne's Revenge	Philip Masters	Intersal, Inc., Florida	FL-USA	1989
SITE ANALYSIS				
Site Mapping	Frank Cantelas	East Carolina University, Greenville	NC-USA	1997
	Philip Masters	Intersal, Inc., Beaufort	NC-USA	2006
	Gordon Watts	Tidewater Atlantic Research, Washington	NC-ISA	1997
	John Wells	UNC-CH Institute of Marine Sciences, Morehead City	NC-USA	2001
	Jesse E. McNinch	College of William and Mary, Williamsburg	VA-USA	2001, 2005, 2006
	Anthony Rodriquez	UNC Institute of Marine Science, MHC	NC-USA	2009
	David Bernstein and Chris Freeman	Geodynamics, LLC, Newport	NC-USA	2006–present
Scour-Burial Modeling	Arthur C. Trembanis	College of William and Mary, Williamsburg, University of Delaware, Newark	VA-USA	2003, 2005, 2006
Sediment Coring	Kelly Gleason	College of William and Mary, Williamsburg	VA-USA	2004
Water Analysis	David Monaghan	Cape Fear Community College, Wilmington	NC-USA	1998
Invertebrate Inventory	Steven J. Hageman	Appalachian State University, Boone	NC-USA	2001
Biological Inventory	Peter Gillman-Bryan	Trulove Fabrications, Wilmington	NC-USA	1998
ARTIFACT ANALYSIS				
General				
Metal ID	James Craig	Virginia Tech University, Blacksburg	VA-USA	2001
	Stacie E. Dunkel	Virginia Tech University, Blacksburg	VA-USA	2002
Wood Fungus	Jan Kolhmeyer	UNC-CH Institute of Marine Science, MHC	NC-USA	2004
Coral Aging	Neils Lindquist	UNC-CH Institute of Marine Science, MHC	NC-USA	1999
Plutonium Tracing	Christopher S Martens	UNC-Chapel Hill	NC-USA	2001
Coal Analysis	Rodd Hatt	University of Kentucky	KY-USA	2014
X-Radiography	Dan Boyd	Davidson University	NC-USA	2014
Concretion	David Krop	East Carolina University, Greenville	NC-USA	2004

Research Topic	Specialist	Affiliation	Region	Published
Ship Structure				
Dendrochronology	Michael G. Baillie	Queen's University, Belfast	N. Ireland	2002
Wood ID	Lee A. Newsom	Penn State University, University Park	PA-USA	2012
	Regis B. Miller	USDA Forest Laboratory, Madison	WI-USA	
Wood Aging	Ann P. McNichols	Wood's Hole Oceanographic Institute, Falmouth	MA-USA	2001
Textiles	Runying Chen	East Carolina University, Greenville	NC-USA	2006
	Adria L. Focht	East Carolina University, Greenville	NC-USA	
Ship's Equipment				
Ballast ID	John Callahan	Appalachian University, Boone	NC-USA	2001
Ballast Origin	Jim Miller	UNC-Asheville	NC-USA	2012
Bells	Joaquín Díaz	Fundación Joaquín Díaz, Valladolid	Spain	2000
	Francesc Llop i Bayo and Francesc Llop i Álvaro	Gremi de Companers Valencians, Valencia	Spain	2001
	Felix López	Spanish National Center for Metallurgical Research, Madrid	Spain	2001
	Alain Jouffray	l'Institut Europeen d'Art Campanaire in L'Isle Jourdain	France	2008
	Joseph Wilde-Ramsing	Independent Researcher, Utrecht	Netherlands	2008, 2016
Horn/Keratin	Anthony Kennedy	East Carolina University, Greenville	NC-USA	2012
Arms & Armament				
Cannon	Ruth Brown and Robert Smith	Private consultant, Yorkshire	England	2007, 2009
Cannon Aprons	Laura Kate Schnitzer	East Carolina University, Greenville	NC-USA	2012
	Timothy Easton	Independent researcher and architectural historian, London	England	2013
Gunpowder Analysis	John Kenney	East Carolina University, Greenville	NC-USA	2014
	Larry Babits	East Carolina University, Greenville	NC-USA	2014
Gunflints	J. Ned Woodall	Wake Forest University, Winston-Salem	NC-USA	2004
Medicine				
Surgical	Linda Carnes-McNaughton	Cultural Resources Management Program, Fort Bragg	NC-USA	2015
Sustenance				
Ceramics	Linda Carnes-McNaughton	Cultural Resources Management Program, Fort Bragg	NC-USA	2008
Bottles	Linda Carnes-McNaughton	Cultural Resources Management Program, Fort Bragg	NC-USA	2008

Table 5.1 Specialists Who Have Contributed Analysis and Research to the *Queen Anne's Revenge* Shipwreck Project *(continued)*

Research Topic	Specialist	Affiliation	Region	Published
Sustenance *(continued)*				
Pewter	Philippe Boucaud	Syndicat Français des Experts Professionnels en Œuvres d'Art, Paris	France	2010
Brick and Tile	Linda Carnes-McNaughton	Cultural Resources Management Program, Fort Bragg	NC-USA	2007
Faunal Analysis	David T. Clark	Catholic University of America, Washington, DC	DC-USA	2005, 2016
Casks	Kimberly Smith	East Carolina University, Greenville	NC-USA	2009
Apparel				
Cloth Seal	Geoff Egan	Museum of London	England	2007
Beads	Linda Carnes-McNaughton	Cultural Resources Management Program, Fort Bragg	NC-USA	2008
Slave Goods				
Pipes	Linda Carnes-McNaughton	Cultural Resources Management Program, Fort Bragg	NC-USA	2007
Coins & Measures				
Survey Chain Tallies	Timothy Guisewhite	Taylor Wiseman & Taylor, NC	NC-USA	2012
Weights	Diane Crawford-Hitchins	Private consultant, Plymouth	England	2009

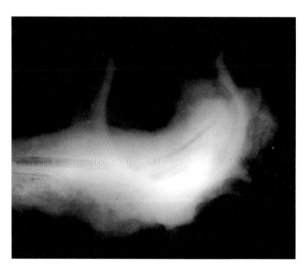

U-shaped mystery metal object in concretion exposed by x-ray image. (Courtesy of the North Carolina Department of Natural and Cultural Resources)

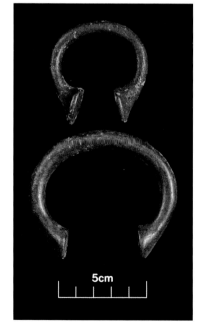

Brass manila associated with the slave trade in the collection of the Hamill Gallery, Boston. (Courtesy of the North Carolina Department of Natural and Cultural Resources)

5cm

the hype was spread by the news media. This led to interest from a film crew doing a story about the science taking place at the *QAR* Conservation Lab as the remains of Blackbeard's flagship were being investigated.

The lab conservator also provided us a copy of the x-ray image and preliminary identification. We couldn't help but wonder if the curious object could be something other than a manila; it just did not look quite right. Various alternatives crossed our minds, such as a pivot mount for a small gun, some type of handle, or maybe an oarlock. We began to gather information on slave manilas and even received several intact eighteenth-century bracelets on loan from the Hamill Gallery in Boston. At the same time, we looked into the other possibilities— gun mounts and oarlocks. The complicating part concerning the oarlock was that this device, as we know it today, wasn't invented until well after *Queen Anne's Revenge* sailed; this implied that it would not have been contemporary with the shipwreck. Yet the object was in concretion, a process thought to take years, if not centuries. How could it be "modern," given its apparent context?

When the day came to break the object free, we were there along with the film crew, looking over Kim's elbow as she carefully and gently removed the surrounding encrustation using a pneumatic drill. Her first observation was to note that the concretion appeared different in color and texture than what normally encased eighteenth-century artifacts. Perhaps the mystery object inside was not so old after all. Within 45 minutes, the U-shaped object was exposed, and we knew the answer. From our research files, out came a photograph of an oarlock manufactured by the Buck Algonquin Company sometime after 1955 and still available today for just $33.99 a pair! It was identical, except the *QAR* oarlock was missing its horn, the part that would have been inserted into a hole on the boat's gunnel. Our inquisitive minds wondered not only how it landed on the centuries-old shipwreck but

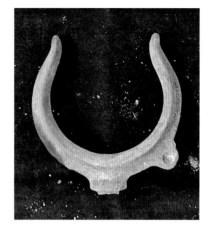

The mystery object unveiled and turned right side up. (Courtesy of the North Carolina Department of Natural and Cultural Resources)

A modern-day Buck Algonquin rowboat oarlock. (Courtesy of Abigail Trumpy, Hydrasearch Marketing and Sales)

what force broke the oarlock in two. It was another line of archaeological inquiry, but one saved for another day.

The main lesson from our story, however, reminded us not to make assumptions (for things might not be as they seem) without thorough research and input from specialists. It also demonstrated that corrosion and concretion could form rather quickly in the right circumstances. And although of interest to us, the whole affair did not impress the film crew, and our *QAR* oarlock discovery never made it into the final cut of their video.

The Sweet Sound of Blackbeard's Bell

DR. JOSEPH M. WILDE-RAMSING

An encrusted, bell-shaped artifact was one of the first objects brought to the surface by divers on the day of discovery. Immediately, there was intense speculation about just how significant this "first find" might be. Could it provide a tell-all clue that would unambiguously identify the shipwreck as *Queen Anne's Revenge*? Or conversely, quickly put an end to that speculation?

The initial cleaning of its surface revealed an embossed inscription "IHS MARIA" and an apparent date of "ANO 1709," neither of which provided definitive answers. The latter provided chronological evidence fitting the 1718 wrecking of Blackbeard's flagship, but the inscription ("IHS," representing the Holy Name of Jesus, and "MARIA," referring to the Virgin Mary) did little to clarify the ship's identity.

A few years later, I was traveling to Madrid and, being fluent in Spanish, was asked to follow up on some preliminary queries posed by *QAR* staff to European bell experts. It was a journey that took me back across the Atlantic to the Old World seeking the origins and history of this intriguing, distinctive artifact. Initial research in Spain's national archives led me to three experts on bells (known as campanologists), two Spanish and one French.[1] They were provided detailed measurements, photos, and scaled drawings of the bell, along with a series of questions designed to elicit the bell's origin, its intended use, and any clues that might clarify its presence on a shipwreck off the coast of North Carolina.

Right away, the bell experts were able to clear up one important observation: The date on the bell was not 1709, as was initially thought, but, rather, 1705. They pointed out that the eighteenth-century stylistic font for "5" closely resembled a modern-day "9"—a small but perhaps significant correction. Otherwise, they were in agreement that it was a rather ordinary bell made by itinerant bell makers for common use. "IHS MARIA" was a familiar Catholic inscription found on bells cast during the seventeenth and eighteenth centuries in Spain and France, which was also a Catholic country.

One of the bell experts, Dr. Francesc Llop i Bayo, requested that a recording be provided to determine its tonal characteristics, and when I returned to the United States, I was pleased to participate in this experience. The subsequent analysis of sound we recorded determined that the *QAR* bell was typical for historic bells of the period, while simultaneously unique. Spanish bell sound analyst Mr. Francesc Llop i Álvaro, Dr. Llop i Bayo's son, pointed out that the sound from a bell was composed of five primary notes and was distinctive to that individual bell. When the bell was rung, he noted, "those five notes produced a remarkable musical effect, giving the sensation of harmony. As time passed, this sound became associated with important ritual acts, both festive as well as sorrowful, and the human ear became accustomed to it, recognized the sound as its own, and took the sound as a key reference point for daily life." This was true whether the ears belonged to townspeople, churchgoers, or shipmates aboard a pirate ship. Dr. Llop i Bayo gave the sound even higher meaning. "Bells represent the living music of the past because they are the only instruments that can retain their original sound throughout the centuries. The restoration of this bell is magnificent, and I suppose that you can still hear its beautiful music. This cultural aspect is of utmost importance because it is the only sound of Blackbeard's ship that we can experience in its original totality."

In the lobby of the North Carolina Maritime Museum in 2002, museum curator Connie Mason, *QAR* volunteers Jim Craig, and Joseph Wilde-Ramsing ring the *QAR* bell for the first time in nearly 300 years! (Courtesy of the North Carolina Department of Natural and Cultural Resources)

1. Bell experts were Dr. Francesc Llop i Bayo, a member of the Gremi de Companers Valencians; Dr. Felix López of the Spanish National Center for Metallurgical Research in Madrid; Joaquín Díaz, Fundación Joaquín Díaz, Valladolid, Spain; and Mr. Alain Jouffray, director of the European Institute of Campanology in France. For a full analysis of the *QAR* bell, see Mark U. Wilde-Ramsing and Joseph M. Wilde-Ramsing, "Report on 'IHS Maria' Bell Recovered from 31CR314," *Bell Tower* 66, no. 4 (2008).

[C H A P T E R   S I X]

An Eye to Detail

Examining Artifacts by Function

We have been fortunate to work closely with the *QAR* conservation team to examine and analyze the latest artifacts extracted from concretions. Before inspection begins, we put on waterproof gloves and plastic aprons to protect ourselves and the artifacts. Most often we work at a designated work table, but on occasion we use the microscopes to examine the cleaned objects. On this occasion, in front of us on the lab table we find an assortment of Tupperware tubs, all labeled "RO" in big black letters to indicate that the artifacts they hold are being treated using "reverse osmosis" baths.[1] Reaching in, we gently pull out several small clear plastic bags, each one labeled with a distinct (catalog) number. They contain individual small artifacts made of metal, but what type and what age has yet to be determined. One by one, the objects, still wet, are placed on a small tray under intense light and, under magnification, are examined for minute details such as maker's marks, modification (like snipping), use wear, and personal initials of the former owner. Details about size and shape and weight are noted. Using sliding calipers and rulers, we quickly record specific measurements so the piece does not dry out and alter the course of conservation already under way. We note every visible detail on analysis forms and add sketches to highlight the notes. Compar-

ative analysis follows, while we attempt to match these objects to others we analyzed from another part of the shipwreck or out of another concretion. During this session at the *QAR* lab, the artifacts turn out to be multiple parts of the hinged lid from a nested weight set. It is a long, meticulous process, a sort of puzzle with no guarantee that the pieces will match or that all pieces would be found. Together with Sarah Watkins-Kenney's conservation team, we seek answers: Where and when was the weight set made? What was it doing on this ship? How was it used, and who used it? Cultural analysis of 300-year-old artifacts takes a wide range of knowledge, a careful eye, and an active imagination to fully interpret them.

Using the guidelines of scientific inquiry, we and our research colleagues often employ the archaeological practice of *inference* (a conclusion derived from observations) and *hypothesis* (a proposed explanation or interpretation) to more fully understand the people of the past. The process of understanding what was found on the site or later extracted from careful laboratory processing of the concretions offers insights into *context* (the exact location where an artifact is found) and *association* (the relationship of one artifact to another) of artifacts found on the site. These concepts enable us

Under the Black Flag, by Jack Saylor (2007), oil on linen. (Courtesy of the North Carolina Office of Archives and History)

to make sense of past human behaviors, much like how a detective figures out a crime scene. The following pages report the rewards of archaeological analysis: a look at the pirates under Blackbeard's rule, plus a glimpse of his conscripted passengers, including the slaves and kidnapped Frenchmen, all of whom exited this sinking ship in June 1718, leaving lots to discover.

Be forewarned: The full and final story cannot be told here today because only 60 percent of the total site has been excavated and a fair amount of what has been brought up remains in concretion and unavailable for our detailed analysis. The quantity, variety, and complexity of the *QAR* artifact assemblage reported here nonetheless permits a fascinating peek at Blackbeard's world. Artifacts of note include three anchors, 29 iron cannons, a variety of lethal cannon shot, the ship's sternpost and a section of hull, two bells, a bronze signaling cannon, over 250,000 lead shot, gun parts, sword parts, tons of ballast stone, 30 pewter plates, med-

Cultural material specialist Dr. Linda Carnes-McNaughton conducting research at the *QAR* Conservation Lab. (Courtesy of the North Carolina Department of Natural and Cultural Resources)

ical equipment, navigational instruments, carpenter's tools, broken ceramics and glass bottles, glass beads, clothing items (pins, buckles, and buttons), four silver coins, and thousands of gold grains. A veritable booty!

For this guided journey through the *QAR* assemblage, artifacts have been separated into broad functional categories based on how items may have functioned on the ship or were used by its crew and passengers. Each section reflects meaningful artifact groupings that have been painstakingly recovered by archaeologists from the ocean floor and by conservators in the laboratory. Collectively they represent the material culture of an intriguing eighteenth-century ship, one commanded by the notorious pirate Blackbeard as he and his accomplices plied their trade throughout colonial America.

Remains of the Ship: Sifting through the Scant Remains

There just wasn't much left of the ship's hull, but that could be expected, considering the bashing it had taken over the years from a turbulent coastal environment. It is fortunate that at least a section consisting of ribs and planking did survive, along with the lower portion of the ship's stern, parts of the iron rigging, and bits of sailcloth and cordage. Together they gave us clues as to how the ship was constructed and rigged for sailing. Associated with the wooden structure was caulking, a mixture of tar and animal hair filler between planks, and fasteners of iron and wood used in hull construction.

Other ship-related accoutrements included pump strainers, a toilet liner, parts of the stern cabin windows, and lots of lead patches for a leaky ship. Rounding out the category were tools to repair the ship. This included a device that baffled us and other researchers as we all waited patiently for the thick layer of concretion to be removed. It exhibited a ratchet and gear mechanism resembling a car bumper jack that if correctly identified meant it was a twentieth-century intrusion into the wreckage with no explanation of how it got there. Further research, however, determined the device was indeed a mechanical jack, contemporary with *Queen Anne's Revenge* and no doubt used by its carpenters to spread heavy timbers or cannon crews to change a broken carriage wheel. There is more about this device in the pages to come.

HULL STRUCTURE AND FASTENERS

All that was left of the ship's hull was a relatively flat section, 31 ft. by 9 ft., with no diagnostic features such as gun ports or keel. The section consisted of 11 frame pairings with individual timbers averaging 7 in. on the side against the hull and 8 in. molded with approximately 22 in. of space between. Hull planks were between 11 and 14 in. wide with a uniform thickness of nearly 3 in. This structural evidence points to a ship that was lightly built and fit the profile of a French privateer during the early eighteenth century.[2]

Our skilled wood specialists, Dr. Lee Newsom from Pennsylvania State University and Dr. Regis Miller of the U.S. Forestry Service, squeezed out even more information by closely examining

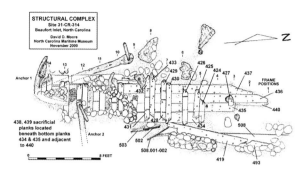

Drawing of wood structure with Anchor A-1 in situ. David D. Moore, illustrator. (Courtesy of the North Carolina Department of Natural and Cultural Resources)

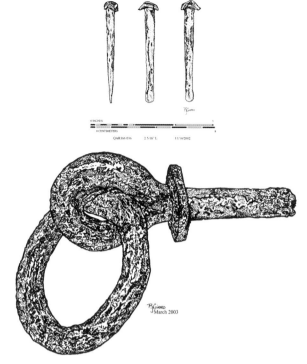

QAR iron fasteners include rose-head, spoon-tip iron nails, and iron ring bolts. Robbie Girard, illustrator. (Courtesy of the North Carolina Department of Natural and Cultural Resources)

samples from various timbers. They determined that most were a type of oak conforming closely to a European species that was heavily used in shipbuilding. That was not the case, however, for the outermost boards, which were Scotch pine, a species common in Scandinavia. These were called sacrificial planking, because the ship's bottom was sheathed with long thin planks less than an inch thick to deter shipworms that much preferred oak and weren't so fond of pine. When the sheathing did become riddled with wormholes or damaged, it was removed and replaced to save the ship's hull. Dr. Michael Baillie, from Queen's University in Northern Ireland, closely inspected growth rings in cross sections of several hull planks, a technique called dendrochronology, and surmised that the ship's construction occurred between 1690 and 1710.[3]

The few handmade iron spikes recovered from the shipwreck provided further construction details. The spikes were used to attach planking to the ship's frames and had been countersunk to reduce drag on the outside of the hull. To minimize leakage, cordage and tar were affixed under the spike heads. Similarly, round wooden pegs, called treenails, trennels, or trunnels, about 1 in. to 1¼ in. in diameter, were driven into pre-drilled holes to help hold the plank and frames together. The fastening pattern of one iron and one wood fastener, which alternated with each frame, was characteristic of

construction patterns by French shipwrights during the early eighteenth century.[4]

Hundreds and hundreds of rose-head, spoon-tip iron nails came from the center of the wreckage. This concentration was thought to have once been a wooden cask of nails probably stored until needed for repairs on the ship. While their quarter-inch shank diameter matched holes found in sacrificial planks, their average length of 2¼ in. would have been a bit short for properly attaching them to the outer hull. When out pirating, however, you make do with what's available to loot.

Larger iron fasteners of several types including eye bolts, ring bolts, very long bolts, flat straps, and various unidentified pieces were found. The bolts with eyes or rings would have been attached throughout the hull of the ship and were invaluable in securing deck equipment during rough weather.

Draft marks visible on the lower portion of the *QAR* sternpost. Jeremy Borrelli, illustrator. (Courtesy of the North Carolina Department of Natural and Cultural Resources)

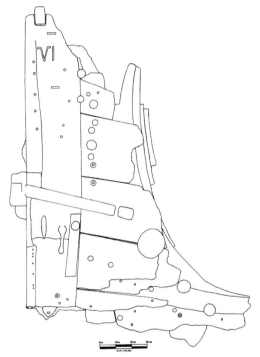

Some of these fasteners may also have come from the numerous wooden gun carriages.

A very significant architectural piece of the ship, the lower part of the ship's stern, was brought to the surface in 2007. This 6-ft.-by-7-ft. composite piece once joined to the keel and supported the massive rudder. On one side, two deeply carved draft marks and the Roman numeral VI denoted the ship's minimum draft of 6 ft. When the distance between marks was measured and found to be 12.75 inches, it became apparent that the increments were closest to an eighteenth-century French foot

(or *pied*) at 12.789 inches, providing solid evidence the vessel was built in that country. *A la votre* Concorde*!*

SAILS, ROPE, AND RIGGING

Three distinct clusters of large rings, ranging in size and number, were found along one margin of the ship's wreckage. Made of thick iron bars formed into large rings, these were lower attachments for the ship's rigging on the port side. Combined with wooden blocks known as deadeyes, they secured a matrix of ropes running up to the ship's three heavy masts and their expansive sails.

To our great amazement, conservators and archaeologists alike, cloth remnants of the sails survived the 300-year burial at sea. The 37 pieces of sailcloth were but an infinitesimal fraction of the fabric required to sail a square-rigger like *Queen Anne's Revenge*. Sailcloth of a coarse linen or canvas was usually made in shipyards, where patterns were cut and stitched together on the floor of sailmakers' warehouses. Edges and seams were creased and sewn over in distinct patterns of stitching to meet the demands of specific sails. Methods of making sailcloth varied through time.

Carefully removed from concretion, one piece of fabric, a mere 2 in. in length, exhibits attributes that are quite revealing. Its vertical stitching, which connects two separate pieces, is known as double-round seaming, standard for square sails during the first part of the eighteenth century. The swatch of sailcloth also exhibits "stuck-stitching" to enforce the seam, which according to literature wasn't introduced until later in the 1700s, making it one of the earliest known examples of this sailmaking technique. Another piece of fabric represents the foot of a square sail and also displays elements of early eighteenth-century sailcloth manufacture. It consists of an 8-in. length of cordage, known as boltrope, attached to the edge of the sail using marlin hitches. Boltropes provided strength along the upper and lower edges of square sails as the wind filled them out. Cordage is a broad term for

Examining Artifacts by Function

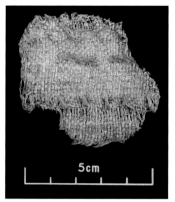

A remnant of fabric and a length of boltrope from *QAR* sails. Jeremy Borrelli, illustrator. (Courtesy of the North Carolina Department of Natural and Cultural Resources)

5cm

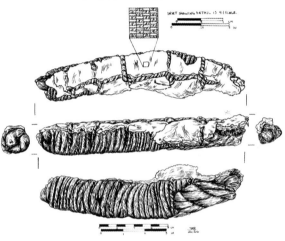

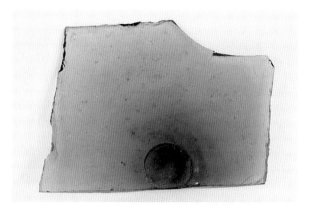

QAR glass panes from the captain's cabin, 4 to 4¾ in. wide and 5 to 6 in. long, were made in French glasshouses. (Courtesy of the North Carolina Department of Natural and Cultural Resources)

flexible stringlike material generally made of hemp and variously referred to as rope, twine, cord, cable, hawser, and lines, depending on size and weave, which were essential for sailing a ship as they fastened, tightened, and adjusted all its moving parts. Most of the fragmentary pieces recovered from the *QAR* site were common three-strand rope (2 to 3 in. in circumference) used for ship rigging. An exception was a relatively flexible and nonabrasive piece of rope found associated with a slave shackle, which is described later in this chapter.[5]

SHIP'S FURNISHINGS

Evidence of cabin windows came from fragments of glass panes blown using the crown method, which was invented in the Rouen region of France in the early fourteenth century. Crown glass exhibits a distinctive central bull's-eye, created when the

blower's pontil rod was snapped off. Finished edges of panes were then snipped to make them squarish, and thin lead strips, known as caming, some of which were also recovered, held the glass pieces in their wooden frames. The unique blue-green color of the *QAR* window glass matched the many shards of French flacon bottles also found in the wreckage, strongly suggesting that both had come from the wood-fired furnaces of Gresigne in Languedoc or the glass factories of Normandy.[6] Evidence of windows was found only in the stern of the ship, where they provided light, albeit heavily tinted, into the captain's quarter.

During our inspection dive of the *QAR* site after Hurricane Isabel passed through the area on September 18, 2003, pieces of a lead sheet full of holes were discovered in a heavily scoured area. We were dismayed that parts of the ship were being dislodged and possibly lost, since most material was much lighter than these lead pieces. Then our attention turned to understanding the object we had recovered, which represented the perforated pieces of a bilge strainer. When in operation, these strainer pieces covered the end of a wooden pump pipe that extended from the deck down into the bowels of the ship. A manually operated suction pump was used to pull water up through the pipe

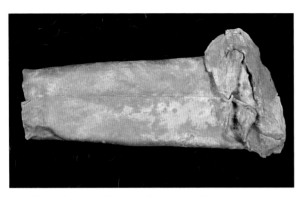

Lead liner for the officers' toilet, approximately 30 in. long with a 12-in.-diameter top opening. (Courtesy of the North Carolina Department of Natural and Cultural Resources)

"head" (the naval term for a toilet). Jokes notwithstanding, this particular artifact above all others found in the *QAR* wreckage is as personal in nature as one will ever get to the infamous pirate captain.[7]

REPAIRS AND MAINTENANCE

Keeping a ship afloat, particularly since it had been at sea for more than a year, must have been a constant challenge for the ship's carpenters. An amazing number of hull patches, over 100 lead sheets of all shapes and sizes, were recovered from the wreckage. It seems that leakage was a very big problem! In one instance, around the rudder straps on the sternpost, lead sheeting was installed at the shipyard. The rest, however, were applied while under way, down in the lowest part of the ship's bilges, where lots of water sloshed about. The goal was to stem leakage using the patches to cover the spaces between plank seams that first had been crammed with caulking and other stuffing, such as rags. The patches of lead were most often strips several inches in width and of varied lengths with parallel rows of nail holes along long edges. Some also exhibited longitudinal grooves down the centers where they were fitted into the hull seams. Based on their distribution, lead patches were used from stem to stern in a constant battle to slow leaks and keep the ship afloat. It was a pirate battle no one hears about.[8]

until it spilled onto the deck and over the side through openings called scuppers. As in household sink drains, the strainer kept debris from entering and clogging the pipe. Manning the pump, especially on a leaky ship like *Queen Anne's Revenge*, was a constant and unpleasant job, assigned to (or forced upon) crew members of the lowest rank.

Another oddly shaped piece of metal caught the attention of *QAR* conservator Shanna Daniel, who subsequently undertook its conservation and analysis. The object was made of sheet lead and slightly rolled into a cylinder shape and somewhat flattened. As Daniel learned, the device played an important role in the everyday routine aboard *Queen Anne's Revenge* (ex. *Concorde*). Its purpose was essential for nautical travelers needing to heed the call of nature, for this was the liner of their toilet, appropriately called the Seat of Ease. The *QAR* sanitary facility, or pissdale, would have been built into a small, enclosed balcony off the stern quarter and used by officers and their guests. The tiny enclosed room was equipped with a wooden seat over a hole lined with sheet lead to carry the waste down and out into the sea. The *QAR* toilet liner was recovered in the very stern of the wreckage, crumpled and folded over. Once Daniel had carefully straightened it out, she and her peers engaged in lively discussions about what it felt like to hold Blackbeard's

Among the most interesting items aboard the ship were the mechanical jack mentioned earlier and another similar one later found among the *QAR* wreckage. Called *crics* in France and wagon or timber jacks in English-speaking countries, they consisted of gears held in a wooden gearbox, a crank handle, and a ratcheted lifting bar with a top fork. Known from the sixteenth century forward, their basic operation was a "rack and pinon" leverage system that converted the rotary motion of the crank handle to the linear motion of the rack, allowing it to lift or spread considerable weight. Jacks were relatively common aboard ships and have been found on shipwrecks contemporary with

Examining Artifacts by Function

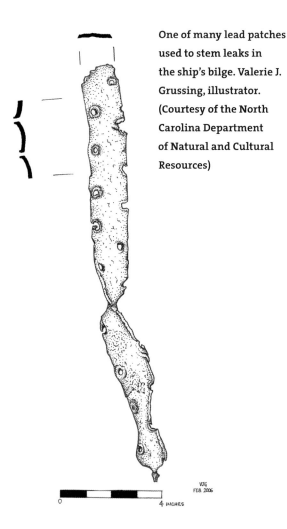

One of many lead patches used to stem leaks in the ship's bilge. Valerie J. Grussing, illustrator. (Courtesy of the North Carolina Department of Natural and Cultural Resources)

X-ray showing the inner workings of the mechanical jack gearbox, approximately 8 by 8 in. wide and 3 in. thick. (Courtesy of the North Carolina Department of Natural and Cultural Resources)

Queen Anne's Revenge.[9] The crank handle and pawl, which was the hook used to lock the device in place, were absent on one *QAR* jack, as was the wooden gearbox casing.

A few hand tools used by carpenters, caulkers, and painters for everyday use have, at least partially, survived. In some cases, epoxy castings of the cavities in the concretion where the tools' iron had corroded away allowed Watkins-Kenney's conservation team to restore them to near wholeness. The assemblage of hand tools contained one very valuable tool, a vice, used to clamp objects needing repair in a fixed position. The two hammers in the group were likely used by carpenters in their constant battle to stem leaks in the ship's lower hull. One aided the ship's caulker in driving oakum

(tarred hemp), or whatever stuffing was available, between the streaks of hull planking. The other, a small claw hammer with a narrow neck and small peened head, was suited for tacking lead patches to the hull. Two gouges, chisels with concave blades, were used to score and shape wood. One retained its wooden handle, which had been wrapped with cordage to enhance the carpenter's grip. Two files have been found. One is a nearly intact flat file with its fine crosshatch pattern used to sharpen gouges and other carpenter's tools, as well as the cook's knives and maybe pirate cutlasses and boarding axes. The second file is a square type with crosshatching on all four sides and used to shape wood.

A curious, oddly shaped stone turned out to be a muller or paint stone used for grinding ores and pigments into dry colorants for paint. The top was dome-shaped to fit snugly into the palm with a flattened grinding surface on the bottom. Most wooden ships were painted for protection against the natural elements of sun and salt water. The paints may have been in patriotic or fanciful color schemes that would broadcast the ship's ownership and intent for all to see. Colors varied throughout the Age of Sail with yellows, blacks, reds, blues, greens, and even

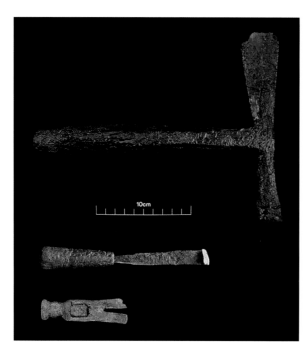

Composite image of *QAR* carpenter tools—caulking hammer, file with wooden handle, and claw hammer. (Courtesy of the North Carolina Department of Natural and Cultural Resources)

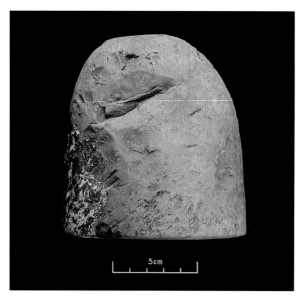

QAR paint muller made of stone. (Courtesy of the North Carolina Department of Natural and Cultural Resources)

white, each holding special cultural meaning that delineated friend from foe.

Finally, a rather interesting device, a curved-neck soldering iron with plumb-bob-shaped head, may have been used by the tinsmith or blacksmith to meld together or join two pieces of metal using a metallic alloy like tin. "Solder" is the Latin term for "to make solid," and solder has been used for a thousand years. Given the variety of gun parts found on this shipwreck, the soldering iron would be a useful tool to have for refitting and repurposing those specific brass items. The delicacy of this tool, however, suggests it more likely served as a cauterizing iron used by the French surgeons to burn human flesh and seal a wound.

Care to learn more about these early ailments and cures? Then continue your steady course straight ahead as we have so much more to tell you!

Sailing the Ship: Equipment and Tools—Tantalizing Clues

From the big, robust iron anchors to the fine and delicate brass mapping dividers, this group of artifacts was essential to plot a sailing ship's way, map its location, and keep it in place. Some are showy and shiny, like the two bronze bells, but most are plain and simple, such as sounding weights that resemble large fishing sinkers and were used to "sound" the depths of water while the ship was under way. Even more mundane were the ballast stones recovered from the *QAR* site. That's where the description and discussion of the ship's equipment and tools will begin.

BALLAST

Tons upon tons of waterworn cobbles served as ballast to keep *Queen Anne's Revenge* (ex. *Concorde*) upright during journeys across the high seas. Those tons of cobbles went down with the ship and remained on the bottom for nearly three centuries. After all that time, they began to move again, one by one, as a result of archaeological excavations:

first to a recovery basket on the bottom, then up the water column 23 ft. to a recovery vessel, then on a short ride to shore, and finally to the conservation lab 80 miles away. Early in the recovery project, some *QAR* ballast stones traveled much farther. Here's how it happened.

Once the ballast stones were retrieved by the divers, we decided to take them to a group of geologists: Dr. Jack Callahan of Appalachian University, Dr. James Craig of Virginia Polytechnic Institute, and Dr. William Miller of the University of North Carolina at Asheville. They weren't marine geologists, but the "hard rock" kind who had agreed to take a look at our seemingly ordinary stones. As we laid them out on the driveway at Callahan's house in Boone, we wondered if it had been worth the effort to drive 300 miles across the state of North Carolina. But then again, this exercise followed a similar pattern for other aspects of the *QAR* project. When specialists couldn't make it to the conservation lab, then we made every effort to carry the artifacts to them. It was our intention to garner the best analysis and research possible for the various bits and pieces, big and small, from *Queen Anne's Revenge.*

But squeezing useful information out of stone, especially ballast, was a long shot, because this essential element of a sailing ship was often exchanged, depending on what cargo was being carried or swapped out. There was a good chance that *QAR* ballast, as with most sailing ships, was a wide mixture of cobbles that had been taken on and off many different ships in various ports around the world for centuries and centuries. There was only a chance that the stones would reveal a pattern or source that held any meaning, but it was still enough to inspire research. So it was on that sunny summer day in the Appalachian Mountains with Callahan, Craig, and Miller we spent the morning examining each rock and placing them in piles, sorted by general type. A basalt here, a gabbro there, and so it went. Sometimes they chipped off a rock's outer cortex (or rind) using a small prospect-

Geologists Dr. Bill Miller, Dr. Jack Callahan, and Dr. Jim Craig analyze *QAR* ballast in Morehead City. (Courtesy of the North Carolina Department of Natural and Cultural Resources)

ing hammer to expose a fresh surface for making a positive identification. At the end of the session, information was recorded, and the stones were repacked for the long drive back to the North Carolina coast and returned to storage at the *QAR* lab.

This was just the beginning of an extensive study to interpret *QAR* ballast, and our colleagues took their job seriously. Not stopping with that first group of rocks, they continued to examine hundreds more to make sure the pattern they were detecting was real. In the end, Callahan, Craig, and Miller studied more than a ton of ballast stones, 2,703 lbs. to be exact, and found them to be surprisingly homogeneous and evenly distributed across the site. Over 80 percent fell into three major types: microporphyritic basalts, porphyritic volcanics, and hornblende gabbros. Rather than a broad mixture of types picked up from generic piles of ballast rubble in many places, it appeared the ballast stones had come from a specific area.

The geology team's goal then was to find that spot, if it was indeed possible, where the *QAR* ballast had last been gathered and placed on board, whether it be in France, Africa, or the Americas. That's when they really got down to work using petrography, bulk chemical compositions, trace elements such as zirconium and titanium, potassium-

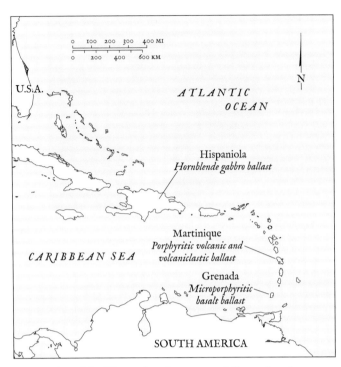

Map of Caribbean showing source of *Queen Anne's Revenge* ballast

QAR ship's bell dated 1705. (Courtesy of the North Carolina Department of Natural and Cultural)

argon and argon-argon radiometric dating techniques, Mössbauer spectroscopy, and 87/86 Sr ratios ("signatures") for distinguishing basalts from one another and to compare to island data.[10] They subjected those common cobbles to every tool they had in their analytic arsenal; it was enough to make one's head spin. Lo and behold, it all paid off! Using the known travels of *Concorde* on both sides of the Atlantic as the potential source(s) of *QAR* ballast, they found likely matches with natural stones from islands of the Caribbean based on age, composition, and variation. Specifically, origins could be tied to Hispaniola (the western half of which was formerly Saint-Domingue), Martinique, and Grenada, France's three primary New World possessions.[11] The slave trading port of Martinique, *Concorde's* destination before being intercepted by pirates, lay in the middle of these islands, thus linking the vessel specifically to the commerce of this area. The trip across North Carolina carrying a bunch of rocks was indeed worth our effort.

SHIP'S BELLS

The larger of two bronze bells, the one which produced the ring tone that reached back in time described earlier, is embossed with "IHS MARIA" and "ANO 1705." It stands 13 in. high and has a base diameter of just over 8 in. Weighing 21 lbs., it is made of bronze, a 79 percent copper and 19 percent tin alloy with traces of zinc, iron, silver, and lead, which is a fairly standard composition for bells of the time. The hanger is called a git top or peg argent, also common on bells of this size and period. On top of the hanger is the casting sprue from the pour hole, which had not been filed off. This feature, along with the unevenly spaced block type letters, indicated to our consulting bell experts that this was not made in a bell factory but, rather, by itinerant bell casters. The iron clapper was lost due to galvanic action, but a casting made of the concretion cavity revealed a length of about 4 in. and a diameter increasing from ⅔ of an inch to

Examining Artifacts by Function

1 ¾ in. A small channel on the underside of the bell provided an attachment for the clapper.[12]

While the IHS MARIA bell was found on the main pile in the middle of the wreckage the day of discovery, a second bell was found in the stern area of the wreckage during excavations in the fall of 2006. It was also made of bronze, although there was less copper and higher amounts of tin and lead in its composition. It measured 4 in. shorter and 6 lbs. lighter than the earlier bell and had a broken hanger. There are no inscriptions on the bell's outer surface; its general style suggests it was manufactured in England during the seventeenth or eighteenth century.[13]

Early on, a few of us on the project speculated that if numerous bells were found, the pirates aboard the ship may have been hoarding them. Bells held monetary value due to their metal, which could be melted down and recast into cannons. With much of the main portion of the wreckage excavated, it seems unlikely more will be found. Thus, it seems logical that the larger of the two, the IHS MARIA bell, was used in the forecastle for signaling and sounding alarms, and the smaller one was used in the stern as a watch bell. By the early

eighteenth century, watch bells were important accoutrements in terms of regulating shipboard activities. Perhaps one day you will be able hear the very sounds that Blackbeard and his crew heard as they went about their daily pirating lives.

ANCHORS

Three anchors have been designated A-1, A-2, and A-3. They are typical in style for eighteenth-century ships, with their long shanks and wooden stocks. The first two anchors were found within the main rubble mound, and the third was approximately 50 ft. forward of the others. They were all quite hefty, with shanks measuring 11 ft. 4 in., 13 ft., and 13 ft. 7 in., respectively.

Ships carried anchors of several sizes that served various functions. The bowers were the largest and, as the name suggests, were carried on the vessel's bow for rapid deployment. Bowers also varied somewhat in size according to their roles. Sheet anchors, also called the best bowers, were the largest anchors aboard and were carried on a ship's starboard bow only to be dropped in extreme conditions. Slightly smaller anchors called lesser bowers were used under normal circumstances. The *QAR* anchors were all likely bowers, although the latter two were slightly oversized for the ship's registered tonnage of 200 to 300 tons burthen. The deposition by *Concorde*'s Lieutenant Ernaut recorded an event early in its last voyage during which the lesser bower was lost. Based on its reported weight, its shank would have measured about 12 ft.[14]

The position of the three *QAR* anchors within the wreckage as it relates to the presumed layout of the ship is telling. Anchors A-1 and A-2 appear within the central mound area intermingled with numerous cannons and the bulk of the ballast stone. It appears that this pair, which according to

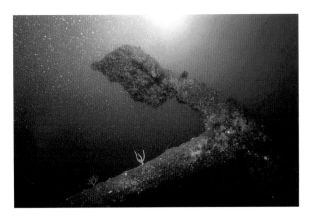

Anchor A-3 standing proudly on the seafloor. Photograph by Julep Gillman-Bryan. (Courtesy of the North Carolina Department of Natural and Cultural Resources)

QAR grapnel anchor being taken off R/V *Shell Point* by UAB archaeological conservator Nathan Henry and *QAR* archaeologist Chris Southerly at the U.S. Coast Guard Station Fort Macon. (Courtesy of the North Carolina Department of Natural and Cultural Resources)

their sizes provided the crew with a sheet anchor and a lesser bower, were an extra set of anchors stored in the hold for future use. On the other hand, Anchor A-3 was located away from the others in what has been identified as the vessel's bow. Being the largest of the three anchors and located in the vicinity of the starboard bow points to it being the sheet anchor. It appears to have dropped straight down onto the seafloor sometime after grounding. Carrying extra anchors and ones that may have been oversized and not originally issued

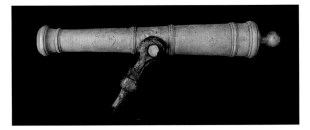

Bronze signaling cannon with pivot mount. (Courtesy of the North Carolina Department of Natural and Cultural Resources)

for the vessel would not be surprising for a pirate ship. It would have been an advantage to cut the anchor cable and leave the anchor behind when unexpectedly confronted by a military ship, especially if there were spare anchors for later use. Historical accounts indicate that pirate crews were apt to take the anchors from ships they captured.[15]

A large, grapnel-type anchor with four arms (flukes) and a shaft of 8 ft. was also found in the main pile, suggesting it was also stored below deck. These types of anchors with their multiple flukes are well suited to rocky bottoms. The grapnel was likely another spare, should the pirate crew need it somewhere along their travels.

SIGNALING CANNON

A nifty little bronze cannon (C-25) only 19 3/32 in. in length has been identified as a signaling or saluting gun.[16] The attached iron yoke would have been used to mount it on the railing of the stern where it was found. The muzzle-loading cannon fired a half-pound shot and, rather than providing firepower as a weapon, was more likely used to signal nearby ships. Signaling cannons were most often intended for personal yachts or naval fleet flagships—indeed quite fitting to be found on Blackbeard's *Queen Anne's Revenge*! It is also rather unique. The general shape of the gun and its muzzle, as well as the two sets of single bands around its barrel, indicates English manufacture, while the less ornate style of the cascabel (knob at the rear) resembles those

Examining Artifacts by Function

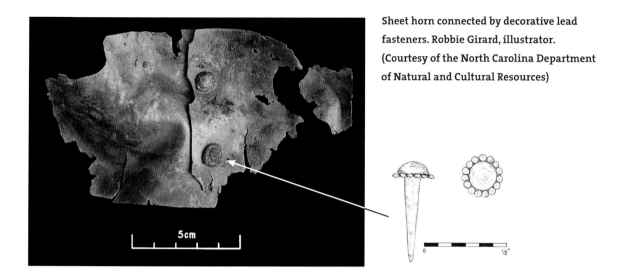

Sheet horn connected by decorative lead fasteners. Robbie Girard, illustrator. (Courtesy of the North Carolina Department of Natural and Cultural Resources)

made in Northern Europe (Netherlands, Denmark, North Germany, and Sweden). Apparently the signaling cannon was prized, since it exhibited evidence of heavy use and repairs, but not so valuable as to warrant taking it when the ship grounded and was abandoned.

ILLUMINATION

To light up the night and the dark interiors of the ship, lanterns, lamps, and candles of tallow were needed on board. Lanterns made of wooden or metal framing would be fitted with small "panes" of sheet horn, which was thin, lightweight, heat resistant, translucent, and most importantly, unbreakable. Referred to as lanthorns, these lighting devices were large and often used to signal other ships or carried on the port side. A possible *QAR* lanthorn is represented by two panes of thin sheet horn (or keratin) riveted together with lead fasteners.[17] The decorative lead fasteners, less than 1 in. in length, are noteworthy. Their heads are domed with a beaded edge and have square-shaped shanks that taper to a soft point. The fasteners were manufactured using a mold much like a gang mold for lead bullets, casting several at a time. Many of the tacks were found loose with shanks crimped, coiled,

or occasionally left straight. They are considered of seventeenth- and early eighteenth-century English origin, based on the few other sites where they have been found.[18]

A second type of lamp was found in the wreckage, evidenced by a small yet symbolic adornment shaped like a hen and made of copper alloy. At first, we speculated that this decorative finial came from the lid of a set of nested weights, also made of copper alloy. A final identification, however, came about when we visited a national naval museum in 2013. There, hanging in the exhibit case that highlighted French and American alliances, was a small eighteenth-century oil lamp, called a gimbal, suspended from an iron hook on a rafter. It was equipped with a small reservoir to hold the oil (likely whale) fitted with two wick portals and a decorative hen finial to hold the wick. We have also found another matching example that was made in St. Etienne, France, a town of origin for one of the French surgeons.[19] This type of lamp would also have been perfectly suited to dispel the darkness from the windowless surgeon's quarters and provide good light for tending the sick and injured. By being suspended, it would swing with the ship's rocking and not tip over.

Brass gimbal oil lamp of French origin with matching decorative hen finial or wick holder, less than an inch tall and wide, from the *QAR* site. (Courtesy of the National Museum of the United States Navy and the North Carolina Department of Natural and Cultural Resources)

NAVIGATIONAL INSTRUMENTS

While candlelight and oil lamps provided guidance in the dark, sailors and pirates needed instruments to guide their ships across oceans and into inlets, to determine their position at sea, and to gauge distances. For many centuries humans have been using celestial signposts such as the sun, the stars and planets, and the curvature of the earth to find their way. Naturally sailors at sea used the same. Durable instruments made of rust-resistant brass (or copper alloy) have been identified from the shipwreck. These include navigational compass parts, numerous dividers (also known as charting compasses), a universal staff mount (for a tripod), two pairs of decorative set screws, a sector, a survey instrument sight, and a logarithmic bar. To jot down position readings when someone was taking measurements, writing tablets made of slate were often used. At the end of the day, permanent readings were recorded in the ship's log by the captain or navigator. Evidence of these writing slates was found in the *QAR* debris, but any logbook was either removed or lost to the sea. To gauge the depth of the ocean and the speed of the ship, sounding weights or leads were required.

Dividers were constructed of two legs held together with a top pin that allowed the legs to be spread wide or narrow at the pivot. Small pieces of steel, or nibs, were placed in the forked ends of each leg to measure and plot points on charts or maps. Three types of dividers were found on the wreckage, some with straight legs about 4 in. in length and some called "bowlegs" with a curved upper portion almost 6 in. in length.[20] Another hinged measuring device from the *QAR* site is called a Gunter's rule or sector, an instrument developed in 1588, which has two arms scaled in logarithmic increments shown in recessed dots and needle holes. The *QAR* example has English inches on one arm, while on the backside of both arms the increments are in slightly longer French inches. The first block is further scaled into 12 increments, and a small set pin holds the arms in

Examining Artifacts by Function

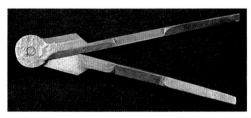

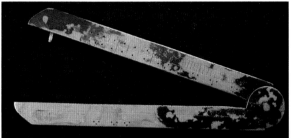

QAR brass mapping instruments include a set of dividers, 3½ in. long minus the nibs (*top*), and a 5-in.-long folding Gunter's rule (*bottom*). (Courtesy of the North Carolina Department of Natural and Cultural Resources)

Components of the brass universal staff mount, approximately 6 in. tall and a socket diameter of 2⅛ in. (Courtesy of the North Carolina Department of Natural and Cultural Resources)

place when closed.[21] The sector was used in tandem with dividers for accurate calculations in scaling to proportion on charts. To plot courses and correlate mapping points, a plane table was needed. This piece of equipment was typically a solid wood table mounted onto tripod legs that could be pivoted in various angles and directions and, when not in use, broken down and stored. Two pairs of decorative set screws, the type used to hold charts, maps, or paper in place on a plane table, have been found. A *QAR* universal staff mount made of brass that likely supported a table or compass has a "rectangular pierced plate with a socket connected to it by a universal ball joint. A worm screw rotates an internal gear, which in turn exerts pressure on a leather gasket, thus fixing the ball in place."[22] A brass sight is also likely associated with a circumferentor. The sight is designed as a longish bar slotted twice for both general and pinpoint aiming; the crosshair elements, as well as the second sighting arm, are missing.

And what would navigation be without the essential compass? A magnetized compass used for sea travel was often housed in a wooden box or case, sometimes with a fitted lid. The compass

card was painted in triangles radiating outward from a central pin. The underside of the card was equipped with two magnetized steel wires. The bowl of the compass would be suspended in the box by brass bands called gimbal rings, allowing it to move with the ship's rocking and swaying, similar to the gimbal lamp. The compass arm or needle was fitted to the central pin floating above the card, and then a glass cover was mounted over the face to prevent damage or interference. The card revolved freely to point to magnetic north. The Lubber Line was positioned in line with the ship's keel, which was always on course.[23] The compass needle and fragments of the gimbal rings are remains of the *QAR* compass.

Beyond knowing landmarks, directions, and winds, understanding the waters and what lay beneath was essential for a ship's pilot. Navigational devices called sounding weights were important tools in determining depth and composition of the seafloor. These lead objects, which came in varying sizes, were molded or shaped into elongated bars, perforated at one end for a rope attachment, and indented at the base for sampling the bottom sedi-

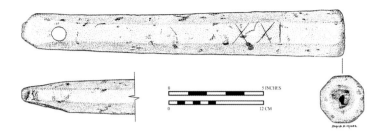

QAR sounding weight with hollow end for sampling the seafloor sediments. David D. Moore, illustrator. (Courtesy of the North Carolina Department of Natural and Cultural Resources)

ments. Depth was measured in fathoms (6 ft.), and thus the rope line was marked off in those increments. Like casting a fishing hook into the surf, the tossing of the lead weights was a ballet of motion set to a cadence of song.

With the free end of the toss line secured to a fixed post on deck, the "leadsman" would swing the tied weight over his head like a pendulum three or four times for greater momentum and distance and then cast the lead as far forward as possible, letting the rope run out until it reached bottom. This action was called "heaving the lead."

Heaving of the Lead

For England when with fav'ring Gale,
Our gallant ship up Channel steer'd,
And, scudding under easy sale;
To heave the lead the seaman sprung,
And to the pilot cheerly sung.
"By the deep—nine!"

And bearing up to gain the port;
Some well-known object kept in view,
An abbey tow'r, a harbour fort,
Or beacon to the vessel true;
While oft the lead the seamen flung,
And to the pilot cheerly sung.
"By the mark—seven!"

And as the much lov'd shore we near,
With transport we behold the roof,
Where dwells a friend, or partner dear,
Of faith and love a matchless proof,
The lead once more the seaman flung,
And to the watchful pilot sung.
"Quarter less—five!"[24]

Deep-sea weights, also known as "dipseys," were heaviest, maybe more than 25 lbs., and could extend to depths of 20 fathoms or more, while the lighter weights, 5 to 10 lbs. were used in shallow waters.[25] To sample the composition of the seabed, tallow was packed into the indentation at the base of a weight, which picked up sands, gravels, or shells from the seafloor. Knowledge of seabed sediments was critical to understanding the submerged landscape of the area and location of impending obstacles, such as sandbars. A log line was also used to gauge the speed of the ship, measured in "knots" by carefully counting fathom markers of the log line coordinated with a timepiece, such as a sandglass, neither of which survivied.

The number of sounding weights carried on eighteenth-century ships varied but normally would have been limited to two, one for inland or coastal waters and the other for water depths farther offshore. Surprisingly, 12 potential sounding leads have been recovered from the *QAR* site. They vary in size, with the largest weighing nearly 40 lbs.! Now that would have taken quite a hardy sailor to heave and retrieve it. Another sounding weight, incised with Roman numerals XXI (21 lbs.), still had the remnants of a rope attached.[26] Much smaller weights, about 3 in. long and weighing 1 lb. each, appear to have been modified or whittled and may have been used as counterbalances for scales rather than as sounding weights. They could have also served as fishing weights or as plumb bobs with surveying instruments. Even if they weren't all sounding weights, it seems that *Queen Anne's Revenge* was clearly overstocked in this department, which points to a practice of hoarding extra tools and implements as the opportunity arose for the pirates.

A Battle-Worthy Vessel: Big Guns and Lots of Ammo

Sailing the high seas in the early eighteenth century required most ships to be battle ready, some more than others. For Blackbeard and a few other captains bold enough to challenge naval authority, augmenting their ships with additional weapons and firepower was of utmost importance. If nothing more, cannons created big blasts meant to intimidate the opponent. An armed vessel's big guns were fitted into wooden carriages set on four wheels operated by rope pulley and tackle systems for heaving out (forward) or retracting (aft) from their respective gun ports. Round cannonballs could punch holes in hulls and splinter railings and decking. Launching projectiles such as double-headed shot to disable sails and rigging, however, was the preferred pirate tactic to slow, not sink, a desired prize ship. At close range, standard rounds of grapeshot were fired at enemy personnel. An unconventional load, called langrage and consisting of bundled iron bolts or bagged bits of lead shot, bent nails, and shards of glass, served the same purpose. Langrage was not a standard naval munition, but a contrivance commonly employed by pirates, privateers, and desperate merchantmen during heated battles.

Basic protocol for firing a cannon required a team of gunners working in quick coordination to fire and reload during battle. One member, called a powder monkey, provided the explosive charge; another packed in wadding, the chosen projectile, and more wadding; and another member using a long-handled wooden rammer would pack it firmly down the cannon tube. Once the fuse was lit using a lintstock (match stick), everyone around braced for the force of the recoil as it fired. And between these quick firings the cannon had to be swabbed clean with a wet sheepskin sponge to extinguish sparks before the tube was reloaded. The touchhole was also cleaned with a vent pick, typically made of nonsparking brass. Other cannon accoutrements

"Twenty-four-pound Truck Gun (1776)," by Edwin Tunis, in his *Oars, Sails, and Steam: A Picture Book of Ships* (Cleveland: World Publishing, 1952), 39.

found on the *QAR* site included wooden tampions used to plug the cannon muzzle when not in use, slivers of wood fashioned to seal touchholes, and removable lead sheets, called aprons, that covered the breech touchholes. All were essential in keeping the barrels and touchholes free of saltwater spray so that the cannons would remain serviceable.

On his newly acquired vessel, Blackbeard set about quickly augmenting the 14 cannons aboard *Concorde* to a reported 40 when he was in full "pirate-power" during the blockade of Charleston harbor. No doubt he quickly filled the French vessel's original gun ports with additional 6-pounders and then added smaller carriage guns as well as rail-guns, at least a few of which were breechloaders, so aptly called "murderers" for effectiveness at close range.

CANNONS

Smoothbore, muzzle-loading ordnance of cast iron or bronze became popular in the mid-sixteenth century and soon reached dominance among the weapons of war throughout Europe.[27] Cannons

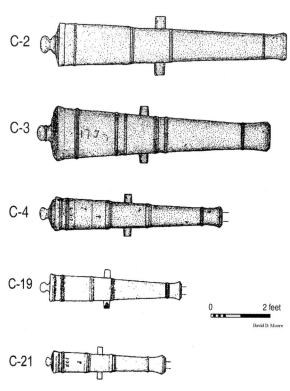

0   2 feet

David D. Moore

Plan drawing of *QAR* cannons: two 6-pounders, one 4-pounder, and two half-pounders. David D. Moore, illustrator. (Courtesy of the North Carolina Department of Natural and Cultural Resources)

remained basically unchanged for nearly 300 years, and manufacturers were known to embellish the large guns with patriotic or spiritual symbols (e.g., fleurs-de-lis, rampant lions, or sea serpents), as well as maker's marks and date of manufacture. By the early eighteenth century, cannon sizes and bores were becoming more standardized, classified by the weight of the iron balls they fired.

Thirty cannons have been recorded for the *QAR* shipwreck. Twenty-four have been raised, of which 6 are fully conserved, and the remaining 18 are undergoing cleaning and treatment at the conservation lab. They are dominated in size mostly by 6-pounders, 17 total, although one or two might be slightly larger 9-pounders. The remaining armament includes four 4-pounders, two 2-pounders, four 1-pounders, and two half-pounders. Each cannon has been numbered sequentially, based on when it was discovered, from C-1 to C-30. Included in this count was the small bronze signaling cannon, C-25, described earlier as part of the ship's furnishings. The discussion below focuses on some of the iron cannons that have undergone cleaning and analysis. All cannons appear to have been manufactured in England or Sweden.

Cannon C-19, a 1-pounder, has very interesting marks on its trunnions—the perpendicular projections that hold the cannon tube upon its carriage. The ends of trunnions are a common place to cast important information. One trunnion reads "713" and represents the date of manufacture in 1713. The other reads "IEC," a maker's mark representing the initials of Jesper Ehrencreutz, the man who oversaw operations at the Ehrendal foundry in Sweden from 1695 to 1722.[28]

Another set of carved numbers made after casting—173—appears on the body of Cannon C-3. It is a Swedish 6-pounder known as a finbanker, based on its shape and reinforcement ring pattern, with manufacture sometime between 1675 and 1700. The numbers likely indicated a weight in French *libre* or perhaps an identification mark by a Dutch trader.[29]

Cannon C-21 exhibits an English proof mark P and the marked weight of 1-3-3 (or 199 lbs.) and was cast in a two-part mold. Its small-bore diameter places it into a half-pounder category. This small cannon is particularly unique because it was made of cast iron rather than bronze, which was standard for the smaller guns. More importantly, it was cast in a two-part mold rather than a single mold. All cannons up to this point were cast solid and required boring out with a huge drilling machine. This is the earliest known example of a cannon being cast in a two-part mold.[30]

AMMUNITION, GUNPOWDER, AND WADDING

The crew felt a bit foolish, but their attempts to clean the barrel of a big 6-pounder were proving very difficult. They cursed the situation. The cannon had been left loaded for way too long in the salt-ridden environment. Chalk it up to pirate neglect. Now they had to clean up the mess and get the cannon wads, ball, and powder charge safely extracted.

These weren't Blackbeard's gunners doing the work, but the *QAR* conservation team of Nathan Henry, Wendy Welsh, and Michael Tutwiler, who were dealing with Cannon C-3, which had rested on the seabed untouched for nearly 300 years. The wooden tampion had long since rotted away, and there was nearly an inch of encrustation lining the inner surface of the cannon barrel. They had devised various makeshift tools to slowly grind their way nearly 6 ft. to where the cannonball was nested. One tool, fashioned from an old iron tie-down used on mobile homes, resembled the gun worm of old. Other cleaning instruments were made from tubes of metal or PVC, slightly undersized to scrape the barrel clean. Often the modified devices became stuck, and it took conservators everything they had to extract them in order to keep cleaning. Cannon C-3 required days upon days of very slow progress to reach and remove the outer hemp wadding, then the six-pound iron ball, the inner wad, and last, a faint trace of the powder charge.[31] More recently, Watkins-Kenney's conservation staff have devised a mechanical boring machine, in some ways similar to those used in yesteryear to manufacture cannons, that makes the work of unloading cannons much quicker, safer, and more accurate.

UAB archaeological conservator Nathan Henry and *QAR* conservators Mike Tutwiler and Wendy Welsh unloading a 6-pounder cannon tube. (Courtesy of the North Carolina Department of Natural and Cultural Resources)

Langrage (three iron bolts) loaded in front of the ball inside Cannon C-19; largest bolt is 8 in. long with a shaft diameter of 1⅛ in. (Courtesy of the North Carolina Department of Natural and Cultural Resources)

The wooden tampions from a couple of the small cannons remained intact, so once they were removed, the bores were quite easy to clean. And sometimes they offered quite a surprise. That was the case for Cannon C-19, which released a puff of centuries-old air as its tampion was being removed. With Cannon C-21, after removal of its tampion and outer wadding, the cannonball simply rolled out its muzzle! Blackbeard's crew must have done a better job maintaining their guns than we first thought.

Additional information comes from cannons that are beginning conservation and analysis. For example, x-raying 6 cannons brought the number of loaded cannons to 9 out of 12, indicating the vessel was battle ready. Those loaded cannons contained a single round shot with wadding holding

A bundle of hemp cordage served as the outer wadding to pack the load in *QAR* Cannon C-19. (Courtesy of the North Carolina Department of Natural and Cultural Resources)

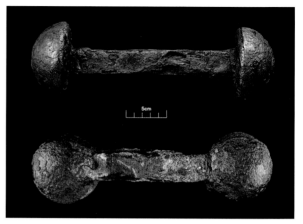

Two of several types of cannon bar shot found on the *QAR* site. (Courtesy of the North Carolina Department of Natural and Cultural Resources)

it in place and some evidence of a powder charge at the breech. Cannon C-19, however, and possibly Cannon C-8, contained a bundle of three iron bolts placed in front of its shot and charge, interpreted as langrage, a nasty load indeed.

Gunpowder made of saltpeter was typically stored in barrels with wooden hoops in a dry hold or armory to prevent it from getting wet. It further needed to be handled with materials that would not spark, like brass, copper, wood, cloth, or leather. Gunpowder could be loaded into paper cartridges or cloth bags and positioned at the rear of the cannon tube, or simply poured in loose. Evidence of all three methods has been found in *QAR* cannons.[32] Wadding was rammed into the barrel to hold the gunpowder in place, followed by the projectile, then more wadding to hold everything in. Dr. Runying Chen, a textile expert from East Carolina University's Department of Interior Design and Merchandising, analyzed the size, twist, and fiber composition of wadding from four *QAR* cannons. All were made from coarse fiber bundles of hemp, perhaps representing scraps of rope lying around the ship. Chen found one exception to be the middle wadding of Cannon C-19, the Swedish 1-pounder that exhibited finer fiber bundles. Rather than hemp, it appears to have been made from ramie, a plant in the nettle

family (*Urticaceae*) and used extensively in Scandinavia and other European countries during the early eighteenth century.[33] Perhaps in this case the wadding and cannon came together as a unit. More often cannon accoutrements lacked uniformity, likely a result of pirates' need to replenish their supplies through plundering ships, or repurposing what they had on hand, like old rope or paper. Making do in order to make war, one might say.

The vast majority of more than 90 loose cannon munitions are solid iron round shot, which correspond neatly in size and number to the frequency of the cannons they fit.[34] The vast majority fit 6-pounders, although a slightly oversized shot may be for a 9-pounder; the rest correspond proportionately to the smaller cannons. There is also a 24-pound cannonball, recovered on the day of discovery. It likely had been shot from nearby Fort Macon during the Civil War and came to rest on the shipwreck during a subsequent period when wreckage was exposed. You may recall what was happening at the *QAR* site in 1927 that might have helped the oversized ball migrate to the wreckage. If not, check back to Chapter 3.

In addition to round cannonballs, other styles of iron ammunition were recovered, collectively referred to as bar shot, which were designed to shred

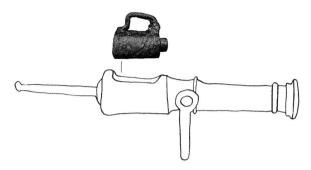

Partially cleaned cast-iron breechblock, 9¾ in. long, showing where it fit on a swivel gun. (Courtesy of the North Carolina Department of Natural and Cultural Resources)

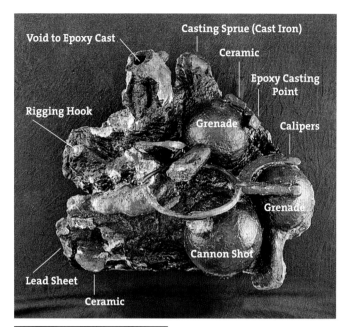

A partially excavated *QAR* concretion containing a variety of artifacts, including the hemispherical calipers, shown after cleaning. (Courtesy of the North Carolina Department of Natural and Cultural Resources)

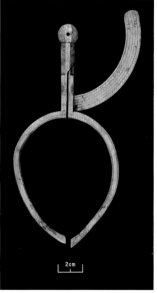

sails and foul rigging. In summary, we know the ship was outfitted with a range of projectiles from standard naval issue to homemade bag shot and bundled bolts.

BREECHBLOCKS

Radiography revealed two iron breechblocks or chamber inserts for a swivel gun. These breech-loaders were mounted into a yoke-like swivel on the ship's railing; similar to a modern oarlock, they could be pivoted in a 360-degree range. Swivel grips or tillers were sometimes fastened to the back of the gun to facilitate quick pivots for oncoming attackers charging from different directions. For rapid firing, several breechblocks were made ready by filling them with gunpowder and shot, kept dry with wooden tampions until put into action. These small cannons were loaded with "base and burr" or "hail shot" for a shotgun effect.[35]

TOOLS TO MEASURE, LOAD, OR EXTRACT

Firing a cannon was an orchestrated event with numerous crew members participating to set commands, action, and timing. In addition to the gunners' team, the cannon with all its parts, munitions in all variety, and gunpowder, several other implements were essential to make this weapon of war operational. Getting the right size ammunition into the right size cannon tube was important. The armorer was in charge of sorting the spherical shot stored in the magazine, and to do this he used tools found on the *QAR* shipwreck. One such measuring instrument is a logarithmic bar, four-sided in cross section and lightweight, with rounded finials at each end. Three of the four sides exhibit scales

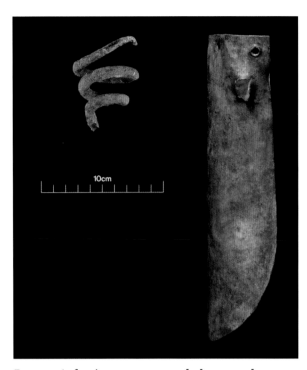

Epoxy cast of an iron gun worm and a brass powder scoop, both missing their wooden handles. (Courtesy of the North Carolina Department of Natural and Cultural Resources)

Tools known as cannon sidearms—the gun worm, powder ladle, rammer, and sponge—were essential to ensuring a successful firing. The powder scoop or ladle, typically made of nonsparking brass or copper fitted to a long wooden handle, was used to place loose powder carefully into the gun tube. Then the wooden rammer, also long-handled, was used to pack the powder and subsequent wadding firmly into place. The *QAR* ladle was crushed when found and missing its wooden parts, but it has since been conserved and extended nearly to its original shape. It measures just under 10 in. and is about 4 in. in diameter, exhibiting five holes unevenly spaced where it was once attached to the wooden plug. There is also one large hole near the top where it was accidentally pierced by a circular object such as the ramrod.

Another component of the cannon sidearms was a gun worm, a corkscrew device essential for extraction of a misfired load from the barrel. Also called a worming iron, the *QAR* example was completely degraded but was resurrected through epoxy casting. Consisting of three spiral coils 3 in. in height and 2 in. in diameter, the tool was made to fit a 1-pounder cannon. It would also have been fitted to a long wooden handle, which is missing. The extraction of powder charges was a dangerous task and likely led to many accidents and fatalities among the pirate gun crew. Volunteers for this duty were rare.

graduated in sets of five, two sides from 0 to 24 and the third side from 0 to 60. It has been identified as gunner's rule, or tally stick, to determine the size of cannon shot.[36] A set of calipers consisting of two arched legs hinged at the top and tapering to a point were designed to measure the diameter of spheres or cavities. Eighteenth-century gunners and armorers used them to measure cannon bores and shot diameters. They are fitted with a graduated arc that provides a direct read of the measurement from increments incised into the metal and relevant to what's being measured.[37] The *QAR* calipers are incised with two sets of numbers and letters on the front and back of the arc. Without maker's mark, we do not know if these graduated increments are intended for a French, English, German, or Swedish scale, or perhaps a combination and designed to be universal.

CANNON APRONS AND MORE

To protect cannon touchholes from sea spray and flying debris and to prevent accidental firing, uniform, flat sheets of malleable lead or leather were cut into rectangular pieces and placed over the breech. The term "apron" for these covers is derived from early gunners' manuals of the late seventeenth century.[38] Aprons were secured by lashes made of leather or rope fitted into two holes drilled on each side of the covers and designed for quick and easy removal. One end was cut into slits creating a series of "fingers," mostly equal in width and length,

Examining Artifacts by Function

A typical *QAR* lead cannon apron, 12 in. long and 8¼ in. wide. (Courtesy of the North Carolina Department of Natural and Cultural Resources)

to ensure a tight fit over the rounded and tapering gun barrel.

The lengths and widths of 13 *QAR* lead aprons are fairly uniform, though in many cases they clearly represent unstandardized, shipboard-fashioned items that could be modified on the spot by the gunner crew as needed. The most re-markable aspect of these cannon aprons, however, is their unique graffiti. Its appearance on these humble touchhole covers reveals more than artistic expression or random doodling by the *QAR*'s gun crew, for these symbols themselves carry profound cultural meanings centuries old.

Cannons were vital weapons needed to complete predatory missions and likewise to provide protec-tion when the ship was attacked. If the vessel was an eighteenth-century naval warship, its mission was to neutralize the opponent through use of force, total destruction, or surrender. For a priva-teering or pirate ship, the objective was purely eco-nomical, to take a prize vessel and all its contents with minimal damage to its hull or function. Can-nons were primarily used by pirates to intimidate, bring the opponent to engage, and slow a vessel long enough to get close for boarding. The face-to-face combat that followed required another arsenal of smaller weapons, which we shall now explore.

"Blackbeard the Pirate" shown with a brace of six pistols, from an engraving by Benjamin Cole in the 2nd edition of Captain Charles Johnson [Nathaniel Mist], *A General History of the Robberies and Murders of the Most Notorious Pyrates* (1725), 70. (Courtesy of the Library of Congress, Rare Book and Special Collections Division, Washington. D.C.)

An Armed Crew: Weapons That Cut, Weapons That Fire

After the smoke cleared from the blasts of cannon fire and the noises of splintering wood subsided, what followed was even more terrifying for the crew of a targeted prize as they were soon overrun by a swarm of pirates with vengeance in their eyes and combat weapons in their hands. Most pirate captains, including Blackbeard, preferred to best any opposing ship by the use of intimi-

Aprons of Lead

LAURA KATE SCHNITZER

Many of the *QAR* cannon aprons have inscribed markings on their surfaces that are not explained by their function as touchhole covers. The markings range from simple linear tick marks to ornate designs and letters. Some markings are obviously incidental, since lead is very soft, but others seem purposely inscribed and artistic. The most intricate markings are made using a repeating series of crescent lines that have been incised in the surface of the lead to form a pattern or symbol. A similar technique, known as "wrigglework" (also referred to as "rockering"), was used to decorate pewter in the seventeenth, eighteenth, and early nineteenth centuries. On several *QAR* aprons, wrigglework-like marks form symbols that resemble the letters M or W or double VV.[1]

Research also revealed similarities between the apron marks and marks carved into architectural timbers of seventeenth- and eighteenth-century English homes.[2] The marks are called apotropaic symbols, and architectural historians believe they were placed around entryways such as door jambs, windows, and hearths as ritual protection from evil. Fear of witches was prevalent for many centuries in England, not just among common people, but also among high-ranking clergymen and government officials. In 1604, a treatise on witchcraft called *Daemonologie* warned the public that supernatural evils gained entry to homes and churches by way of any unprotected thresholds. It seems logical that a ship's gunport could also be considered an unprotected threshold. Mariners were and still are notoriously superstitious, and there are hundreds, if not thousands, of customs that ensure safety at sea. Perhaps the crew of *Queen Anne's Revenge* sought to protect themselves by using the same apotropaic symbols that might have protected their homes on land.

Some well-known apotropaic symbols include multifoils (some are hexafoils), overlapping circles with petal-like formations inscribed within them, and symbols to invoke protection from the Virgin Mary (MARIA). This practice appears to have begun during the pre-Reformation era (based on datable examples from structures) and apparently lingered on in certain realms of

dation, which if successful would save lives and munitions. But when bluffs like raising flags (red or black) or sending a few shots over the bow were not heeded, pirates set their sights on "boarding." The first action might be a few more cannon shots to disable the opponent's rudder, block and tackle, or masts. There was great tactical skill involved to challenge an opposing ship without directly ramming it or crashing into it, which could result in sinking and losing the prize and everything in it. The consequences might also severely damage the pirate craft. Rather, the desired outcome was to halt progress long enough to come alongside, which then allowed some crew members to hurl grappling hooks over the opposing ship. Using the attached ropes, they could then pull in close, holding that position while their comrades gained access. Clenched in their hands, and sometimes teeth, personal weapons were essential for survival, defense, and warfare. Pirates were experienced combat craftsmen seeking protection from *maleficum* (or evil-doings). Originally created by carpenters, plasterers, potters, and blacksmiths, the symbols were adopted by later craftsmen as powerful and meaningful protective glyphs. These include M for Mary; W, which is actually interlocking Vs for Virgo Virginium; R for Regina; and formations of lines radiating out from a single point, which are thought to be stylized Ms. The hourglass (vertical glyph) or butterfly (horizontal glyph) symbols, along with "feathered arrows" are also found, not as a Marian invocation but as a general charm to ward off evil. Marks similar to all of these can be found on the *QAR* aprons.

1. Laura Kate Schnitzer, "Aprons of Lead" (M.A. thesis, East Carolina University, Greenville, N.C., 2012).

2. Ibid. Timothy Easton, "Ritual Marks on Historic Timber," *Weald & Downland Open Air Museum* magazine, Spring 1999, 22–28; Timothy Easton, "Apotropaic Symbols and Other Measures for Protecting Buildings against Misfortune," in *Physical Evidence for Ritual Acts, Sorcery, and Witchcraft in Christian Britain: A Feeling of Magic*, ed. Ronald Hutton (London: Palgrave Macmillan, 2015), 39–67.

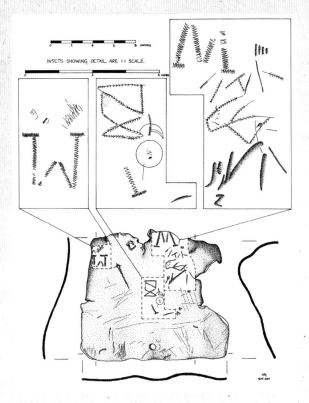

QAR lead cannon apron with incised apotropaic marks. Valerie J. Grussing, illustrator. (Courtesy of the North Carolina Department of Natural and Cultural Resources)

fighters armed with pikes, boarding axes, cutlasses, daggers, pistols, and blunderbusses. Some pirates carried multiple firearms, since each gun only fired a single shot; Blackbeard is known to have carried a complement of six pistols, "three braces," suspended from a baldric (an elaborate holster), along with extra powder and shots.

Most close-combat weapons had specific purposes: Blunderbusses, although unreliable, issued a wide blast of small shot; axes were used to scale the high sides of ship or masts; grenades were tossed onto the decks for smoke and shrapnel; daggers and short swords were preferred for quick stabs and thrusting—longer swords could get caught on the ropes or clothing; and pistols were the most personal of weapons. Pirates who had sea-service muskets supported the boarding party, typically shooting from fixed positions along the ship's gunnel or, better yet, from the yardarms and masts, since from there they could reach targets farther

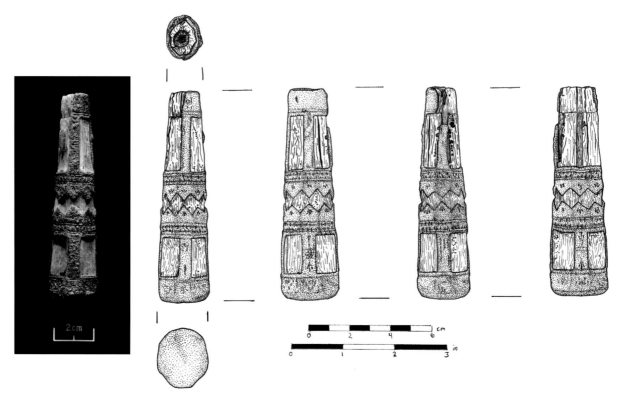

Handle made of boxwood and pewter for a bladed dirk. Jeremy Borrelli, illustrator. (Courtesy of the North Carolina Department of Natural and Cultural Resources)

in the distance. These men were the sharpshooters of their day. All weapons were kept in serviceable condition; repairs were often needed due to the corrosive effects of the saltwater environment. Blackbeard considered the upkeep of firearms of such importance that he coerced Jean Jacques and Claude Deshayes, *Concorde*'s two gunsmiths, to sail with him.[39] Pirates depended on guile, skill, and proper arms to successfully disarm opposing crews. Our understanding of these conditions, coupled with the implications of what was left in haste when *Queen Anne's Revenge* was abandoned, provides us with an intriguing glimpse of pirate warfare.

BLADED WEAPONS

Handheld weapons with sharpened blades were choice and effective once combatants were close enough to use them. Two *QAR* bladed weapons

have been identified; one is most likely the handle for a dirk, and the other represents elements of short swords. No portions of their forged iron blades have survived.

Dirks were short thrusting daggers commonly found among sailors or naval personnel; they were easily stowed and kept handy and alternately used for fighting, eating, and recreation. A dirk was also more affordable than a sword for the average sailor or pirate. The handle or grip for the *QAR* dirk is composed of a wooden core made of European boxwood.[40] The outer grip is made of pewter that has been elaborately engraved with decorative elements of trefoils, diamonds, and dentate patterns with a zigzag border treatment. This handle appears to have come from a very personalized and portable weapon or tool (such as the surgeon's cauterizing iron) that has no comparable examples from other archaeological sites or collections. Why was it left

Examining Artifacts by Function

behind? Its owner must surely have been distressed to lose it.

Short swords, also known as hunt swords, are represented by three identifiable parts: a scabbard clip, a quillon block, and an antler grip. The latter two items are possibly from the same weapon. The U-shaped scabbard clip, also called a frog, held the scabbard, or sword's sheath, to a belt or holster. Made of cast brass, it is flat on the back and decoratively embossed on the front. The quillon block, or sword's cross guard, is one of the most spectacular finds from the site. The design, made of cast brass then finely carved on each side of the quillon block, exhibits the Romanesque draped bust of a male figure in the center, the head adorned with a garland wreath and framed by foliage and scrollwork. The sides are not identical and reflect slightly different tooling by the artisan. Experts on French weaponry agree this male figure likely represents Louis XV, the child monarch who took the French throne at age five in 1715. A similar one from *Machault* is referred to as the Royal Sword, which featured the young king, "Louis le Bien Aimee" (Louis the Beloved). These were popular weapons among French gentlemen of the era.[41] Was this a Frenchman's prized possession or a pirate's prize, or both?

About 25 ft. from the quillon block, another unusual sword part was found, a beautiful sword handle made of hartshorn (antler). The grip's end is capped by an embossed pommel with alternating cherub or child faces, fleurs-de-lis, and diamond shapes encircling a center hole, which once held a small capstan rivet.[42] This decorative motif is considered to be French in origin. It appears that this handle may have once joined the quillon block, as they are nearly identical in dimensions. Short swords were gentlemen's property, but in the eyes of pirates they were not only pretty but quite useful in close combat. If, however, a blade broke and could not be refitted into the handle and quillon block, then it was likely discarded despite its decorative beauty, for above all, pirates needed functioning weapons—no matter how you cut it.

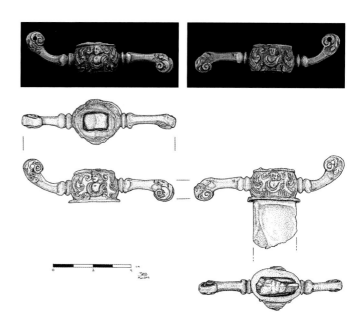

Brass quillon block from a Frenchman's short sword. Jeremy Borrelli, illustrator. (Courtesy of the North Carolina Department of Natural and Cultural Resources).

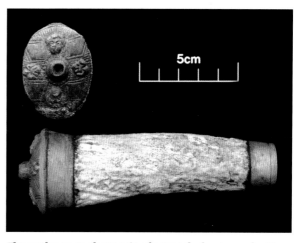

The antler or staghorn grip of a French short sword with decorative brass pommel. (Courtesy of the North Carolina Department of Natural and Cultural Resources)

Grinding stone, 17 in. diameter and 3 ¼ in. thick, used for sharpening bladed weapons and tools. (Courtesy of the North Carolina Department of Natural and Cultural Resources)

SHARPENING STONES

Fine-grained stones of various sizes were vital necessities aboard a pirate ship. Pirates needed a way to sharpen bladed weapons and many of their tools (e.g., axes, adzes, and chisels), or they would quickly have become ineffective and ultimately useless. The grinding stone was a large, heavy, disc-shaped stone with a square central hole through which an axle passed and was mounted to a wooden frame. Grinding wheels, including the one from *QAR*, were made of sandstone. Generally, they required two people to operate, one to crank the wheel and the other to hold the tool at an angle to the turning stone, all the while dribbling water onto the edge to prevent sparking, which was certainly to be avoided on a wooden ship.

For smaller bladed weapons and tools, a whetstone was employed and used often, as is evidenced by the one recovered from the *QAR* wreckage. It was used for fine-tuned sharpening after blades were run across the larger grinding stone. The fine-grained stone was laid flat and braced, and then the blade would be run across its surface at a slight angle, often after the stone was lightly lubed with sperm whale oil. This process was repeated for both sides until the blade felt sharp to thumb pressure, ready for action.

FIREARMS

Brass gun parts from the *QAR* site were few, since personal weapons no doubt were considered worthy of removal when the call "Abandon Ship!" was sounded. What appears in the archaeological record are mostly gun parts that were either broken or showed signs of extensive repairs, indicating onboard activities to keep weapons serviceable. Pirates acquired an assortment of firearms from the ships they took, so reuse and recycling of available parts to match different makes and models challenged the gunsmiths. *QAR* gun parts include a musketoon barrel, a flintlock firing mechanism, several trigger guard parts, three buttplates, and two serpentine sideplates. In addition, a silver gun worm and chain of a musket tool kit have been recovered. In early 2016, a nearly whole pistol was recovered from a concretion in the lab; this small-arms weapon has been tentatively identified as a sea service pistol dating ca. 1710–20, or a James II dragoon model, slightly earlier. Both would be of British origin.

The brass barrel of a musketoon, also called a blunderbuss, was among the first artifacts found on the site in 1996. This type of firearm was a preferred weapon of the seventeenth and eighteenth centuries for use on ships. It was a shoulder-fired flintlock musket used to fire scatter shot at close range in confined spaces. It was an effective anti-personnel weapon, similar to today's sawed-off shotgun. The tubular musketoon barrel from the *QAR* site was marked with several identifying symbols of great interest. The letter V beneath a crown reveals that the weapon had been "viewed" (inspected) prior to testing. The letters "GP," for "Gunmaker's Proved," indicate that it was test-fired. A third mark on the gun barrel represents the maker's mark or initials, in this case "T H," which repre-

Brass barrel of a blunderbuss or musketoon, 27⅛ in. long with a bore diameter of 2½ in. (Courtesy of the North Carolina Department of Natural and Cultural Resources)

sent an as yet unidentified London gunsmith who made the piece sometime between 1672 and 1718.[43]

One iron lock mechanism from a flintlock musket exhibited various elements, including the lock plate, main spring, tumbler, part of the sear spring, most of the hammer (cock), the frizzen pan and part of its cover, and the jaw screw. The hammer resembles a dog-lock mechanism from a French weapon; however, it had been repaired with a different type of hammer, and a small piece of lead shot was crammed into the hole where a dog-latch would have been fastened. The firing mechanism of the gun also appears to be jammed in a half-cocked position and only partially engaged. No doubt this factored into the decision to leave it behind. The reworked piece represents elements of two types of guns, an English trade musket, ca. 1700s–1720s, and a French naval musket, ca. 1710s.

Two brass serpentine sideplates were found, one fancier than the other. Both are of stamped brass construction, decorated on the outward side, flat and plain on the underside. The fancier *QAR* sideplate is engraved with scales and scrolls and a detailed face. The second sideplate is more stylized with a less ornate wave flare. These ornamental pieces of "musket furniture" were mounted onto the wooden stock with small screws. Popular among colonial arms traders who catered to American Indians, muskets, also referred to as Trade Fusils among the English, Dutch, and French (Canada), were fitted with sideplates exhibiting serpentine motifs from 1675 to 1875.[44] A nearly identical match for the second sideplate can be seen on an English Hunting/Trade musket, 1700–1720s.[45]

Three brass buttplates, so named because they fit the butt end of a wooden rifle stock, have survived. The only whole buttplate has three countersunk

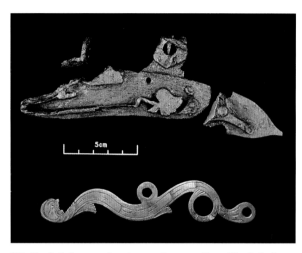

Flintlock firing mechanism and serpentine sideplate from *QAR* muskets. (Courtesy of the North Carolina Department of Natural and Cultural Resources)

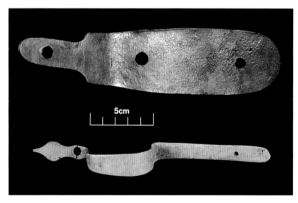

Brass musket components include a buttplate (*top*) and a trigger guard (*bottom*). (Courtesy of the North Carolina Department of Natural and Cultural Resources)

A delicate chain was likely part of a sailor's musket tool kit. Jeremy Borrelli, illustrator. (Courtesy of the North Carolina Department of Natural and Cultural Resources)

mount holes for attachment to the wooden stock and matches those used on a 1716 French Contract Grenadier Musket.[46] The other buttplates are partial and show extensive modifications. All had flat heels, a characteristic of sea service muskets that kept them seated in arms racks and easier to reload with the butt against the wooden deck.[47]

Brass trigger guards, the narrow strip of metal that fits on the underside of a musket or pistol to protect the trigger, have also been recovered. Of the three *QAR* representatives, two are made up of broken pieces; the whole one shows signs of soldering to weld two slightly different pieces together, which were then filed to smooth out the rough edges. As with other few gun parts, they match firearms of the 1716–17 French model or English trade guns of 1710–30.[48]

Three artifacts are elements of a musket tool kit, which was kept handy while under fire. Often these multipurpose tool kits were fastened to the shooter's crossbelt. Items in the kit included a vent pick, a brush, and a worm. Each item was attached by a lightweight chain or leather thong. Recovered from

the *QAR* site, a small piece of brass wire, pointed at one end, was identified as a vent pick or prickler, used to clear the touchhole. Another item was a silver or white brass gun worm used to clean the bore of the barrel. It is broken, revealing five pieces of small lead bird-shot still attached. The third item was a 1-ft.-long section of brass wire chain made of woven and twisted figure-8 links that likely served as an attachment for the vent pick or gun worm.[49]

GUNFLINTS

Without gunflints there would be no spark, and without a spark there would be no ignition of the gunpowder to combust and fire the lead bullets. These small pieces of stone were specifically shaped to fit in the adjustable jaws of the flintlock cock. When the trigger was pulled, the cock projected the flint downward against a steel frizzen directing the spark into the waiting pan of gunpowder. Gunflints were beveled on the edge facing the frizzen to create successful sparks; these edges would have been retouched several times during the use-life of a gunflint. In the seventeenth and eighteenth centuries, most gunflints originated from high-quality chert deposits located in England, Scandinavia, and France. They varied in shape (e.g., spall, prismatic, or blade) and color (e.g., gray to black to honey color).

A total of 27 gunflints have been recovered, of which only 7 have been fully analyzed.[50] Light to dark gray in color, they are spall- or wedge-shaped flints, which were common throughout the seventeenth and eighteenth centuries. During the pirates' golden days, spall gunflints and strike-a-lights (used with a striker steel to start fires or light candles) were virtually identical in shape. A few of these smaller *QAR* flints may have served as strike-a-lights or pistol-size flints. Some also appear unused or pristine, while a few show evidence of resharpening by knapping. Several large pieces of flint along with numerous small flakes and chips suggest that knapping for gunflint production was done on board the ship.

Examining Artifacts by Function

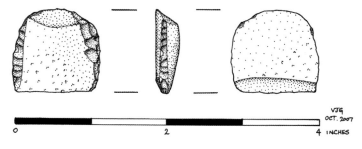

During excavations, the *QAR* dive team was excited to discover a cache of related items that may have been contained in a small personal box. The lid was made from a wooden slat, and the contents included three gunflints, a handful of lead bird-shot, chert chips from sharpening the gunflints, and a bent pewter spoon, which may have served as a powder scoop. Since these items were left behind, at least one pirate was at a loss to keep his munitions handy, his powder dry, and his flints sharpened for action.

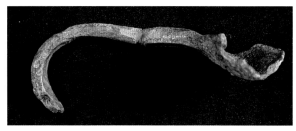

Modified pewter spoon, shortened and bent (3½ in. long), found with gunflints may have served as a gunpowder scoop. (Courtesy of the North Carolina Department of Natural and Cultural Resources)

AMMUNITION

By far the most abundant artifacts are small-caliber rounded lead shot, more than 250,000 so far! Almost every excavation unit contained some amount of lead shot plucked out of sediments by divers, hidden in concretions, or sucked up from the bottom and captured in the sluices. The greatest concentration of small shot, however, was in the stern area, suggesting this was the location of the gunroom where munitions were securely stored. Lead shot would have been shipped and stored in wooden kegs or barrels or cloth sacks, most of which would have deteriorated. Still some evidence of woven cloth bags was found adhering to *QAR* lead shot concretions, which may reflect storage practices. Another use has been posited: The cloth bags may have held lead shot to fire out of cannons at oncoming invaders. Bag shot of this kind were found in cannons recovered from the *Whydah* shipwreck site.[51]

Larger caliber lead shot used for muskets (0.45 to 0.70 caliber) and for pistol shot (0.20 to 0.40 caliber) were made using a hinged mold, called a

QAR lead shot sorted by diameter: (*left to right*) small caliber, musket, pistol. (Courtesy of the North Carolina Department of Natural and Cultural Resources)

gang mold, which could produce a dozen or more shot in one pouring (of molten lead). Many of the *QAR* shot exhibit scrap lead or "sprue" as a result of this casting technique. Smaller caliber shot (0.15 to 0.20 caliber) was most often produced by a method invented by Prince Rupert in which the molten lead was poured through a colander and allowed to drop several feet into a pool of water, which immediately cooled the lead drops into spheres.[52] Appropriately called Rupert shot, most exhibit a small dimple

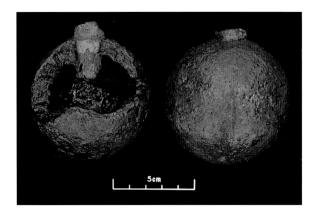

Cast-iron grenades with wooden plugs. (Courtesy of the North Carolina Department of Natural and Cultural Resources)

"The Combatants Cut and Slashed with Savage Fury: Blackbeard and his gang engage in a savage fight on the deck of a ship," by Howard Pyle (1901), in *Howard Pyle's Book of Pirates*, ed. Merle De Vore Johnson (New York: Harper and Brothers, 1921), facing p. 146; originally published in Woodrow Wilson, "Colonies and Nation," *Harper's Monthly Magazine*, May 1901.

on one side from the drop-trail cooling. Lead shot of various diameters was often mixed and used in scatter loads for cannons and musketoons, which is likely the case for the majority of the *QAR* shot. It does appear, however, that most of the molded shot is relatively large, made for muskets rather than pistol shot.[53] There is still much to learn about the uses of lead shot carried aboard this once heavily armed, ready-to-rumble battleship.[54]

GRENADES

The arsenal of *QAR* iron grenades totals 22; 10 are out of concretion, and the rest are visible in x-rays. These explosives are hand-sized and spherical and reveal imperfections of casting, which was more or less intentional so that the walls of the grenade would shatter into small pieces upon explosion. They were fitted with wooden fuses made of beech.[55]

Grenades were used for antipersonnel warfare. They were common aboard ships and preferred by pirates. Historical accounts document successes and failures of grenade warfare, the worst case being the occasion when a grenade dropped below deck and exploded the powder magazine. The action has been summed up this way: "When a pirate crew suggested grenades against an armed mutineer in the ship's hold, the quartermaster wisely elected to engage the mutineer in close

combat, instead of conducting the *tedious* business of randomly dropping in grenades through the deck boards."[56] The grenade itself could be just as dangerous to the user as to the intended victim. Loading a grenade and trimming the fuse so it would ignite at just the right time was vital; otherwise the intended target could simply pick it up and lob it back . . . just like in the cartoons. "Uh-Oh! Better Run!"

In addition to the cast-iron shells, another type of "impromptu" grenade was used by Blackbeard

Examining Artifacts by Function

Queen Anne's Revenge *Sick Bay: French Surgeons at Work*, original oil painting by
Virginia Wright-Frierson (2016), Mark Wilde-Ramsing and Linda Carnes-McNaughton
private collection. (Used by permission)

during his final battle, as reported by Lieutenant Robert Maynard. "Captain Teach's men threw in several new fashioned sort of grenadoes, viz. case bottles filled with powder, and small shot, slugs and pieces of lead or iron, with a quick match in the mouth of it, which being lighted without side, presently runs into the bottle to the powder, and as it is instantly thrown on board, generally does great execution, besides putting all the crew into a confusion."[57] Great confusion indeed; chaos and blood is more like it! The case bottles used for this purpose may very well have been liter-sized French flacon bottles, for which thousands of shards were found on the *QAR* site. Assuming a case or two were carried away from the sinking ship, these improvised, hand-propelled bottle bombs would have caused great confusion and piercing shrapnel during Blackbeard's final stand. With Maynard's men hidden below deck prior to boarding Blackbeard's sloop, the improvised grenades were not

enough to turn the tide and save the pirate captain's life.

Throughout the life of the ship's service, the surgeons on board were kept busy, not only during times of conflict, but with an array of injuries and ailments produced from everyday life on the sea. Now let's move on to the next section to find out what tools, procedures, and remedies the ship's medical staff had at their disposal.

Mariners' Maladies: Keeping the Crew Healthy

It was paramount for a captain to keep his ship in good working order and his crew healthy. Moreover, on a slave vessel, providing care and provisions for enslaved Africans ensured that they would arrive in the Americas in good enough health for sale. The group of artifacts in this section includes some of the equipment and materials needed to practice

The Duties of a Ship Surgeon

DR. LINDA F. CARNES-MCNAUGHTON

Medical treatment for the sick and injured on board a pirate ship was challenging in the best of times. Ship's surgeons of the early eighteenth century administered to chronic and periodic illnesses, fevers, wounds, amputations, burns, toothaches, and other indescribable maladies. The chief surgeon, assisted by his aides, cared for officers, sailors, and passengers, who in the case of slave ships were the cargo. Contagious diseases (e.g., smallpox, diphtheria, measles, strep throat, consumption, and syphilis) impacted everyone on board the ship due to the close quarters. In this period, prior to the Age of Enlightenment, when the beginnings of germ theory appeared, medicine was more art than science. Practitioners treated visible symptoms without understanding the underlying causes of most ailments, obvious wounds being the noted exception. Diseases went by descriptive and colorful names such as "violent bilious fever," "putrid sore throat," "pain in the bowels,"

"phlegmatic constitution," "bloody flux," and "the great pox." Medical philosophers considered disease to be the imbalance between the Four Humors—air, water, fire, and earth—as indicated by the body's dry, moist, hot, or cold condition, respectively. Consequently, treatment was geared toward gaining a proper balance of the humors through bleeding, sweating, vomiting, and purging by the patient.

The chief surgeon provided his own equipment and recipes for medicines, while the ship's owner or captain was required to stock the medical chest. Contents of the medical chest included compresses, needles, ligatures, splints, ointments, compounds and chemicals for medical mixtures, scales and weights, dose cups, and mortar and pestle for grinding ingredients. Surgical instruments would have included pliers, extractors, scalpels, syringes, clysters, catheters, tourniquets, trepanning saws, amputation saws, bleeding basins, and irons for cauterizing wounds.

medicine in the early eighteenth century on board an oceangoing ship. These items testify to the more personal aspects of the crew and passengers, what ailments or traumatic wounds they suffered, and what equipment was required to administer medications and treatments. Surgeons and their aides were important personnel on the ship, so it was no surprise to learn that Blackbeard retained the chief surgeon and his two assistants from *Concorde* when he stole the ship.[58] It is also likely that because the French crew and enslaved Africans suffered extreme illnesses and mortality before the pirate captain took the ship, Blackbeard needed to restock the ship's medicine chest. This reality was played out later when he blockaded the port of Charleston, South Carolina, demanding and receiving crucial medical supplies.[59]

Most of the artifacts related to medical practices on the ship were considered "capital equipment" and property of the surgeon; thus most of them possess French maker's marks. Conversely, the supplies needed to treat the ill and wounded, such as compounds, liquids, mercury, sulfur, and cloth bandages, called clouts, were expendable. They also would not have survived the marine environment for 300 years.

Historical records from the *Seaman's Vade Mecum* of 1707 outline the contractual duties of the ship's captain, the surgeon, and his aides:

1. The Surgeon must practice the art of healing by operations and treat wound, fractures, and disorders.
2. The Surgeon must be approved by two Master Surgeons before boarding a ship.
3. The Ship Owner must provide a medical chest, stocked; surgeon must provide his own tools.
4. The medical chest must be inspected by the Chief Surgeon & Apothecary prior to departure, or be fined.
5. The Ship's Captain must verify the Surgeon's certificate (proof) and approve the chest contents or be fined.
6. The Chief Surgeon is to inform the Ship's Captain of any contagions on board in order to take precautionary measures (isolation, quarantine, or removal from the ship).
7. The Surgeons are not to be paid by any crew members or receive favors, or be fined.
8. The Surgeons are not to leave their vessel in which they are engaged prior to completion of the voyage or be fined (the largest fine of all).

Contract provision 8 is an important consideration and may shed new light (or an alternate interpretation) on the "retention" or "kidnapping" aspect of the three French surgeons after Blackbeard and his crew stole *Concorde*.

MORTAR AND PESTLE

Together the mortar and pestle were essential tools for surgeons and apothecaries alike. Used to grind various raw ingredients in preparation for compounds needed to treat topical wounds and internal ailments, they were also unbreakable. Made of cast copper alloy (or brass), the *QAR* set survived burial at sea, although the mortar certainly took a beating during Hurricane Ophelia in 2005. And

The brass mortar and pestle were recovered separately from the *QAR* site. (Courtesy of the North Carolina Department of Natural and Cultural Resources)

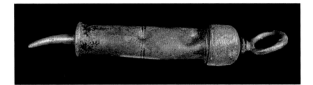

Urethral syringe, 6½ in. from nozzle tip to plunger ring, from the French surgeon's kit. (Courtesy of the North Carolina Department of Natural and Cultural Resources)

though important to the surgeons on board, they were left behind in the shuffle to escape the sinking ship. The mortar is 4½ in. in height and 5 in. in diameter. Neither piece exhibits a maker's mark or features to assign it as French or British. Moreover, their styles have remained unchanged for hundreds of years, for even today a mortar and pestle set remains the universal sign for pharmacy.

URETHRAL SYRINGE

QAR archaeological conservator Wayne Lusardi identified a pewter syringe, which surfaced during the early years of recovery, as French-made based on its Paris trademark (the letter P) with a 1707 date.[60] The distinct maker's mark on the plunger ring is that of St. Laurent Chatelain, a martyred saint who was burned alive.[61] The particular angled funnel, or nozzle, identifies it as the type used to administer mercury into the male urethra, as this was a common eighteenth-century treatment for syphilis. Once the artifact was stabilized in the lab, Lusardi extracted the contents from the syringe plunger and sent it off for chemical analysis, which confirmed traces of mercury. As a treatment, mercury was applied as a liquid using the syringe or mixed in a compound and applied topically to exposed sores or blisters. Though it was effective in reducing the symptoms of syphilis, it was certainly not a cure, since most patients eventually suffered lead poisoning from it—proving the old adage that the cure is sometimes worse than the disease!

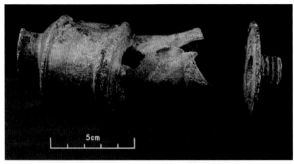

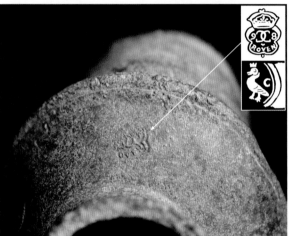

Pewter clyster, 12 in. long (estimated) with 2-in.-diameter cylinder, with French maker's mark. Philippe Boucaud, illustrator. (Courtesy of Philippe Boucaud and the North Carolina Department of Natural and Cultural Resources)

PUMP CLYSTER

During the eighteenth century a prevalent method of administering medicines was via enemas or clystering, a method that has been in use for centuries. Depending on the nature of the ailment, various compounds and concoctions were mixed and injected into the patient to remove blockage, relieve ailments, cleanse the colon, and allow more rapid absorption of the liquid medicines into the body's system. A specialized tool, known as a pump clyster, was used for administering this treatment.[62] Portions of three pewter clysters were found in the stern section of the *QAR* wreckage, where we presume the surgeon's sick bay was located. The first clyster has parts of the cylindrical chamber, with

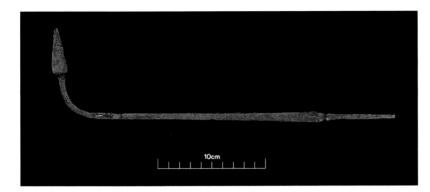

Wrought iron cauterizing tool with a pointed tip, known as an olive or acorn. (Courtesy of North Carolina Department of Natural and Cultural Resources)

a threaded top and a pumplike handle or plunger at one end and a tapered nozzle on the other end. On the second clyster, two manufacturer's marks are visible. One is the guild mark of Rouen, year 1698, and the other mark represents the CANU family of pewterers, who operated from 1659 to 1701.[63] The mark also shows a small duck, which is a subtle joke on the family's name, as CANU is French for duck. The third clyster is currently undergoing conservation but may reveal additional manufacturing marks. Chemical analysis of residues from the cylinders may also provide identification of the medicaments being used aboard *Queen Anne's Revenge*.

CAUTERIZING IRON

Another unusual tool made of wrought iron has been tentatively identified as a cauterizing iron used to seal wounds by burning. This delicate implement has a bent-neck arm about 10 in. long with a plumb-bob triangle-shaped head on one end and a tapered rat-tail tang on the other end, designed for an interchangeable wooden handle. French surgeons of the day used a variety of cauterizing irons with different shaped heads for singeing various open wounds. The wooden and pewter grip previously described as a dirk handle may in fact be part of a surgeon's cauterizing kit.

NESTED WEIGHTS

Used by apothecaries and surgeons to measure ingredients for medicines and by merchants, and

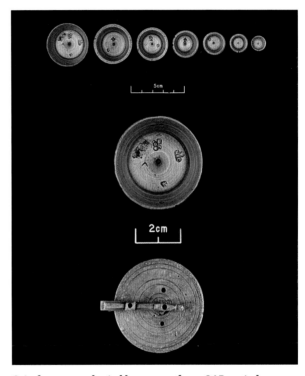

Set of seven graduated brass cups from *QAR* nested weight set with close-up view of the set's lid and the largest cup showing the maker's mark and city stamp. (Courtesy of the North Carolina Department of Natural and Cultural Resources)

certainly pirates, for precious metals, weight sets were common on most ships of trade. Parts from two *QAR* sets of nested weights are really quite sophisticated. Their unique design is a compact assemblage of graduated cups that "nested" tightly inside one another, with the largest or "master" cup having a hinged lid to keep all smaller cups intact.

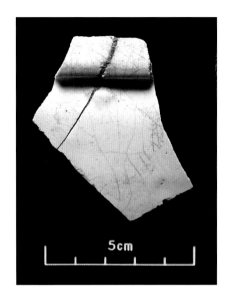

Fragments of a tin-glazed galley pot or jar from the sick bay. (Courtesy of the North Carolina Department of Natural and Cultural Resources)

All are made of cast brass. The weight of the master cup is equal to the sum of all smaller cups, and the weight of the second-largest is equal to those it contains, and so on, until there is just a small single disc of the lightest weight. Each of four cups from one set of *QAR* nested weights exhibits fleurs-de-lis marks stamped on its interior, along with the number 1, 2, 4, or 8 corresponding to its size. The fleur-de-lis symbol has been the nationalistic cultural emblem of France since the thirteenth century. We were able to identify a unique touchmark seen on the master cup as a rectangular cartouche (scroll) with initials N and C separated by a small dot, representing the town of Montpelier, France, the source of its manufacture.[64] Nested weights of this type were also known to be made in Nuremburg and were sometimes generically referred to by that name. A complete set of nested weights (eight cups) similar to the *QAR* set was found on the 1629 wreck of *Batavia*, implying minimal changes in their use and design had taken place.

APOTHECARY JARS OR GALLEY POTS

Also called ointment jars, these small ceramic pots would have been filled with unguents, salves, balms, and potions for medical use. They would have been kept in the surgeon's chest and refilled as the need

occurred. Most were covered with a small piece of cloth, tied securely with cotton twine under the rim. A few small potsherds found on the shipwreck likely represent small apothecary jars of French origin, based on the pinkish-colored clay, which is characteristic of faience, a type of tin-enameled earthenware unique for that country. Being very fragile, galley pots would not likely survive intact on shipwreck sites, but in a few instances, they have been found with residue of the original greasy ointments.[65]

"BLEEDING" PORRINGER

For centuries dating back to ancient Greece, Egypt, and parts of Europe, medical practitioners performed "bloodletting" as a treatment for ailments believed to be caused by an imbalance in the natural humors of the body. This practice was accomplished by the use of live leeches, aka sanguine suckers, placed directly on the patient's skin. These segmented worms were allowed to engorge on blood and then were removed to be stored until needed again. Using another tried and true technique, the blood could be "let" by venesection, the practice of slicing into a vein or artery and allowing life's liquid to flow into a container of some type. Special bladed tools called lancets or scarificators were used to make a thin slice into the vein. The release of blood from the patient reduced blood pressure by reducing volume and was thought to be useful; however, once again it was a cure that often proved more harmful than the ailment, if not fatal. In a few eighteenth-century illustrations, double-handled pewter porringers were seen as the container of choice for this bloodletting. A crushed pewter porringer of this description from the *QAR* site may have once served this purpose, although it had been repurposed to fit as a lid for a food canister, as evidenced by its altered shape and rat gnaw marks visible on its rim. A maker's mark on the handle, "I M" separated by a fleur-de-lis set within a cartouche, is similar to styles and marks from southern France dating to 1675–1700.[66] Further-

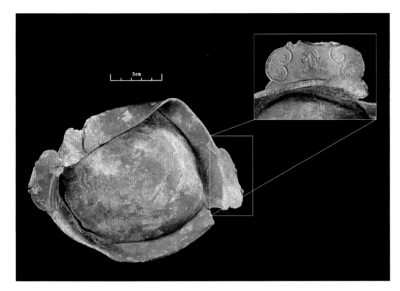

QAR double-handled pewter porringer showing maker's marks, and "Armamentium Chirugiae," woodcut by Ioannis Sculteti (1693). (Courtesy of the North Carolina Department of Natural and Cultural Resources)

more, the ropelike design around the foot and rim was a recurrent motif on porringers from Metz, France. On the exterior base, initials "D V" were found double-stamped, which may indicate the original owner's name.[67]

NEEDLE AND SCISSORS

These simple tools, which have not changed in style for many centuries, were essential to a surgeon's kit. For most open wounds and amputations, a threaded needle and scissors were required to close wounds. Ligatures or waxed shoemaker's thread was used to compress the wound and suture the opening. Topical ointment and salve would be used to dress the wound before bandaging. According to eighteenth-century illustrations, suturing needles came in a variety of shapes and sizes.[68] A needle from the *QAR* site may have been used by a surgeon or a sailmaker. Being made of silver suggests its place in the surgeon's kit; however, its length at 5½ in. makes it better suited for sailmaking than sewing up flesh wounds. Regardless of who used it, the silver needle would not rust or corrode while in the marine environment. Also found in the *QAR* wreckage were the eyelet handles from a pair of iron scissors, preserved through epoxy casting, that also could have been used by a surgeon to clean

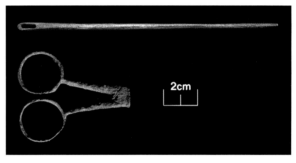

A large silver needle and steel scissors (epoxy cast) were part of the surgeon's or sailmaker's kit. (Courtesy of the North Carolina Department of Natural and Cultural Resources)

up suture threads, or by a sailmaker to snip loose threads or cut away sections of cloth.

Sustaining the Crew: Eat, Drink, and Be Merry

Feeding a hungry crew was the responsibility of the ship's cook, and the job could be life-threatening at times. If provisions ran low or food stores rotted and became inedible, the cook's head might be on the platter instead of a piece of salted meat! He, along with the steward, was responsible for stocking the larder and ship's hold with enough provisions for a scheduled voyage at sea. Sometimes

Tales of Pirate Repasts

DR. DAVID T. CLARK

Years of tedious, painstaking archaeological recovery from the *QAR* shipwreck produced a wealth of amazing artifacts, including hundreds of broken animal bones. Once teased from dense concretions and cleaned of encrusted layers, they were analyzed by zooarchaeologists to determine animal species, skeletal part, and dietary significance. Since most refuse or garbage would likely have been thrown overboard, the following account, though enlightening, is nevertheless incomplete, given the limited inventory of preserved bone. What we do know is Blackbeard and crew ate a meat diet of mostly beef and pork supplemented occasionally by fish and fowl. And the numerous small shattered and splintered bone fragments are the resulting by-products of meat processing indicative of long-term, onboard butchering. Butchers and cooks aboard ship used cleavers and axes to reduce bulk meats to piecemeal-size portions for use in potage (stews), which extended the available meat stores to feed hundreds of hungry pirates.

Cattle yielded more meat than pigs by size alone. Evidence from bone growth patterns showed all butchered cattle were young, less than 14 months old. Butchers cleaved center shafts into "short rib" portions for boiling and use in stews prepared in large cauldrons. Nearly all beef portions (leg extremities, ribs, back) constituted low-yield, lesser-quality meats. Exceptions included the hind leg rump meats, truly a "cut-above" other meat rations.

Also popular aboard the ship was pork. Compared with cattle, pigs were more ship-friendly because they were smaller and also served as onboard garbage disposals consuming anything in sight with their powerful grinding teeth and massive jaw muscles. Pig bones included numerous skull fragments, but more common were foot bones. Eaten boiled or stewed, pigs' feet were apparently very popular. Considering the pig head, butchers cleaned it to remove thick, juicy cheek meats around the jaws and skull. Preparation of head meats required special skills and knowledge, as the pigheadedness of tough meat attachments often proved challenging for a novice butcher. Since all pork bones represented low-yield, lesser-quality cuts, it seems safe to say, "Blackbeard and crew warn't eatin' high on the hog!"

Additional evidence of the pirates' diet centered on meager morsels of fowl and fish found on the shipwreck. Bird bones consisted of small shattered pieces of leg shafts. Though chicken and other fowl were popular for meat and eggs, their thin, delicate bones did not survive the rigors of the harsh ocean environment. Similarly, the remains of fish were few, mostly unidentifiable pieces of skull, backbone, and fin rays. Undoubtedly, however, fish provided a staple food source for the pirates.

Last but not least, a few domestic rat bones surfaced from the wreck, representing stowaways that, quite literally, went down with the ship. This nonedible, diminutive seagoing scavenger left its telltale teeth marks on several bone fragments and one pewter porringer. Such scavenging was only possible when bone refuse and foodstuff were left exposed for prolonged periods on the ship. As offensive as rats may have been, their presence contributes to a greater knowledge of onboard human activities.

Though delicate and fragile in nature, these 300-year-old animal bones, preserved under extraordinary conditions, represent a unique "taste of the past." Faunal analysis provides a glimpse of the dietary lifeways of Blackbeard and his crew while aboard *Queen Anne's Revenge*.

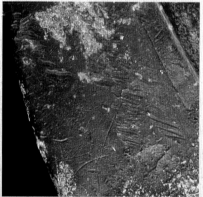

Pewter porringer with rat gnaw marks. (Courtesy of the North Carolina Department of Natural and Cultural Resources)

called victuals, most foods were various stages of "dry" or desiccated items, like hardtack, meat jerky, and dried beans or potatoes, which had to be reconstituted with some liquid (in other words, boiled beyond recognition) to become edible. Potages or stews were the common communal meals, which allowed the slimmest amounts of poor cuts of meat to go a long way. Fishing, turtling, and shooting or netting birds also augmented the mariner's diet in the early eighteenth century; the quarry was eagerly consumed when brought on board.[69] Meats were mostly salted and stored in barrels below deck, while vegetables like potatoes and peas were dried and packed in sacks, kegs, or ceramic jars. Wooden cages held chickens or other domestic fowl until time for consumption. Pigs often roamed the decks, scavenging everything in their path. Live cattle, if available, were tethered or corralled above or below decks. The fact that livestock were aboard *Queen Anne's Revenge* is collaborated by Henry Bostock, who reported the pirates taking 4 beeves and 35 hogs from his sloop *Margaret*.[70] Animal bones also provide archaeological evidence of the pirates' eating patterns and preferences.

Sailing the seas and stealing ships could be a thirsty business. Besides the essential fresh water, often stored in barrels, beverages of choice were typically alcoholic, such as rum, wine, gin, brandy, and beer. These liquids were stored in glass bottles (of round or square shape), ceramic jugs, wooden kegs and barrels, gourds, or personal-sized leather botas. As Blackbeard noted in his "travel log," when the rum was all out, the crew were sure to get mean and surly.[71] Celebrations after taking ships that provided ample amounts of alcohol, which often took place on nearby shores, included much drinking and drunkenness. Rum and brandies that originated in the tropics were the favored drink, while wines and gins often came from cooler latitudes of England, France, and Spain, a tradition which continues today.

Liquids such as oils and vinegars would also have traveled in jars or bottles. Rationing of provi-

sions was the job of the captain and cook, to make sure that victuals and beverages lasted until the port call was reached or the next prize was stolen.

So where did the cook prepare all these meals? Oceangoing ships were generally equipped with a galley and built-in cookstove, sometimes located on the second deck with the exhaust vented via hole or pipe through the upper deck. Most often, the galley stove was built of brick pavers, like the ones found on the *QAR* wreck. These were set into a wooden box for support and were designed to hold large cauldrons for the preparation of communal meals to feed the crew and cargo. Wood was the fuel source. As with any hierarchical society, including pirate crews, eating habits reflected social status among the group, so while the crew ate common gruel or stews served in cups or bowls, the captain, officers, and preferred guests were likely fed meals individually prepared for them and served in their cabins on dinner plates. Archaeological evidence offers insight into this social activity of taking a meal.

COOKPOTS

Cooking stews (or potages) and gruels for large numbers of people aboard ship required an assemblage of large metal containers that fitted onto the galley stove. Sheet metal cooking pots were common on ships because they were lightweight and durable and traveled well nested in stacks. They were popular trade items in colonial America and Africa but do not often survive on shipwreck sites. Evidence in the form of a bail ear for handle attachment and several copper rivets represent at least one copper kettle that was left behind on *Queen Anne's Revenge*.

More durable were cast-iron cookpots, which were standard for most galleys on wooden ships and have changed very little in the past 300 years. Two styles have been recovered. The first is round-bottomed with angled ear lug handles on opposite sides and would have rested on short tripod legs. This pot design, which was patented by Alexander Darby in England in 1707, according to some

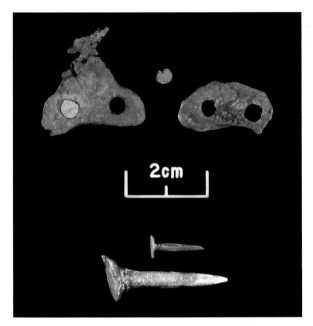

Evidence of a copper kettle, shown by rivets and bail ears. (Courtesy of the North Carolina Department of Natural and Cultural Resources)

Plan and profile views of a nearly whole stove brick, originally 8¾ in. long, 4 in. wide, and 1 in. thick; note the finger ridges on the top surface. (Courtesy of the North Carolina Department of Natural and Cultural Resources)

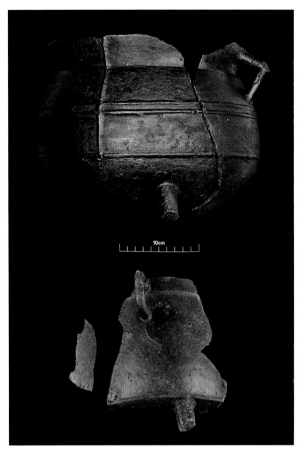

The two iron cookpots from the *QAR* site were identified as a British Darby (*top*) and a French saucepot (*bottom*). (Courtesy of the North Carolina Department of Natural and Cultural Resources)

launched the Industrial Revolution because of its global popularity.[72] The second iron cookpot is taller and more cylindrical in shape, with opposing ear lug handles and taller tripod legs. Similar pots, called saucepots, have been found on French colonial sites in America.

GALLEY BRICKS

Several whole and fragmentary thin bricks are believed to be the insulating liner for the galley stove. Made of a reddish micaceous clay, the bricks had very rounded edges because of extensive use. The average dimensions for the 10 *QAR* bricks are consistent with the historic French unit of length

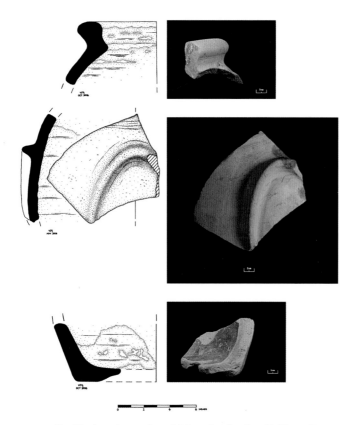

Profile drawing and matching sherds of an Italian oil jar. Valerie J. Grussing, illustrator. (Courtesy of the North Carolina Department of Natural and Cultural Resources)

(*ligne*) and closely resemble those found at Old Mobile, a French colonial settlement.[73]

CERAMICS

Containers made of clay, called ceramics, are by far the most studied artifacts from archaeological sites for a number of reasons: They usually survive harsh conditions and are thus well represented; they are readily recognizable by style, date, and function; they reflect the economic status of the consumers; and moreover, they are directly related to humans, as they reflect specific foodways. Put simply, a lot can be told about people from their broken dishes. The ceramic pieces recovered from the *QAR* wreck-

age are from all over the world and represent forms of jars, jugs, bowls, plates, and one teapot. Most were used for food preparation, consumption, and storage, but a few small jars made of tin-enameled earthenware likely held medicines and salves in the sick bay.

To date, 17 individual ceramic vessels have been identified. Some are represented by a single sherd, while others have dozens from which to reconstruct their original shape. Fragmentary evidence was recovered from three large earthenware jars that would have been used to ship food items in bulk quantities. One form, known as an olive jar, became so ubiquitous in the sixteenth to eighteenth centuries that it has been referred to as the "cardboard box" of its day. Originally used to ship olives in brine or oil, they were often repurposed for holding dried foods like beans or chickpeas, corn, flour, vinegar and wine, and for nonfood contents such as tar, pitch, soap, and lead shot.[74]

Over 50 sherds from a single earthenware jar were found scattered across the *QAR* wreckage. Manufactured in the Montelupo region of Italy, this large oil jar was unglazed on the exterior and lead-glazed on the interior and was once used for shipping and storing liquids. It held several gallons of olive oil and stood 2 ft. tall with mouth diameter of 12 in. These behemoth jars from Italy were often covered on the outside with a raffia grass harness used to move them around. Traces of white paint still visible on the exterior of this jar indicated it too once had a shipping harness, which long since rotted away. A second large earthenware jar may be French in origin, based on the mottled yellow and green lead-glazed interior and pinkish-red clay body. It would have been used for storage of foods as well. The third container, the olive jar, was likely manufactured in Spain, where thousands upon thousands of these shipping containers were produced. The jar was perfectly suited to carry dried foods, given its unglazed and porous body, which allowed airflow to reduce mold growth.

Examining Artifacts by Function

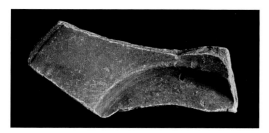

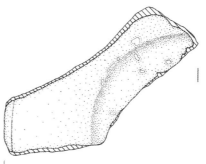

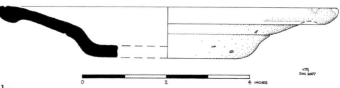

Shallow earthenware plate from the Saintonge region. Valerie J. Grussing, illustrator. (Courtesy of the North Carolina Department of Natural and Cultural Resources)

Among other coarse earthenware ceramics found on the wreckage were two small bowls and a plate related to individual dining. These are glazed on the interior with a green copper-oxide and lead mixture characteristic of Saintonge pottery made in southwestern France. They would have been used for service of meals to the French surgeons and, no doubt, the pirate captain and his guests. One bowl rim is also decorated in a slip-trail circle and dot motif, dateable to the early 1700s (see the bowl pictured at the end of Chapter 7). Saintonge wares, which have been recovered from the *La Belle* shipwreck in Matagorda Bay, Texas, are not often found on land sites in American colonies, but examples have turned up at the Trudeau site (an Early French-Indian contact period settlement) in Louisiana, at the Old Mobile site in Alabama, and at French Canadian settlements of Quebec City and Fortress of Louisbourg.[75]

To complement French table wares, a small sherd of Chinese porcelain from a teapot lid revealed that someone onboard *Queen Anne's Revenge* enjoyed the occasional cup of tea. This blue-on-white floral, hand-painted porcelain piece was made in the Kangxi region of China between 1662 and 1722. The social ritual of taking tea was gradually spreading across Europe and into the American colonies by the early 1700s, and though tea and porcelain were still costly import items,

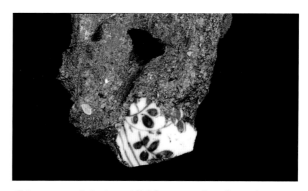

Chinese porcelain teapot lid fragment, less than 1 in., shown in concretion. (Courtesy of the North Carolina Department of Natural and Cultural Resources)

they were in high demand in the Atlantic market. Despite its size, the porcelain piece speaks volumes about social status, international trade, and refined drinking practices.

For storage and dispensing of stronger beverages, stoneware jugs were popular, and Germany was the favorite market for these types of containers. At least six salt-glazed stoneware jugs have been identified by various pottery pieces; all exhibit a light gray to tan color, characteristic of salt-glazed stonewares from the Siegburg region of Germany.

QAR pewter plates, partial spoons, and a crushed porringer. (Courtesy of the North Carolina Department of Natural and Cultural Resources)

Two large potsherds, one the mouth and handle and the other the base, represent two of the six German salt-glazed stoneware jugs, which ranged in capacity from 5 to 10 gallons. (Courtesy of the North Carolina Department of Natural and Cultural Resources)

Two jugs exhibit the potter's distinctive finger impressing along the strap handle terminals; however, none exhibited manufacturing marks to identify a specific potter or market.

PEWTER WARES

In addition to ceramic plates, pirates used less-breakable wooden trenchers (which don't survive burial at sea) and plates made of pewter, a soft metal composed of varying amounts of tin, lead, antimony, zinc, and some copper and silver. Pewter wares were also used as a commodity in the African slave trade, which may explain why they are found on the QAR site, considering the ship's former service. Pewter was created as a composite metal, and the quality varied from source to source until pewterers' guilds were formed to standardize its composition and use in England by the fourteenth century. Because pewter wares (including plates, porringers, tankards, and utensils) were unbreakable and rust-free, they have often been recovered on shipwreck sites, such as *Whydah* and *Henrietta Marie*. The word "pewter" is derived from the French term *"peautre,"* traced back to 1229, when it appeared in its early form in Europe.[76] By the seventeenth century, England and France were major production centers and suppliers for worldwide markets due to their access to the source of raw ores used to produce pewter. Since production of pewter wares was regulated and documented for over 400 years, they are also very datable. In addition to maker's marks (or touchmarks), hallmarks, and owner's marks (usually initials), numerous decorative elements of pewter wares changed over the years as styles evolved and foodways changed.

During the early days of exploration, we were delighted to discover recognizable pewter items amongst the generally amorphous QAR debris. Despite being torn, folded, scratched, and punctured, they were all returned to relatively good shape during conservation by Watkins-Kenney's team. A total of 35 individual pewter vessels have so far been recovered. Twenty-one are plates, 13 are larger dishes, and 1 was a porringer, previously described as part of the surgeon's kit. Historically, the term "plate" was used for smaller, individual service flatware measuring 7 to 11 in. in diameter. Dishes

Examining Artifacts by Function

were larger pieces, some over 18 in. in diameter, used to hold communal food from which individuals helped themselves. Five different, identifiable maker's marks have been found on 11 *QAR* pieces of pewter flatware, all English. Three plates bear the touchmark (a double-headed eagle) identified with Henry Sewdley of London, dated 1709. Two plates have been struck with the touchmark of George Hammond (a right arm and hand holding a two-edged dagger), who registered his mark in 1695. His mark was also found on several pewter basins found on the wrecked English slaver *Henrietta Marie*, lost off Key West, Florida, in 1700.[77] Three plates and one dish exhibit the touchmark of "IO STILE," identified as John Stile(s), dated ca. 1689. The name appears above a feathered crest bracketing an eagle clutching a snake, and three other marks (a leopard face, a rampant lion, and an eagle atop a snake). Another plate is stamped by the touchmark of Timothy Fly (with a small fly motif), who worked in London ca. 1712. A single pewter plate bears the touchmark of William Smith of London, ca. 1693. Finally, an unusual and most personal dish exhibits "LONDON" on the underside and "B s A" on the topside edge, representing a man's initial B, a woman's initial A, and their surname letter of S, suggesting this was a wedding piece.[78] The French maker's mark and initials on the single porringer were previously described with medical instruments.

Because pewter is a "soft" metal, a few *QAR* flatware pieces exhibit cut, stab, or slash marks from use, perhaps a testament to the tough meats or poor job by the cook, or both. There are also puncture marks that penetrated several pieces as if they were attached to a wall or mast using a nail or spike. Historical research suggests that large pewter dishes were sometimes hung up as "message boards" to convey information, such as the famous 1616 Dirk "HARTOG" plate found hammered to a tree in Western Australia, to document his arrival and departure.[79]

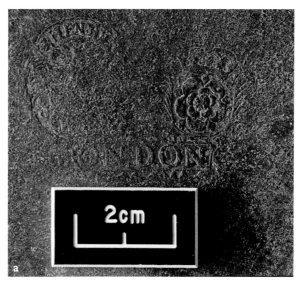
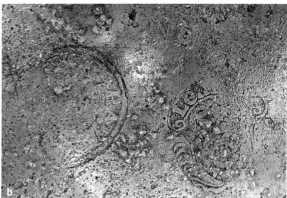

Dateable touchmarks found on *QAR* pewter plates: (a) Henry Sewdley, (b) George Hammond, and (c) John Stiles. (Courtesy of the North Carolina Department of Natural and Cultural Resources)

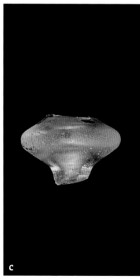

STEMWARES AND BOTTLES

Despite the turbulence at sea combined with the fragile nature of glass containers, we were fascinated to find four intact wine bottles and the fragments of four stemware glasses on the wreck site. The stemware glasses speak to a level of fine dining that was common amongst eighteenth-century gentlemen, including officers, their guests, and French surgeons aboard the pirate ship. Even better, they are datable and traceable to a specific country. And best of all, the nearly whole pedestal square-stem (Silesian) wineglass, one of the most unique items found on the wreck site, represented a major political event: the crowning of a British monarch, George I of Hanover, who came to power in 1714 after the death of Queen Anne. Its delicate stem is embossed with crowns and diamonds to mark the occasion. If only we could have been there to see this—Blackbeard enjoying the irony of drinking his wine from this souvenir for a king he despised and then throwing back his head in robust laughter. Or perhaps Stede Bonnet claimed this piece as his, given his penchant for the finer life of luxury goods and his gentlemanly status.

The three remaining examples of glass stemware are referred to as blown baluster style, with simple curved stems, outward flaring bowls, and small circular feet. The two smaller ones date to ca. 1701–10 in a style based on intact matching examples from the Museum of London collection.[80] The third, with a teardrop-shaped air bubble inside its blown-glass stem (or annular knop), dates ca. 1691–1725.[81]

The pirate captain's table likely held one or more distinctive rounded, dark green bottles from England that contained wine or other distilled beverages popular in the eighteenth century. One bottle is noted for its squatty bottom, irreverently

QAR stemware with comparable museum examples (measurements provided): (a) George I coronation stemware (ca. 1714), 6 3⁄16 in. tall; (b) baluster stemware (ca. 1701–10), 7 19⁄32 in. tall; (c) annular knop of baluster stemware (ca. 1691–1725), 8 3⁄16 in. tall. (Courtesy of the North Carolina Department of Natural and Cultural Resources and Museum of London by permission)

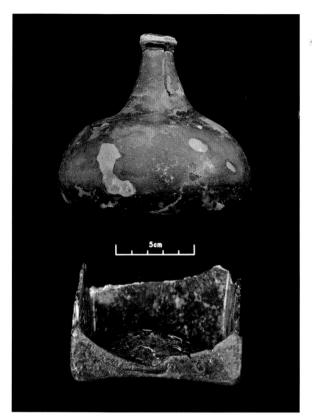

QAR wine bottle called "Queen Anne" style (ca. 1714) and the base of a dark green case gin bottle. (Courtesy of the North Carolina Department of Natural and Cultural Resources)

Neck and base shards from French flacon case bottles, averaging 1 quart capacity, 8⅝ in. tall, and 2¾ in. square base. (Courtesy of the North Carolina Department of Natural and Cultural Resources)

called a Queen Anne style and dating to 1714, while the other three are slightly earlier.[82] Dozens of glass fragments from other wine bottles have been recovered as well as hundreds of "case" bottle shards; remember, glass does break. Case bottles derive their name from the wooden shipping containers used to transport them; thus they are square-shaped and flat-bottomed. The most common of all glass fragments are from a type of case bottle known as flacons, which were manufactured in France and noted for their vivid blue-green color, which coincidentally matches the ship's window panes.[83] They held a variety of liquids, such as household products, toiletries, perfumes, oils, and occasionally spirits.[84] As mentioned earlier, they were also the perfect size for use as homemade

grenades. After all, pirates could be very resourceful when cornered.

UTENSILS

Among the artifacts related to eating and cooking activities were metal utensils needed to mix, stir, baste, cut, and serve foods. Portions of eight spoons, six pewter and two silver, have been recovered. One long silver tube shaped like a cannon with its cascabel finial created great speculation when it was hauled up from the seafloor. Some thought it was a musical instrument (like a flute), some ventured it was a distaff tube, while others simply scratched their heads and wondered. Eventually we were able to identify it, appropriately, as the cannon-shaped handle from a large basting

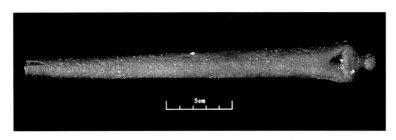

Silver cannon-shaped handle for a basting spoon. (Courtesy of the North Carolina Department of Natural and Cultural Resources)

pip

Hanoverian pewter spoon handle with distinctive pip, 5¼ in. long (mended). (Courtesy of the North Carolina Department of Natural and Cultural Resources)

spoon, popular in England and the colonies from the 1690s to 1710s.[85] The handle was made hollow to reduce heat transfer from the detachable bowl, which has yet to be found.

Six pewter spoons, represented by two whole, two handles, and two bowls, collectively exhibited elongated bowls, rat-tail terminals on the back, and sculpted handles. One spoon exhibited a small "pip" on the top of its upwardly curving handle end, a feature common on Hanoverian-style flatware, dating to ca. 1710–30s. Another was incised with a personalized X on its handle. Spoons were personal gear for individual eating, and if a sailor owned one, he stowed it in his gear or trouser pocket, which may explain why some handles were purposefully shortened. Lastly, a bent white metal spoon found in context with several gunflints and lead shot appeared to have been modified for use as a scoop for gunpowder.

CASKS AND KEG TAP

Casks made of wood were the most common form of shipping containers used in the Age of Sail to store foodstuffs, drinking water, grog, and a vast array of other supplies, such as nails, lead shot, tar, and pitch. They also carried trade items like glass beads, axe heads, weapons, and tools. From the

largest (tuns and puncheons) down to the smallest (bidons and monkeys), with barrels and kegs in between, wooden casks came in various sizes dependent on volume. They were fastened with wooden hoops or iron hoops, depending on availability, cost, and content of container (e.g., liquid or dry).

Although only nine wooden staves and two head-pieces were recovered, casks of various sizes were found among 183 iron hoop fragments, which often were only represented by concretion and voids, since the iron was totally rusted away. For those, conservators reclaimed their original form through epoxy castings. One complete set of iron hoops consists of a bundle of 7 with varying diameters. The remaining fragments represented at least 18 sets of hoops, many of which could have been in storage for use later by the cooper, a practice called shooking. The majority of casks were concentrated in the bow section, which corresponds to the galley, cooper's work area, and forward storage area.[86]

For casks filled with liquids like beer or wine, the contents were dispensed using keg taps made in two pieces; a hollow tube, inserted into the cask bunghole, was regulated by a valve or stopcock, placed at the dispensing end, which opened or closed to control the flow. A beautiful *QAR* brass stopcock lever shaped like a fleur-de-lis is similar

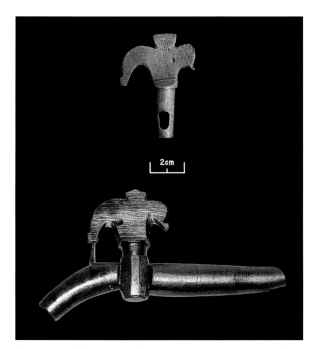

The stopcock from a *QAR* keg tap and an intact example from Fort Michilimackinac, an early French settlement site. (Courtesy of the North Carolina Department of Natural and Cultural Resources and Michigan's Mackinac State Historic Parks)

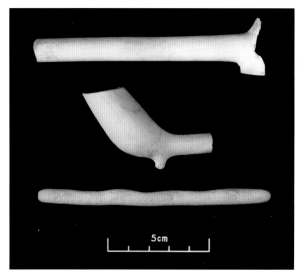

Fragments of kaolin tobacco pipes showing different styles, one with a flattened heel and one with an elongated bowl and spur heel, and a possible pipe tamper. (Courtesy of the North Carolina Department of Natural and Cultural Resources)

to some found on eighteenth-century French settlement sites.[87] The short arm indicates the valve is closed; the long one, open.

PASTIME AND PROCUREMENT FOR PIRATES

During long voyages at sea, crews spent time crafting tools to procure food from the sea, or items for personal use and exchange. For entertainment and socializing, pirates played games (although gambling was often discouraged), danced, and sang songs, but mostly they drank and smoked pipes of tobacco, if available. Pirate captains knew the importance of keeping ample spirits on hand, for without it, their crews were likely to get restless and uncontrollable.[88]

Among items related to leisure activities from the *QAR* artifact assemblage are a few lead pieces flattened and shaped into gaming chips of square

or round shapes. Six square-shaped pieces weigh between 12 and 32 grams, and two are incised with an X on one face. One of those was done using the wrigglework technique similar to that seen on cannon aprons. Dozens of similarly shaped and scored gaming pieces were found on the pirate ship *Whydah*.[89] Checkers, sennet, and draughts were popular board games of this era.[90]

Tobacco, which was introduced to Europe in late 1570, was enjoyed by New World explorers on land and at sea, and the culture of pipe-smoking evolved over time as availability and fashion regulated.[91] *QAR* pipes were made of white clay (called kaolin) in a two-piece mold in which the stem, bowl, and

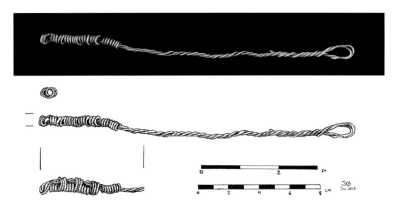

Brass wire fishing hook leader line. Jeremy Borrelli, illustrator. (Courtesy of the North Carolina Department of Natural and Cultural Resources)

heel/spur were contiguous. One of the 35 tobacco pipe fragments was a nearly complete pipe with a flattened heel, but it was missing part of the bowl. It dated to 1680–1710, based on style. Collectively, the bore diameters of all pipe stems, using several dating techniques, provided a relative manufacture date of 1710.[92] A curious, elongated artifact from the *QAR* site was made of hand-formed, fired white clay with brown staining on one end. This has been tentatively identified as a tamper, used to pack shredded bits of tobacco into a pipe bowl before lighting up.

To augment the pirate's diet of dried and salted meats and hardtack, those who had time and inclination also went fishing overboard, vying for any fresh "catch of the day." Though no metal fishing hooks have been found, evidence for this pastime aboard *Queen Anne's Revenge* was identified by an intricately woven piece of copper wire known as a fishing hook leader line, about 8 in. long. As was common in the eighteenth century, fishing hooks had their "tads" squared off without holes for lines, so the practice of securing the line to the hook was done by hitch knots using wire or rope. Similar leaders have been found in abundance at Fort Michilimackinac, a French settlement trading post.[93]

Imagining how pirates acted and carried on seems easy nowadays, what with the hundreds of movies, books, and reenactments. There is even a Talk-Like-a-Pirate Day to practice how they spoke.

Please keep that image in your mind as we move on to explore the personal gear and apparel pirates and their passengers left aboard Blackbeard's abandoned vessel.

Clothing and Adornment: Wardrobes for Pirates

Life at sea, whether for a pirate, sailor, passenger, or enslaved African, offered its own unique subculture of customs and traditions, often separate from those of landsmen or planters of the eighteenth century. Historical accounts and personal journals as well as ships' logs provide rich texture to the world of mariners and their "closed communities" formed on board a ship. Even before there was mass communication as we know it today, those who sailed were cultural transporters of ideas, carrying customs of their homelands around the world and bringing back curios and stories of exotic cultures.[94] Ships, their cargos, and their crews' clothing and personal belongings were all material expressions of their mother cultures set afloat on vast oceans only to touch down in ports in different worlds. Clothing and adornment highlighted these differences. These items are very personal and sometimes can be tied to specific owners, which is the case for *Queen Anne's Revenge*.

QAR artifacts identified as clothing elements, given the corrosive marine environment, predominantly include items of hard material, principally

Examining Artifacts by Function

"Captain Keitt," by Howard Pyle (1907), in *Howard Pyle's Book of Pirates*, ed. Merle De Vore Johnson (New York: Harper and Brothers, 1921), 212, 213; originally published in *Harper's Monthly Magazine*, August 1907.

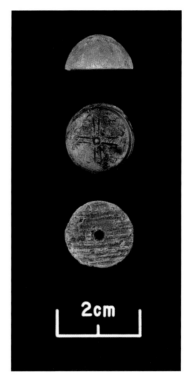

The profile of a two-piece dome button (*top*), the decorative face of a second dome button (*center*), and a wooden button core from the French passementerie style (*bottom*). (Courtesy of the North Carolina Department of Natural and Cultural Resources)

metal, shell, glass, or bone. They were principally used as fasteners—buckles, buttons, hooks, and pins—needed to construct, alter, or mend clothing, especially during long months at sea. Others served as adornment for clothing or personal appearance, like jewels, spangles, and beads, the latter being the most prevalent decorative items. All in all, they offer us a modified glimpse of the personal apparel and adornment, assuming pirates and passengers had ample opportunity to gather their belongings and get off the sinking ship.

BUTTONS AND SLEEVE-LINKS

These items are separated by size and type of device, with buttons generally being the larger of the two. Twelve buttons and two pairs of sleeve-links have been found, of which nine buttons and the sleeve-cufflink pairs are brass, two buttons are pewter, and one is wooden. Regarding the buttons, several are indicative of eighteenth-century styles, including one of two-piece construction with domed face and bone back. Another jacket button is much fancier, with an engraved decorative front or face, a soldered loop, and a convex back. Others have a flat face and are called "coin-buttons."[95] A large wooden button with a central hole may represent the back of a two-piece metal button or the core of another type of decorative fastener once covered with silk, woolen, or golden threads. These were part of a French cottage industry called passementerie popular during the 1600s to 1800s. Rarely found on shipwreck sites, buttons of this type have survived and been found on land sites of the early 1700s.[96]

The Pirates "Stript Them Naked"

DR. MARK U. WILDE-RAMSING

Queen Anne's Revenge served as a pirate ship for six months, a period that was bookended by two significant piratical events: in the beginning, the ship's capture from the French and, near the end, the blockade of Charleston, purportedly for a chest of medicine. While the two incidents provided a ship and later needed medical supplies, it is also known that Blackbeard and crew came away with a lot of money, totaling hundreds of thousands in today's dollars. Both times, another commodity was also targeted: the clothes off the backs of the officers, passengers, and seamen they held.

In his official deposition concerning the taking of *Concorde*, Lieutenant Francois Ernaut testified that prior to releasing the French crew, the pirates "grabbed all their clothes and togs making them naked."[1] At Charleston, the *Boston News-Letter* reported that detained passengers were not freed until the pirates "stript them of all their Cloaths."[2] This apparently was nothing new for pirates under Blackbeard's command. In October 1717, he and Captain Benjamin Hornigold detained a vessel from which "they took . . .

from him about 3 Cask Sugar and most of their clothes at the same time."[3]

The importance of receiving clothing is emphasized in the second Article of Consent under another pirate captain, Bartholomew Roberts: "Every Man to be called fairly in turn, by List, on Board of Prizes, because, (over and above their share) they there on these Occasions allow'd a Shift of Clothes."[4] It seems sea rovers favored a change in their wardrobes whenever possible, since by the very nature of their business, they were not able to return to major ports where they might replace worn and torn garments. Refurbishing apparel was routine, for while a prize ship seldom held significant amounts of gold or valuable cargo, nearly all could provide the basics: food, liquor, ship's equipment, tools, and personal items.

The procurement of clothing, however, was more than a simple necessity. The vast majority of early eighteenth-century pirates were common seamen who did not have the means or wherewithal to sport fancy attire. As freebooters, they now had access to silk scarves,

Sleeve-links are made of two small buttons joined with a single wire loop that functioned like a cufflink of today's fashion. They are often decorative and made of copper alloy or pewter. The *QAR* sleeve-link sets are decorative and identify with

QAR sleeve-links, one pair with a scrolled motif (12 mm diameter) and the other exhibiting a faceted face (15 mm diameter). (Courtesy of North Carolina Department of Natural and Cultural Resources)

Examining Artifacts by Function

gold earrings, silver spangles, fancy sleeve links, shiny brass buckles, and other pieces of finery. Stealing these items from ships' officers and wealthy passengers and wearing them defiantly allowed the men aboard *Queen Anne's Revenge* to project a persona that expressed disdain for authority and the social norms of the day.

1. Francois Ernaut, "Deposition regarding *La Concord de Nantes* Plundered and Taken by Pirates," Série B 4578, Folia 56v & s, April 17, 1718, Archives départementales de Loire-Atlantique, Nantes, France.

2. *Boston News-Letter*, July 7, 1718.

3. *Boston News-Letter*, November 25, 1717.

4. Captain Charles Johnson [Nathaniel Mist], *A General History of the Robberies and Murders of the Most Notorious Pyrates*, reprint of the 3rd edition with introduction by David Cordingly (London: Conaway Maritime Press, 1725), 180.

"Kidd on the Deck of *Adventure Galley*," by Howard Pyle (1902), in *Howard Pyle's Book of Pirates*, ed. Merle De Vore Johnson (New York: Harper and Brothers, 1921), 84–85; originally published in *Harper's Monthly Magazine*, December 1902.

status dressers, perhaps the French chief surgeon. One set with an embossed scrolled motif and beaded edge and the other set with a faceted cut face are similar to types found on other French colonial sites.[97]

BUCKLES AND FASTENERS

Like the buttons, 21 *QAR* buckle parts, which include frames, tangs, and pins, reflect both fancy and ordinary attire. Most appear to be from shoe or knee buckles, based on size and shape.[98] Two are made of silvered or tinned metal, and the rest are copper alloy or brass. Four distinct styles have been noted: the simple rectangular frame dating ca. 1710–30, the stud-chape knee or shoe buckle dating 1660–1720, a "spectacle" knee buckle frame dating 1630–90, and two loop-chape silvered shoe buckles dating 1690s–1720s. We were most excited with the stud-chape buckle because it had a partial maker's mark NOSS set in a cartouche, which

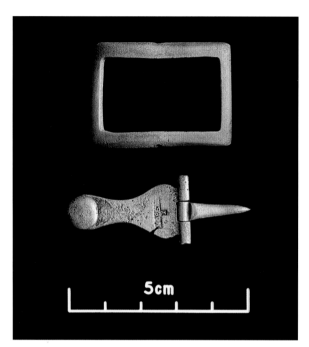

Examples of brass buckles showing assorted styles, one rectangular frame minus its tang and another stud-chape tang with no frame. (Courtesy of the North Carolina Department of Natural and Cultural Resources)

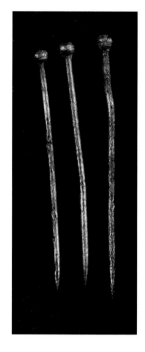

Close-up view of *QAR* brass pins with wound heads. (Courtesy of the North Carolina Department of Natural and Cultural Resources)

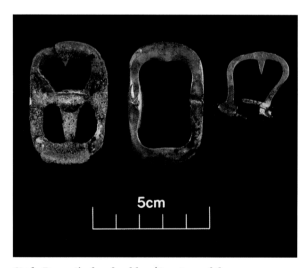

Stede Bonnet's shoe buckles. (Courtesy of the North Carolina Department of Natural and Cultural Resources)

was common during the early eighteenth century. We are still searching for its maker.[99]

Also of particular interest are two matching shoe buckles made of silvered or tinned metal, one of which is hand-engraved with the stylized initials of the owner, "S. B.," which only match the initials of Stede Bonnet among the known crew aboard *Queen Anne's Revenge*. Bonnet, known as the Gentleman Pirate, was a "guest" aboard Blackbeard's flagship. He may have been caught off guard with the sudden demise of *Queen Anne's Revenge* and left behind his extra pair of shoes or perhaps, he fled shoeless.

PINS, HOOKS, AND CLOTH SEALS

Down amongst the heavy cannons and tons of ballast stones, the smallest of artifacts from this shipwreck settled into the sediments on the ocean floor. During careful archaeological excavation emerged humble straight pins, hundreds of them. Made of brass, these delicate yet durable artifacts were essential in the creation, alteration, and mending of clothing and items made of fabric, especially on long voyages at sea. Perhaps straight pins were

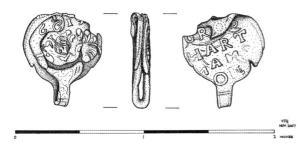

Lead shipping seal for a cloth bale with lettering of manufacture and market. Valerie J. Grussing, illustrator. (Courtesy of the North Carolina Department of Natural and Cultural Resources)

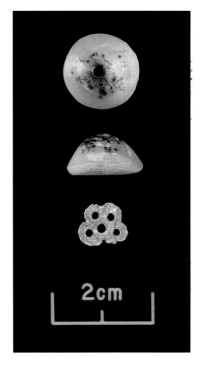

Top and profile view of a blister pearl with a central perforation, and a decorative silver spangle. (Courtesy of the North Carolina Department of Natural and Cultural Resources)

especially valued by pirates as they attempted to refit clothing they had stolen. The design was simple, a narrow-gauged wire shank, pointed on one end with a triple knot of wound wire as a head on the other end. In eighteenth-century Europe, the manufacturing of pins and needles was a well-developed industry, and their design lasted until mass-production arrived a century later. *QAR* straight pins average ¾ to 1 in. in length.

Another clothing item from the *QAR* site was a 1-in.-long hook fastener made of brass wire commonly called a "frog" because of its shape. It was used in tandem with a brass "eye," a design we still see in use today on many clothing items.

An unexpected artifact that relates to cloth manufacturing was also pulled from the *QAR* wreckage. It was a shipping seal, or market tag, made of two lead discs connected by a narrow strip. The soft metal was stamped with shipping or manufacturing data. Merchandise, including cloth, was often bundled into bales and held in place with cords or metal bands and then secured with crimped and stamped lead seals. Arriving at its destination with its seal intact indicated the package had not been tampered with. Our consulting expert on bale seals, the late Geoff Egan, interpreted the seal's embossed letters, "GROS/MART/NARB/ON," as merchandise intended for the "Great Market at Narbonne," France.[100]

JEWELRY

Items deemed valuable are the very things that no one, especially pirates, would leave behind on a sinking ship. We are not surprised, then, that only a few pieces of manufactured jewelry have been discovered so far, excluding the tiny glass beads associated with enslaved Africans that will be discussed in the pages to come. Six items of individual jewelry include a blister pearl, a silver spangle, a clipped segment of a gold ring band, and three snipped pieces of African gold jewelry called Akan. All are small but culturally intriguing.

Pearls are gems derived from the deep sea instead of the deep earth. They are known for their luster and durability and have been treasured by many cultures throughout history. In some cultures, it was *the* gem; in England, the sixteenth century was known as the Age of Pearls, and only kings, queens, and people at court were allowed to wear them.[101] The one recovered from the *QAR* site is a type known as a blister pearl for its hemispherical shape, domed on one side and flattened on the other. Called mabes for the silver-tipped or

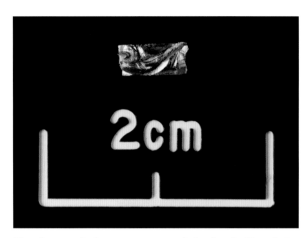

Tiny fragment of a rococo engraved ring band, clipped at both ends. (Courtesy of the North Carolina Department of Natural and Cultural Resources)

mabe-winged oysters that produce them, they come from the Caribbean in the region of Panama and Venezuela.[102] The *QAR* pearl is pierced with a single hole for stringing on a gold wire or, based on use wear from abrasion, more likely sewn onto clothing. Another piece for adornment on clothing is a small, flat, silver spangle with five holes. Its origin is unknown.

The first of the clipped gold pieces is a small part of a ring band with an engraved rococo design. The curved floral design was popular following the Baroque period of the late 1600s. Less than ¼ in. in length, it appears to have been cut at each end, purposefully reducing it in size for distribution with gold dust amongst the pirates. Three fragments from gold beads, so small they required a magnifying glass to examine them, exhibit elements of design known for eighteenth-century Akan jewelry made in Ghana. These pieces, along with brass and glass beads, were associated with *Concorde*'s enterprise in the African slave trade, which is revealed just ahead. . . . Please read on.[103]

Slave Goods: Evidence of a Former Mission

The former service of *Queen Anne's Revenge* as a ship for transporting enslaved Africans is revealed by a group of discrete artifacts related to that business. Most are European manufactured glass beads that we know through historical accounts were sometimes given to the enslaved Africans and thus collectively carry information about the slave trade. A few other recovered items were made in Africa and provide information on traditional customs of adornment, the origins of Akan jewelry, and unique aspects of powdered glass beads.[104]

AKAN JEWELRY

Three tiny fragments of gold jewelry of African origin have been found at the shipwreck. Each of these pieces was made using the lost-wax casting method in which sheets of gold metal are molded over special shapes created from wax and thread. Originally, they were parts of gold beads used by African elites as necklaces, earrings, and headpieces, or were sewn onto clothing. Made of pure gold, they are also very thin, bendable, and non-corrosive. More importantly, each piece represents but a fragment of the original whole bead, which had been clipped or snipped into smaller pieces for their monetary value. Thousands of pieces of Akan gold jewelry (of similar threaded and molded design, of African origin and craftsmanship) were found on the shipwreck *Whydah* (1717) and during the excavations at Elmina, once a base for trading gold, ivory, and slaves, in present-day Ghana.[105] As early as the 1680s, gold was an important cultural commodity among the African tribes of the Gold Coast, particularly the Asante.[106] It was used for jewelry and regalia of the Akan royals, as well as a form of currency, and the Europeans recognized its importance in early trade relations. Not only was it valued for its purity and high price, but culturally the African tribes prized it for its symbolic relationship to the sun.[107] In honor, kings and queens wore

Negres a fond de calle (Negroes in the cellar of a slave boat), by Johann Moritz Rugendas (ca. 1830), painting at the Museu Itau Cultural, Sao Paulo, Brazil.

gold adornments and gold dust on their faces and bodies to enforce their divine status of wealth. This belief may also explain why, in addition to pieces of gold beads, most glass beads from *Queen Anne's Revenge* are also gold in color.

BEADS

Portable, desirable, and durable, beads find their way into many archaeological sites. The history of glass bead making is well known and documented among historical archaeologists by various typologies, chronologies, and comparative studies currently in use. Bead size regulated how the ornaments were used, either for clothing or strung for adornment, such as in necklaces and earrings. Glasshouses in Amsterdam and Venice produced beads of all varieties and colors for global trade and exportation for more than three centuries. Asso-

Whole Akan gold beads strung in a necklace. (Courtesy of Museum Liaunig, Austria)

X-ray image shows leaded glass beads locked in concretion. (Courtesy of the North Carolina Department of Natural and Cultural Resources)

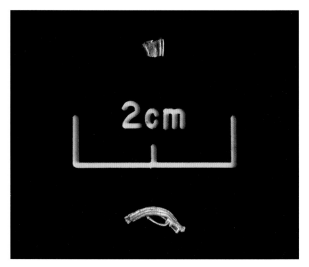

Tiny fragments of Akan gold beads, clipped into small pieces. (Courtesy of the North Carolina Department of Natural and Cultural Resources)

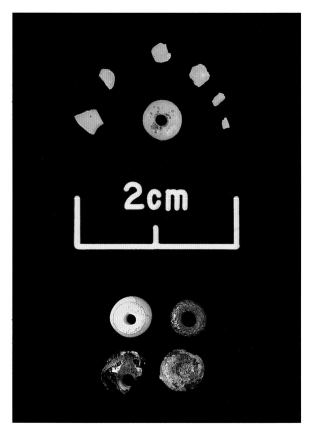

Trade beads of white-, blue-, black-, and gold-colored glass. (Courtesy of the North Carolina Department of Natural and Cultural Resources)

ciated with trade activities, beads occur in a wide variety of contextual sites and ranges, beginning with the earliest contact period in North America. We have learned that as popular trade items, glass beads were shipped to all parts of the globe.

Colored glass beads have been recovered throughout the *QAR* site, and many thousands appear still locked in concretions. They are strong reminders of the ship's original function as transport for enslaved Africans. Women and girls were sometimes provided beads, known as "reward-incentive" items, to string and otherwise occupy their time during the Middle Passage.[108] Most of the 45 whole glass beads available for analysis were made by drawn-tube construction and are mono-chromatic in color and medium in size (⅛- to ¼-in. diameter). Based on their combined attributes, they range in date of manufacture from the 1680s to the 1750s. Some of the beads are colored opaque white or opaque blue, and a few are black (or translucent dark burgundy, tinted by manganese oxides). The vast majority of all other drawn glass beads are a translucent color called "bright yellow gold."[109] This particular color was achieved by the addition of sul-fides or antimony to the molten glass. Interestingly, over time in the abrasive salt water, the outer surface of these beads turned sooty black. Their true

Examining Artifacts by Function

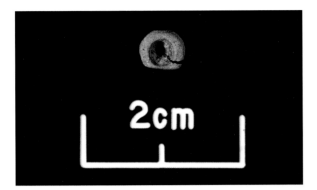

Unique powdered glass bead from Ghana, partially split and damaged, is approximately 6 mm in diameter and 3 mm thick with a 3 mm bore diameter. (Courtesy of the North Carolina Department of Natural and Cultural Resources)

color only emerges when the exterior patination is removed. The *QAR* site has produced hundreds of similar bead fragments, and many more remain locked in concretions.

One unusual whole bead appears to have been made of fired powdered glass and has an oversized central perforation and three flattened sides. This bead was not made in Europe. After comparative research, we found similar beads that had been excavated from land sites in African graves dating in the 1690s to 1710s, and their source of manufacture has been attributed to Ghana or the west coast of Africa.[110]

Four small brass beads have also been discovered at the site. These barrel-shaped (or biconical) adornments have relatively large holes, a result of the lost-wax casting technique of manufacture. Three have coiled brass wire still attached and looped at one end, as dangles for jewelry or attaching to clothing. They were likely made by the goldsmiths in the style of Akan beads and jewelry, which coincidentally are still produced in West Africa.[111] Beads made of metal (brass, gold, or silver) were popular among Africans, who wore them strung or suspended in clusters as noisemakers or charm bracelets to ward off evil spirits and invite good luck.

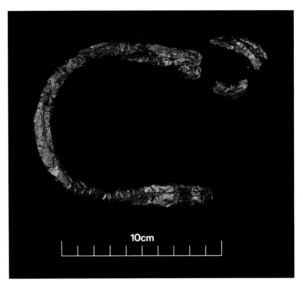

U-shaped portion of *QAR* leg iron. (Courtesy of the North Carolina Department of Natural and Cultural Resources)

SHACKLES

To restrain enslaved Africans, shackles or leg irons were commonly used.[112] Historical documents sometimes refer to them as bilboes, a name derived from the Spanish region of Basque, where they were invented. Generally, shackles were made of two U-shaped iron straps with holes in the ends through which an iron rod was inserted perpendicularly and then padlocked. They were made in varying sizes to fit men, women, and even children and were fitted to the ankles, most often while the person was barefooted.

Portions of two shackles have been found on the *QAR*. They are U-shaped to fit the ankle and are made of a ½-in.-diameter iron bar forming a 4-by-4½-in. loop. One is additionally wrapped with hemp rope and was, you might remember, originally misidentified as a cargo hook. The single-strand hemp cordage, which was relatively flexible, was likely applied to resize the shackle for a smaller ankle. While these restraints were most often used on enslaved Africans, they may also have been used for miscreant pirates as a form of corporal punishment when they overdrank or became greedy.

Coins, Currency, Weights, and Measures: Accounting Matters

Pirates were merchantmen from the get-go, with a slightly different attitude or method to acquiring goods. They had a penchant for gold and silver. On a wrecked pirate ship, one might expect to find a treasure chest filled with coins, and lots of them. This is our classic image of a pirate, stealing treasures and then burying the chest in a secret location known only by coded maps or messages. It is pirate legend and lore, a story told again and again. But sometimes that reality played out, like the treasures found during excavations of the pirate ship *Whydah*, which went down in a ferocious storm. And the same goes for the famous *Atocha* and the 1715 Spanish fleet wrecks, where thousands upon thousands of coins and jewels were salvaged.

Well, sorry, golddiggers, that is not the case for *Queen Anne's Revenge*—not because the treasure wasn't on board but because the loss of Blackbeard's flagship was not a catastrophic wrecking event but a slower, low-impact loss. No one was killed, and it seems there was ample time to remove almost everything of value before the ship sank beneath the waves. Rather, the valuables that remained for us to find centuries later may simply have "fallen between the cracks" and been forgotten. On the other hand, specific tools used to measure pirate gold and coins were left behind, apparently not worth the effort to grab when abandoning ship. Let's take a closer look at this situation; but we warn you, when it comes to booty, you may need that spyglass to catch a glimpse of it!

COINS

Four coins have been observed through x-radiography, and of those, three have been removed from concretion and carefully examined by numismatists and other scholars to identify the metal, value, country of origin, and year of mint.[113] All are "cob" style, made from silver rolled into cylinders of

Close-up of both sides of a silver one-*real* coin, 16.6 mm to 19.1 mm diameter, 1.75 mm thick, and weighing 1.1963 grams. (Courtesy of the North Carolina Department of Natural and Cultural Resources)

prescribed size and weight, then sliced into wafers and snipped into shape. Both faces of each coin are stamped with mint marks indicating date and amount. The *real* (plural *reales*), which means royal in Spanish, was the central unit of currency for Spain and its global colonies for centuries, beginning in the mid-fourteenth until the early nineteenth century, and was widely adopted in international trade and commerce. One *real* was one-eighth of a silver Spanish dollar, thus known as a "piece of eight," which weighed one ounce, or 28 grams. Other increments of *reales* were four, two, and one-half.

The largest of the *QAR* coinage is a Spanish one *real*, and the two smaller ones are thought to be one-half *real*, based on their diminutive size. All are in very poor condition, having suffered from centuries in seawater. Despite this, the one-*real* coin reveals several exciting features. One side bears the knobbed cross (of Jerusalem) enclosed by a tressure (the thin border of a shield), and on the backside is the shield of Philip V (1700–1724) and the letters M, a small o, and I (a period font for the initial J). The first two letters indicate the coin was minted in Mexico City; the third letter likely denotes assayer Jose Eustaquio de Leon, who worked there from 1705 to 1723.[114] Though mere pocket change, these coins reflect the type of currency expected to be on an early eighteenth-century pirate ship.

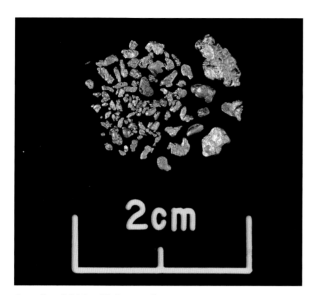

Sample of *QAR* gold dust and nuggets.
(Courtesy of the North Carolina Department of
Natural and Cultural Resources)

GOLD DUST

The most popular form of currency used during
this era, however, came in the form of gold nuggets
and dust, geologically called grains. Pirates stole
gold by the bagful. The French slave traders on
the *Concorde* reported that when Blackbeard and
his men confiscated their ship, they also stole over
20 lbs. of gold dust.[115]

Research by geologist Dr. Jim Craig tells us
that the *QAR* dust and nuggets are placer gold.
Since mingled in the dust were snippets of gold
Akan jewelry, it was most likely mined from
streams in the gold beds of Africa. African gold was
"treasured" by international pirates because of its
purity and consistency of quality; it is not called
"the gold standard" for nothing. One thing is for
certain: Gold would not be naturally occurring in
Beaufort Inlet, and so what was sifted from *QAR*
sediments must have been aboard the pirate ship.
Nearly 15,000 gold grains have been extracted using
macro-archaeology methods (e.g., panning or sein-
ing sediments) developed by *QAR* archaeological
conservator Franklin Price.[116] Sounds like a lot?

Well, unfortunately, the average weight of one grain
of gold is only about one-six-thousandth of a gram,
making the total weight for recovered *QAR* gold
dust just 20.8 grams, a minuscule amount compared with the 9,072 grams that were taken when
Concorde was captured. Perhaps the gold dust we
found during archaeological recovery had spilled
during transactions and fell into the cracks of the
floorboards. Or perhaps it was someone's secret
stash, hidden in a crevice somewhere, that they
could not retrieve on that fateful day when the
ship was lost.

WEIGHTS

For merchants, surgeons, and pirates alike, making
sure quantities were accurate, or nearly so, was
a valuable business principle. Standardization of
weights was still in its infancy during the early eighteenth century, and there was noticeable variation
from country to country, market to market. And
then, of course, there was also fraud and forgery to
consider. Throughout Europe, efforts were made
to establish standardized weights, made of brass
or bronze, that were verified accurate by specific
trade officers and then stamped to indicate what
municipality had issued them. The brass nested
weight sets used by surgeons that we described
earlier reflect those initial efforts at standardization
and custom office marks. Coin weights were often
impressed with a unique design specific to the coin
being verified (through counterweight), such as the
celebrated Queen Anne coin weight for one guinea
described at the beginning of Chapter 2. Recognizing the symbols and images used on weights was
important during times of global exchange and illit-
eracy.[117] No matter the difficulties, pirates preferred
the basics of gold.

Coin weights from France, Germany, Italy,
Holland, and Belgium were typically square in
shape, while those from England were rounded,
hexagonal, or quadrangular. Rounded weights
from England were often fitted with a top finial

Knobbed round weights. (Courtesy of the North Carolina Department of Natural and Cultural Resources)

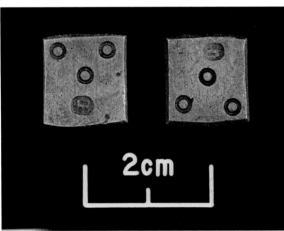

Square weight, front (*left*) and back (*right*). (Courtesy of the North Carolina Department of Natural and Cultural Resources)

for easier lifting and placement.[118] Of the five *QAR* coin weights, one is square and four are round; all are made of brass. Two of the round weights have knobbed finials and were used to verify coins of 8-*real* and 1-*real* value. Cast and tooled, they would have been part of a set held in a wooden box, along with a scale balance or beam. The weights are stamped on the face with the numbers 8 and 1, respectively, along with roman numerals to identify the pennyweight, which is a unit of weight based on the Troy ounce used for gold. A pennyweight is equal to 24 grains, usually marked as "dwt." The weights also exhibit the letter R, for *real*, and grain weight marks; thus they are likely of English origin.[119] Another round coin weight is knobless and simply stamped with a "¼" mark on the top, possibly representing one-quarter ounce and thus the avoirdupois metrical system widely used in English-speaking countries. The square coin weight is also English, indicated by the three dots stamped on its face to represent three pennyweights, in addition to a passant lion, which served as a verification mark used by the Goldsmith's Company Assay Office in London.[120]

SURVEYOR'S CHAIN TALLIES

Perhaps the most unusual measuring device in the *QAR* artifact assemblage is represented by small, oddly shaped, flat brass tags that have been identified as tally markers for a land surveyor's chain. This type of geodetic measuring device was invented by an English mathematician and clergyman named Edmund Gunter and was used to measure linear feet and distances (e.g., 80 chains equaled one mile, or 5,280 ft.). A full chain was composed of 100 metal chain links totaling 66 ft. in length and typically carried a set of nine tally markers, or brass "tellers," set at 10-link intervals.[121] Markers were specially shaped to indicate how many links they marked; two tags each had one to four "fingers or lobes," with the ninth tag a 0-lobe marker, normally located at the center of the chain.

Examining Artifacts by Function

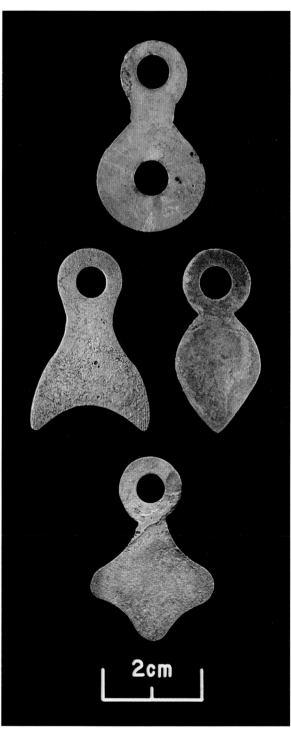

The *QAR* brass tallies include one 1-lobed, three 2-lobed, one 3-lobed, and one 4-lobed tally, and two rounded circles (for 0-lobe or center), representing one full Gunter's chain, and perhaps a second, given the extra 2- and 0-lobed tallies.[122] All tallies were found near one another, and the chain's iron links, which did not survive, have been observed in concretion. Surveyor's chain sets were often stored in a bundle secured by a leather strap. Why these elements of land surveying equipment were even on *Queen Anne's Revenge* is anyone's guess, adding to the mystique surrounding life aboard a pirate ship.

Brass tallies 1, 2, 3, and 0, from a Gunter surveyor's chain. (Courtesy of the North Carolina Department of Natural and Cultural Resources)

A Tale from the High Seas

Archaeological Interpretations

Soon after the discovery of the debris site in Beaufort Inlet in 1996, we confirmed that it represented the remains of a sunken ship, answering the most basic question. Throughout the years that followed, nothing in the rubble altered the assumption that it was the remains of *Queen Anne's Revenge*, Blackbeard's flagship. While no single item, such as a ship's bell, dinnerware, or a piece of equipment, clearly linked the ship with that identity, the preponderance of evidence was strong: correct time period and affiliation, a vessel profile that matched descriptions, and the right location and orientation. Despite using the best tools available to us, we were still cautious, since our evidence remained largely circumstantial, and we know that archaeology cannot always produce absolute truths. However, we also know that when assumptions are tested using hypotheses and theories, such a preponderance of evidence allows us to make statements about the past with an elevated level of confidence.

Over the years, when pressed by reporters, we made declarations of how certain we were that the ship was *Queen Anne's Revenge*, starting with 90 percent for the *New York Times* at the 1997 announcement of the discovery.[1] Through the ensuing years, the percentage of certainty has increased to nearly 100. Yet, as sometimes happens, in those early days of work on the shipwreck, our theories were questioned by others who saw it differently. Not until we published a 2012 article in the *Journal of Historical Archaeology* with our colleague Dr. Charles Ewen that presented overwhelming circumstantial evidence did the professional archaeological community fully accept that the ship's identification was correct.[2] Still, with media hype and the occasional professional challenge, we were driven to provide more proof. What transpired was a collaborative effort with input from experts in their various fields to gather a tremendous amount of solid scientific information related to the shipwreck's identity. The process turned out to be gratifying, for often the same findings were applied to other lines of research. For example, the signaling cannon not only provided a date of manufacture, ca. 1700, coinciding with the time *Queen Anne's Revenge* sailed, but the cannon's condition provided indications regarding its value to the men aboard. The fact that the bronze piece showed extensive repair spoke to the resourcefulness of pirates as well as their inability to pull into a port and buy (or steal!) a new one. Because they liked to shoot it, the cannon was worth fixing. On the other hand, when fleeing the ship after it wrecked, the crew chose not to take the small cannon with them.

Archaeologist Chris Southerly hands up a pewter plate recovered from the stern area of the *QAR* site. (Courtesy of the North Carolina Department of Natural and Cultural Resources)

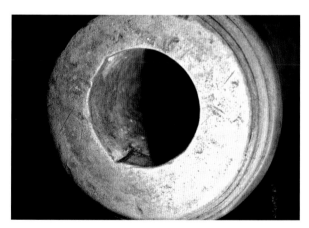

The interior of the *QAR* signaling cannon barrel exhibits deep scarring from use. (Courtesy of the North Carolina Department of Natural and Cultural Resources)

So, even though it was portable, its usefulness was diminished as the pirates scrambled to get off the sinking ship.

In the pages that follow, we offer a summary of evidence to give you an understanding of why the wreckage in Beaufort Inlet has been linked definitively to Blackbeard and *Queen Anne's Revenge* (ex. *Concorde*). Then we will discuss how selected artifacts reflect life aboard the ship for the pirates, the kidnapped Frenchmen, and the enslaved Africans, all on board the ship. As you will read, the position of artifacts across the wreckage provides some indication of work activities and social arrangements. Their distribution also reveals how the ship went down and the events that occurred in the moments, hours, and days that followed. Items that seem to be missing, versus those left behind, reveal what was important to crew members as they were forced from the ship. With a little over 60 percent of the *QAR* wreckage excavated, a broader and more complete picture of the vessel and its crew will emerge in time. Here's what we know so far.

If It Looks Like a Pirate Ship, It Probably Is!

TIME PERIOD

Except for a few intrusive items, the *QAR* artifact assemblage includes 45 individual or classes of datable artifacts entirely made up of late seventeenth- and early eighteenth-century items. None of their manufacture dates is later than the sinking of *Queen Anne's Revenge* in 1718, a finding that would counter the site's hypothetical identity. Key among the datable relics are the ship's bell cast with a date of 1705 and the Swedish cannon with 713 embossed on its left trunnion, indicating a date of 1713. The King George drinking glass was made for his coronation in 1714, and the Queen Anne coin weight was cast during her reign from 1702 until her death in 1714.

Radiocarbon dating and dendrochronology results support vessel construction between 1690

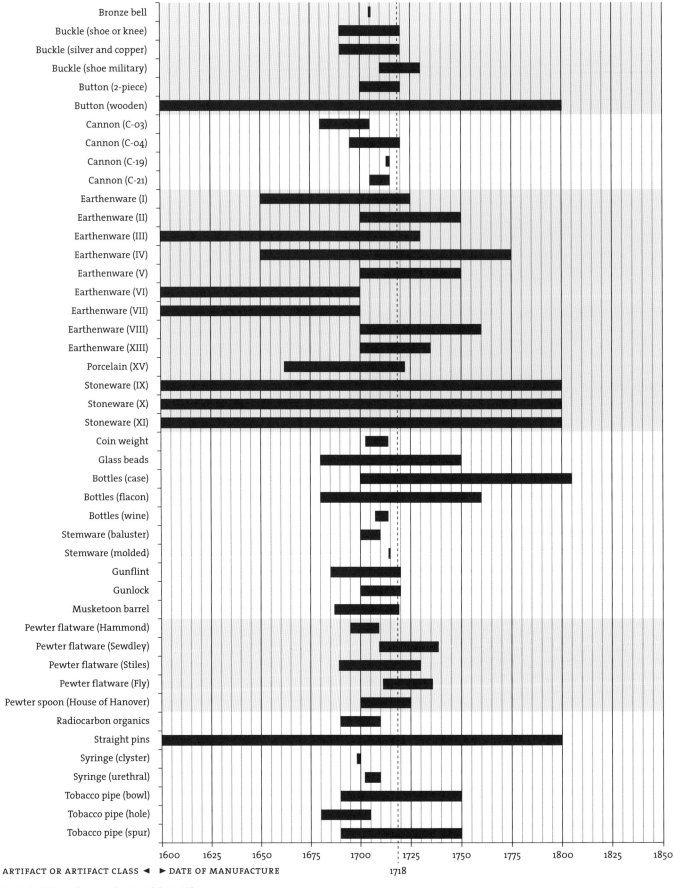

ARTIFACT OR ARTIFACT CLASS ◄   ► DATE OF MANUFACTURE

1718

Period of Manufacture for Datable Artifacts

and 1710. Many other items also provide a general period of manufacture. All the iron cannons, the signaling cannon, and the blunderbuss barrel were made prior to 1718. Thirty-some pewter dishes exhibit marks from five different London pewterers who were in business during the late seventeenth to the second quarter of the eighteenth century. A similar date range has been assigned to the pewter spoon with the rat-tail handle and the cannon-shaped handle of the silver basting spoon. The remaining dates, or range of manufacture, derive from the pieces representing ceramic vessels, glass bottles, tobacco pipes, and clothing items. Among them are the intact wine bottle with the "Queen Anne" shape.

Collectively, all datable artifacts provide a mean manufacture date of 1708. Artifact use-life varies depending on durability and composition of the artifact. For instance, ceramic tableware only lasted a few years, while pewter wares were likely useable for several decades.[3] Viewing the datable assemblage as a whole, we can reasonably conclude that the shipwreck was lost within a decade or so of 1708 and shortly after the years 1713 to 1715, based on the Swedish cannon (C-19) and the King George I coronation glass, a defining period that includes the sinking of *Queen Anne's Revenge*.

CULTURAL AFFILIATION

It comes as no surprise to us that artifacts from this vessel are international in origin, for the early eighteenth century was a time of expanding trade and globalization. Artifacts have been sourced to England (wine bottles, stemware, tobacco pipes, coin weights, survey chain, small weapons, silver spoons, and pewter platters); France (window glass, bottles, surgical instruments, keg tap, navigational instruments, nested weights, oil lamp, weapons, dinnerware, and clothing items); Africa (powdered bead, gold dust, and jewelry); Germany (salt-glazed stoneware jugs); China (hand-painted porcelain); Italy (oil jar and glass beads); Spain (silver coins and olive jars); Sweden (cannons); Holland (glass

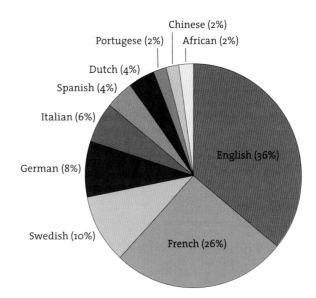

National Affiliation of *Queen Anne's Revenge* Artifacts

beads); and the Caribbean islands (anchor stock and ballast stones). English and French goods, however, dominate the collection, each approximately one-third of the total. Overall, artifact affiliations neatly fit the historical profile of *Queen Anne's Revenge* (ex. *Concorde*) as an early eighteenth-century former French slave ship commandeered by English pirates, who cruised the Caribbean taking and robbing numerous vessels for a period of months before unceremoniously grounding and abandoning their ship on the outer shoals of Beaufort Inlet in June 1718.

SHIP'S PROFILE

As we pointed out earlier, there is not much left of the wooden ship to study. Aided by specialists, we have pieced together all the evidence before us and find that the vessel's profile fits historical descriptions of Blackbeard's flagship. A distinct cluster of ship's rigging elements lies in the middle portion of the site and represents the mainmast, while two other groups are forward and aft, confirming a three-masted vessel. Three large anchors found within the main wreckage are rated for a vessel of 250 to 350 tons and are within the range, albeit a bit large, for what *Concorde* might carry. The size

Cannon C-19 and C-21, likely added to *QAR*'s armament after capture, are sown here undergoing cleaning. (Courtesy of the North Carolina Department of Natural and Cultural Resources)

of timbers and fastening pattern of the surviving hull structure suggests the wreck was of French construction. Observations and measurements taken on the 29 iron cannons denote a ship equivalent to a late seventeenth- or early eighteenth-century sixth-rate English or French light frigate, which was *Concorde*'s initial service. Actually, Blackbeard's flagship may have been even more powerful, based on South Carolina attorney general Richard Allen's statement that "Thatch the Pirate came and lay off this Harbour with a Ship of forty Guns mounted, and one hundred and forty Men, and as well fitted with warlike Stores of all forts, as any Fifth-Rate Ship in the Navy."[4]

LOCATION

Historic accounts place the grounding of *Queen Anne's Revenge* on the outer bar of Beaufort Inlet. While no charts exist from the time Blackbeard attempted to bring the ship through the inlet, maps drawn 20 years later provide reasonably accurate depictions of the inlet's physiography. When the location of the shipwreck is transposed onto those charts, it plots out on the outer ebb tidal shoal or "bar" at the seaward entrance to historic Beaufort Inlet.

While evidence points to the correct time period, the correct profile, and being in the right place, the case for the ship's identity might not be totally convincing, or hold water so to speak, if it were not accompanied by *QAR* historian Dr. Lindley Butler's assessment of shipping along the North Carolina coast in the first quarter of the eighteenth century. He tells us that a 200- to 300-ton ship armed with dozens of cannons would not typically have sailed to and from Beaufort because, truth be known, it was a backwater place with little commerce. The vast majority of vessels engaged in trading there during the eighteenth century were small sloops bound to and from New England ports. Is it possible that an unnamed eighteenth-century vessel was lost without any report by authorities, its owners, or local inhabitants? Slim chance. Is it possible that a vessel that fits that archaeological evidence could have sunk without record at this location, while the remains of *Queen Anne's Revenge* lie elsewhere in Beaufort Inlet? Not really. Extensive remote sensing surveys and site identification virtually eliminate that possibility. Although we can never be 100 percent sure, we are now very confident that Blackbeard's flagship has been found. If it walks like a pirate and talks like a pirate, then shiver me timbers, chances are it is!

How the Ship Went Down

The old ship in Beaufort Inlet, now a weatherworn debris field, holds enough spatial integrity to allow us to infer what happened when it wrecked as well as to surmise shipboard activities while it was afloat. The site best fits a type of shipwreck that sank and deteriorated in place rather than one strewn across the seafloor during a violent storm. As such, it retains structural elements, some organic materials, and a variety of other artifacts in a scattered but ordered spatial distribution depending on weather and oceanographic conditions. With this type of slow-wrecking event, there is a high probability that vessel remains and artifacts will survive intact. As sands shift due to storms or sea-bed currents, however, some or all of the remains may be re-exposed and eventually entirely lost.[5]

Based on magnetic gradiometer surveys together with archaeological test excavations, we find the *QAR* wreckage is contained within an area approximately 200 ft. in length (north and south) and 75 ft. across. Thus, the site's footprint is only twice the actual size of the ship, indicating it deteriorated in place. This scenario is supported by the results of intense magnetometer surveys conducted in the area that reveal no wreckage on the shoreward side of the shipwreck, where predominant winds and currents would have driven debris. The *QAR* represents a low-impact wrecking rather than a catastrophic loss that might scatter wreckage over greater distances.

Looking at various signature artifacts found within site boundaries, we can say with reasonable certainty that the ship was pointed shoreward, as would be expected for a vessel heading into the inlet, when its captain miscalculated and hit the outer shoals. The offshore end of the *QAR* wreckage is thought to be the vessel's stern, based on items traditionally associated with the ship's officers' quarters, including pewter ware, scientific and medical instruments, lead shot, and gold dust. Conversely, a large anchor at the shoreward end represents the ship's main anchor, once located on its starboard bow. Cannons are in paired sets along the site's western edge, indicating the vessel rolled onto its port side sometime after grounding.

Over 100 lead hull patches used to stop leaks in the vessel's lower hull are distributed down the length of the ship's wreckage, providing further evidence that the vessel deteriorated in place. Additionally, 183 separate iron hoop fragments have been recovered, and another 18 complete sets were recorded in situ. While there has been some debate whether these were extra hoops in the cooper's inventory, a portion were likely in use, representing as many as 150 casks. If that is true, the presence of intact wooden containers suggests that sea

Conglomerate of rigging elements from the ship's main mast that deteriorated in place on the *QAR* site. Photograph by Julep Gillman-Bryan. (Courtesy of the North Carolina Department of Natural and Cultural Resources)

UAB archaeological conservator Nathan Henry inspects the fluke of Anchor A-3 with a shaft nearly 13 ft. long. Photograph by Julep Gillman-Bryan. (Courtesy of the North Carolina Department of Natural and Cultural Resources)

Blackbeard Rants as Stede Bonnet Reposes, painting by
Virginia Wright-Frierson (2017), Mark Wilde-Ramsing
and Linda Carnes-McNaughton private collection.
(Used by permission)

conditions at the time of wrecking were not strong
enough to wash them ashore. Instead they became
waterlogged and settled in place, where they consequently rotted. It's apparent from archaeological
evidence that *Queen Anne's Revenge* grounded and
was abandoned, as reported by eyewitnesses. It
will probably never be known whether Blackbeard
ran his flagship aground on purpose, as Bonnet's
men accused him of doing, or simply miscalculated
while attempting to reach safe harbor inside Beaufort Inlet. Either way, the ship hit hard and fast on
the sandbar and could not be freed.

Life on a Pirate Ship for All Those Aboard

PIRATES

Because the *QAR* wreckage is relatively concentrated, the distribution of its artifacts reflects the
ship's layout and related activities while afloat.
Despite historical accounts that pirates were a
democratic bunch who shared and shared alike,
it appears Captain Thache maintained traditional
hierarchal control from his cabin in the stern. This
area contains artifacts befitting the officers, including fancy dinnerware and most of the gold dust
and few coins that remain after the ship's abandonment, apparently having fallen behind furniture or
between the floorboards. By contrast, the absence
of valuables in any form is noticeable in the forward sections of the ship, where the common pirate

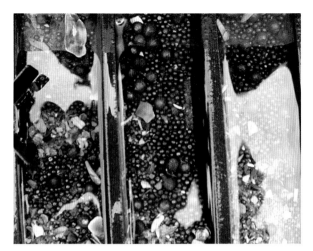
Thousands upon thousands of *QAR* lead shot were captured in dredging sluices. (Courtesy of the North Carolina Department of Natural and Cultural Resources)

sailors would have congregated, suggesting that whatever booty they may have had, albeit minor, was taken with them. *One for all, and all for one!* Well, not so, according to archaeological evidence from *Queen Anne's Revenge* and the corroborative testimony by Bonnet's men, who said Blackbeard took all their money and left them with nothing.

Perhaps more telling is the large amount of ammunition, over 250,000 lead shot, also found near Blackbeard's cabin. It is likely he kept it under his control to minimize threats to his command. The ship's heavy armament of at least 29 cannons, not including the signaling cannon, lots of ammunition, and the makings of scatter shot for disabling ship's sails and maiming enemy personnel point to a ship set on a predatory mission aimed at capturing, not sinking, targeted ships. Particularly lethal to enemy personnel when fired at close range were the breechloading swivel guns, called murderers. Two *QAR* breechblocks confirm the use of these antiquated yet very effective weapons, which pirates were known to prefer. When we look at what firearms were left behind, we are struck by what we see: gun parts from an assortment of weapons, most of which reveal heavy wear and repairs. It is

clear the gunsmiths on this ship were not only busy but forced to make do with whatever they had on hand.

The presence of several classes of artifacts appears out of the ordinary and may reflect pirate behavior. This is seen in the multiple sets of navigational instruments, presumably taken from prizes and maybe used to help negotiate unfamiliar waters or kept as curiosity booty. The number of sounding weights, quadruple what was normal, points to a secondary use other than determining water depths. Perhaps they represented a source of raw lead, to be melted down into patches for the leaky vessel or some other repair work, or as ammunitions. Lead served as the eighteenth century's duct tape when it came to fixing things. There are also multiple numbers of scale weights that apparently represent a preoccupation related to money (coins and gold dust), administering medicines, or both.

THE FRENCH PRESENCE

Goods manufactured in France are strongly represented on the ship because it was originally from that country and because 14 of its crew members continued to sail with the pirates. The majority had professional skills: surgeons, carpenters, a pilot, a cook, a gunsmith, and a musician. Medical instruments made in France are likely the property of chief surgeon Jean Dubou and his assistants, Marc Bourneuf, Nicolas Gautrain, and Claude Deshayes (originally a gunner turned surgical aide). Being men of status, they were more refined and better educated than the regular crew, which is reflected in artifacts associated with them. French-related clothing items include silver buckles and gilded buttons. Of the few weapons left aboard were a decorative short sword and a dirk that the Frenchmen likely carried. The Saintonge tableware was likely used by the French surgeons and perhaps by Blackbeard and his officers. *Concorde*'s kidnapped second cook, Georges Bardeau, remained in the galley using French-made storage jars and copper and iron cooking pots to feed his countrymen, pirates,

Close-up of the bleeding porringer showing "DV" initials stamped twice on the base. (Courtesy of the North Carolina Department of Natural and Cultural Resources)

African oarsmen (detail), *The Marooning of Ignatius Pell and Other Crewmen by Blackbeard*, oil painting by Virginia Wright-Frierson (2017), Mark Wilde-Ramsing and Linda Carnes-McNaughton private collection. (Used by permission)

and Africans alike. Could the personalized initials DV incised on the bottom of the French porringer have originally belonged to Charles Duval, the pilot from Port Louis, or perhaps his compatriot Rene Duval, the carpenter from Nantes? With the majority of these items coming from the stern section of the ship, we surmised that the Frenchmen aboard *Queen Anne's Revenge* were treated and quartered well.

THE AFRICAN PRESENCE

Archaeological evidence related to Africans on board the pirate ship is but a small fraction compared with the English and French presence, despite *Concorde* starting out carrying 516 men, women, and children from Africa. Those objects include a few pieces of clipped Akan gold jewelry, an abundance of small glass trade beads, one powdered glass bead, and a couple of iron shackles used for restraint. The presence of these items is but a

whisper from the many unfortunate people who were snared in an assault by pirates. Associated with the enslaved was gold jewelry, once magnificent body adornments worn by Akan royalty. With complete disregard for the artisan's craft, Frenchmen, pirates, and African slave traders clipped the finery into small pieces, sacrificing beauty for pure monetary value (gold weight). The vast amount of Italian and Dutch glass beads accompanied slave operations, since they were likely provided to women and girls as incentive rewards to string and sew as a way to occupy their time aboard ship. Given the many beads left behind, enslaved Africans were in no position to manage their meager possessions as the ship was abandoned. On the other hand, of the hundreds of shackles that were likely on *Concorde* at the time it left Africa, only two have been found. They must have retained their value as restraining devices for those in bondage. This suggests that Africans remained enslaved regardless of whether the ship was controlled by the French or by English pirates.

Historical records shed some light on the relationship between Blackbeard and Africans. From the testimony of *Concorde*'s Captain Dosset, the pirates retained 157 Africans along with the black musician after taking control of Dosset's ship. Of those, Dosset reportedly recovered 61 Africans on the shores of Grenada and 15 others from the slave market at Martinique. Another 5 Africans were later given by Blackbeard to 4 men of the *Great Allen* as a reward for joining the pirates and helping secure the ship's valuables. The pirate captain was still interested in Africans when he removed 14 enslaved individuals from a vessel just days before the loss of *Queen Anne's Revenge*. After the wrecking, he reportedly left Beaufort Inlet with 40 whites and 60 blacks. It is apparent that Blackbeard dealt in slaves, kept some aboard as menial laborers, and perhaps elevated a few to crew status, depending on their ability to fight or sail, coupled with a loyalty to the freebooters' cause. The latter is demonstrated by five Africans captured during Blackbeard's epic battle at Ocracoke, including Caesar, who was set to blow up the pirate's sloop if he hadn't been stopped by Lieutenant Robert Maynard's men.[6] This embracing of the pirates' cause may or may not have been the case for the black musician, who was married in France and forced to join the pirates.

Abandoning Ship: Crew Priorities Revealed

Artifact patterns related to people facing disaster, whether it is a burning building today, a prehistoric pueblo in a desiccated landscape, or a ship rendered useless on a sandbar, provide archaeologists with similar clues reflecting how fast the abandonment took place, how things were prioritized, and who in the group had special status. The following discussion focuses on choices and options and who made them during the loss of *Queen Anne's Revenge*.

Neither historical records nor archaeological evidence provides specifics on what actually happened when the ship ran aground. It is known from firsthand accounts that a second ship, *Adventure*, also grounded and was lost. That left Bonnet's

Queen Anne's Revenge aground in Beaufort Inlet. Bernie Case, illustrator (1999). (Courtesy of the North Carolina Department of Natural and Cultural Resources)

Revenge and the fourth vessel in the flotilla, a small, unnamed sloop, to pick up the stranded sailors. No doubt ships' longboats were also used to ferry men to the rescue ships or to shore. The disabled flagship grounded in shoal waters on the seaward side of the inlet over a mile from shore and was likely subjected to constant pounding from wind-driven waves, made worse at low tide when the vessel heeled over hard to port. Therefore, decisions by the crew on what to take from the ship were likely made in haste, since their primary concern was to transport everyone to safety. They were successful in that historical accounts report no loss of life, and archaeologists have found no evidence of human remains. Since few personal items and serviceable weapons were found, it's a good bet sailors escaped with the shirts on their backs, weapons in their hands, and coins in their pockets. Or it is more likely the valuables were probably only in Blackbeard's purse!

Some items that were useful to the pirates as they went about their business of navigating, plundering, and dividing the booty were expend-

A heavy grinding stone left behind on the *QAR* site was recovered by archaeologists on June 1, 2006. (Courtesy of the North Carolina Department of Natural and Cultural Resources)

able when the men no longer had their battleship. Pirates chose to leave navigational instruments, including all those sounding weights, plus a trove of weighing and measuring instruments. Excepting the casks, many of these things could have been easily removed. There is a theory regarding abandonment behavior known as Zipf's principle of least effort. It suggests that one factor in whether something is taken relates to its size and weight (bulkiness).[7] At the *QAR* site, the many large, heavy artifacts left on board, such as cannons and anchors, although of value for use or sale, were simply too cumbersome to remove, given the circumstances. The same goes for the mechanical jacks and grinding stones, while other items, like the bells, may have been too firmly attached.

Ownership, wear, replacement costs, and utility also had some bearing on human behaviors during the wrecking process. With only 29 iron cannons of the 40 reported for Blackbeard's flagship found so far, and prospects not good for finding the rest, it is suspected that at least some were removed, those being the portable rail guns. Yet the bronze signal-

ing cannon was left behind, apparently too worn to bother with. What about all those medical instruments? Were the conscripted French surgeons just happy to get off the ship? Did the pirates not allow them to remove their medical kits? Was it every man for himself? There is so much that can be learned about the people, the ship, and all that was taking place aboard *Queen Anne's Revenge*. To tease it out of the archaeological record, a theoretical lens, such as abandonment theory, is particularly useful. As excavations and conservation expand the body of evidence, much more will be explored and learned. What now looms over the horizon?

Where the Real Treasure Lies: Full Recovery, Answering Broader Questions

The importance of archaeological investigations conducted at the *QAR* site cannot be overestimated. Full-scale recovery of the vessel from the seafloor using today's exacting archaeological standards and modern technology, when successfully completed, will place it among the world's most important wooden shipwreck recoveries, in the company of *Mary Rose* in England, *Vasa* in Sweden, and *La Belle* in Texas. First and foremost, these ship-named projects have been leaders in the science of conserving waterlogged and salt-impregnated artifacts, by far the most difficult aspect of underwater archaeological recovery. The task of overseeing the condition of treated artifacts, whether they are on display or in storage, goes on in perpetuity. It is estimated that three or four years of field operations will be needed to bring up the remaining 40 percent of the *QAR* site, depending on how aggressively we are able to proceed, which ultimately depends on available funding. Yet that is only one-tenth of the journey, for after the recovery of artifacts from the ocean floor is complete, conservators will be around for a very, very long time cleaning, stabilizing, curing, analyzing, and monitoring the assemblage of artifacts.

The scientific implications of bringing up every artifact associated with *Queen Anne's Revenge* are broad and far reaching. It is often said shipwrecks are time capsules that provide an assemblage of artifacts from a moment in history. As has been evident throughout this book, all of that eighteenth-century, pirate-associated, internationally affiliated cultural material gives specialists a lot to study for years to come. They will recognize many things, scratch their heads on a few, and on occasion have a eureka moment, such as realizing the *QAR* half-pounder English cannon was cast using a two-part mold, the earliest known example for such a small iron gun. When excavation and artifact analyses are finally completed, we and our archaeological colleagues will have a rich and full palette with which to paint the *Queen Anne's Revenge* canvas. Everything that has been hinted at, explored, expressed, and hypothesized will become more focused.

Complete excavation of a scattered wreck is unprecedented, since these types of sites have, by and large, only been sampled or at most partially excavated. In North Carolina, for example, more than 1,000 shipwrecks have been reported and entered in the state's database. The majority have been barely touched, and none has been fully explored because funding has not allowed it. Yet the mere power of pirates, especially one called Blackbeard, has gotten the *QAR* project this far and will likely provide enough wind in its sails to ensure that all evidence will be recovered, analyzed, and conserved, and a good portion will be displayed. Consequently, making a clean sweep of the seafloor will enhance future researchers' ability to maximize sampling strategies on shipwrecks that are historically important but are limited by lack of funding. To add to this excitement is the possibility of discovering and exploring a second ship from Blackbeard's fleet, David Harriot's *Adventure*, which lies "within gunshot" of the *QAR* site.

Behold, scallywags, untold treasure still remains hidden in the waters off Beaufort!

QAR chief conservator Sarah Watkins-Kenney and East Carolina University graduate student Jim Parker inventorying a small artifact storage tank. (Courtesy of the North Carolina Department of Natural and Cultural Resources)

Full recovery operations with *QAR* archaeologists Nathan Henry, Josh Daniel, Franklin Price, and Chris Southerly and Captain Julep Gillman-Bryan (*background*). (Courtesy of the North Carolina Department of Natural and Cultural Resources)

What Happened to Blackbeard and All Those Pirates? The Rest of the Story

So hoist up the John B's sail
See how the mainsail sets
Call for the Captain ashore
Let me go home, let me go home
I wanna go home, yeah yeah
Well I feel so broke up
I wanna go home.[8]

In parallel with the long-running news segments of noted radio broadcaster Paul Harvey, we now wish to give you "The Rest of the Story," which involves more tales of survival, success, and disappearance of the other pirates following the loss of *Queen Anne's Revenge* and *Adventure*. While we may never know for certain whether the wrecking was accidental or a preconceived plot by Captain Thache and his confidants, we are curious to learn the fate of everyone on the scene that fateful day in June 1718. As they watched the two ships falter and keel over, hundreds of men, reportedly 320 in all, were subsequently cast on the desolate shores of North Carolina.[9] A portion were in Thache's party who fled the scene in their smallest sloop; members of Stede Bonnet's crew were put ashore, were later rescued, and then went back out to sea. According to their respective narratives, the trajectories of both pirate captains, in relatively short order, led to their deaths. Thache and some of his crew died at Ocracoke, and Bonnet was hanged in Charleston, along with dozens of his followers. By all estimates, however, this is a fraction of the crowd who abandoned the two ships at Beaufort Inlet. What happened to the rest of the pirates, in addition to the Africans and Frenchmen sailing on *Queen Anne's Revenge* and the three sloops in its fleet? Where did they end up and why? Historical records, local folklore, and a dose of imagination provide some clues toward answering these questions. But first, here's a recap of what happened to Blackbeard, Bonnet, and their men.

Capture of the Pirate, Blackbeard, 1718, painting by Jean Leon Gerome Ferris (1920). (Courtesy of WikiCommons)

After Captain **Edward Thache** (aka Blackbeard) left Beaufort with 40 white men and 60 Africans, he took the king's pardon from North Carolina governor Charles Eden. For the next five months, he used the fledgling Carolina colony, principally Bath and Ocracoke Island, as a base of operations to continue pirating while local officials looked the other way. Specifically, Thache and a dozen or so men captured the French merchant ship *Rose Emelye*, which he reported to authorities was adrift at sea with no one aboard and a cargo of cocoa and barrels of freshly refined sugar.[10] Reporting the ship as "abandoned," he was able to stay within the measure of the law. Thache sold or gave away its cargo for his financial well-being. His life came to an end on November 22, 1718, when Virginia governor Alexander Spotswood sent an invading force south, and out of his colonial jurisdiction, to confront the pirate band. The nine others killed alongside Thache were **Philip Morton**, gunner; **Garrott Gibbons**, boatswain; **Owen Roberts**, carpenter; **John Philips**, sailmaker; and common sailors **John Husk**, **Joseph Curtis**, **Joseph Brooks Sr.**, **Thomas Miller**, and **Nathaniel Jackson**.[11]

The Taking of Teach the Pirate: 1719

So each man to his gun,
For the work must be done
With cutlass, sword, or pistol.
And when we no longer can strike a blow,
Then fire the magazine, boys, and up we go!
It's better to swim in the sea below
Than to swing in the air and feed the crow,
Says jolly Ned Teach of Bristol.[12]

An intriguing story surrounds another man aboard *Queen Anne's Revenge* at the time of its sinking; he is **Edward Salter**, the cooper on the merchant ship *Margaret*. When the vessel was stopped by the pirates on December 5, 2017, Salter was forced to join them. Six months later in Beaufort, it seems that Salter may have been among one of the favored 40 whites who accompanied Thache to Bath. Months later he was picked up there by the Virginia militia when they invaded the town looking for pirates. Not only did Salter apparently beat a charge of piracy then, but eight years later, in 1726, he was in a financial position to purchase Governor Eden's former residence. Remember that stone wharf that we found during the Bath field school described in Chapter 1? The one that Blackbeard walked up when he visited the governor? Well, as it happened, Salter came to own it and the associated brick warehouse. During the 1984 archaeological excavations of the warehouse, researchers also unearthed a vault containing a wooden coffin complete with a human skeleton. Forensic specialists determined the remains were those of a male Caucasian of European descent, 40 to 42 years old, matching Salter's description.[13] The irony lies in that this same wealthy merchant, who served as the colony's powder receiver for the port

"One More Step, Mr. Hands," painting by N. C. Wyeth (1911), in *Treasure Island*, by Robert Louis Stevenson. (Courtesy of WikiCommons)

of Bath when he died in 1735, had been thick in piratical activities nearly two decades before under the reign of Blackbeard.

Among the other pirates surviving the fight at Ocracoke or swept up in Bath by Governor Spotswood's dragnet were **James Blake**, **Joseph Brook Jr.**, **Caesar**, **John Carnes**, **Stephen Daniel**, **Thomas Gates**, **John Giles**, **Israel Hands**, **Richard Greensail**, **John Martin**, **Samuel Odel**, **Joseph Philips**, **James Robbins**, **Richard Stiles**, and **James White**.[14] These men were put on trial in Williamsburg, and with the exception of Odel, who was acquitted, all were convicted of piracy and sentenced to be hanged. A few, as we know for Hands, were spared the gallows through a timely extension of England's amnesty program for pirates. Captain Hands reportedly returned to London and was reduced to begging on the street, only to rise to fame

Marooned, by Howard Pyle (1909), oil on canvas, Delaware Art Museum, museum purchase, 1912. (Used by permission)

posthumously as the right-hand man to Long John Silver in Robert Louis Stevenson's *Treasure Island*.

Henry Man (Inan), **William Stoke**, and **Adolf Van Pelt** were cornered and captured in Kiquotan, Virginia, along with **William Howard**, quartermaster aboard *Queen Anne's Revenge*. These men were convicted of piracy and then also freed due to the king's extended "Act of Grace."[15] Family lore, perhaps stretching the bounds of longevity, claims that 40 years after his trial, Mr. Howard purchased Ocracoke Island and lived there until his death, when he would have been in his nineties.[16] Another man, **Richard Hyde**, as reported through less-than-reliable sources, was known to have been a "disciple of Black Beard, the pirate." Hyde apparently escaped capture by heading west and becoming a frontier trader whose dealings may have taken

him into Indian country as far away as Mississippi. He reportedly had his ears "clipt off by the Muskhoge" for sexual indiscretions with their women, before his death in June 1719.[17] **John Rose Archer**, who may not have been at Beaufort, reportedly "learnt his art as a pirate in the excellent school of the notorious Blackbeard." After working as a New England fisherman for a time, he once again lapsed into piracy in 1723 when his boat was captured by Captain Phillips and he remained aboard serving as quartermaster. A short while later, the pirate ship and the crew were captured. Archer expressed regret for his decision a few minutes before he was hanged for piracy on June 2, 1724.[18]

A day or so after the wrecking of *Queen Anne's Revenge*, Captain **Stede Bonnet** sat in the cabin of his ship *Revenge*, soon to be renamed *Royal James*,

Archaeological Interpretations

and with his quartermaster **Robert Tucker** and boatswain **Ignatius Pell**, conceived a plan to continue their predatory calling. Their scheme was to first receive amnesty through King George's pardon from Governor Eden and then sail to St. Thomas in the Danish West Indies, where they would receive a letter of marque for privateering. Needless to say, things didn't go as planned. After Bonnet left for Bath to apply for the pardon on behalf of himself and crew, Thache ransacked *Revenge*, taking 14 men and all of their arms and money; most devastatingly, he emptied the ship of its remaining food supplies. Adding insult to injury, the remaining crew was then marooned.

Eventually, Bonnet returned and rescued his men, and they left Beaufort with a vengeance for Thache. Soon reality set in, for they had nothing to eat and began a six-week spree attacking ships along the Atlantic seaboard. Their binge ended on September 27, 1718, when Bonnet and crew were cornered at the mouth of the Cape Fear River by a naval contingent from South Carolina under the command of Colonel William Rhett. **Thomas Wallace**, **William Heron**, and **James Robinson** were killed, and the rest were captured and put on trial. Stede Bonnet and the following men were convicted of piracy and hanged in Charleston: **Alexander Amand** (Annand) of Jamaica; **Job Baily** (Bayley) of London; **Sam Booth** of Charleston, South Carolina; **Robert Boyd** of Bath Town, North Carolina; **John Brierly**, alias Timberhead, of Bath Town, North Carolina; **Thomas Carman** of Maidstone in Kent, England; **George Dunkin** of Glasgow, Scotland; **William Eddy** of Aberdeen, Scotland; **William Hewett** (Hewet or Hewit) of Jamaica; **Matthew King** of Jamaica; **John Levit** of North Carolina; **William Livers**, alias Evis, of Dublin, Ireland; **Zachariah Long** of the Province of Holland; **John Lopez** of Oporto, Portugal; **William Morrison** of Jamaica; **James Mullet**, alias Millet, of London, England; **Neal Patterson** of Aberdeen, Scotland; **Daniel Perry** of Guernsey (British possession); **Thomas Price** of Bristol, En-

"The Hanging of Stede Bonnet in Charleston, 10 December 1718," engraving in Captain Charles Johnson [Nathaniel Mist], *A General History of the Robberies and Murders of the Most Notorious Pyrates* (1725), Dutch version. (Courtesy of WikiCommons)

gland; **John Ridge** of London, England; **James Robbins** of London, England; **Edward Robinson** of Newcastle-upon-Tyne, England; **George Ross** (Rose) of Glasgow, Scotland; **William Scot** of Aberdeen, Scotland; **John Williams Smith** of Charleston, South Carolina; **John Thomas** of Jamaica; **Robert Tucker** of Jamaica; **Henry Virgin** of Bristol, England; and **James Wilson** of Dublin, Ireland.

According to records of the South Carolina trials, a few men who sailed with Bonnet before and after the wrecking of *Queen Anne's Revenge* were not hanged.[19] These included **Thomas Nichols**, who was never a willing participant aboard the pirate ship. Nichols reportedly kept to himself and let it be known that he would escape the pirates if ever given the chance. He was nearly killed by Bonnet for refusing to fight during their final battle, but with a pistol cocked at his temple, Nichols was spared when Bonnet's attention turned toward his mortally wounded friend. During the South Carolina trials, testimony that kept Nichols off the gallows was principally provided by **David Harriot**, as he was a key witness giving state's evidence in order to save his own neck. This likely would have gotten him off, but he was housed with Bonnet during the trial and was persuaded to join him during an escape attempt. The breakout was ill fated, for in short order they were located, and in the ensuing skirmish Harriot was shot dead. **Ignatius Pell** also testified against the pirates, which led to his acquittal. Yet, in a macabre twist, Pell turned out to be the worst, most vicious pirate of them all, as reported by newspapers on April 25, 1724.

> We have Advice from New-England, that the Pyrates keep still in Action upon the Coasts of America; a Sloop of 12 Guns lately took a Ship call'd the *Eagle*, Captain Collins, the Pyrate was commanded by one Pell [Ignatius Pell], formerly Boatswain under Major Bonnet, and an Evidence against him when the said Major was try'd: The *Eagle* fought the Pyrate for some time, but being boarded and overpower'd with a superior Number of Hands, she was obliged to yield to their Mercies. which prov'd unheard of Cruelties, they hack'd and hew'd the Men in an inhumane Manner, and the Master they cut in Quarters alive, and hang'd them up at the Main Yard.[20]

Much less is known about the 14 Frenchmen who were forced to join or went willingly when Thache and crew took their ship *Concorde*. Based on the vessel's pay record, the 2nd cook, **Georges**

This slip-trailed decorated Saintonge bowl fragment made in France, and the only one of its kind found on the *QAR* site, represents the Frenchmen who continued aboard as their ship sailed off course and was lost in a remote place in the Americas. (Courtesy of the North Carolina Department of Natural and Cultural Resources)

Bardeau, arrived back in France by May 1718, a month before *Queen Anne's Revenge* was lost at Beaufort. Perhaps his French cooking wasn't up to pirate standards and he was let go or otherwise escaped, making it back home well before the others. Two Frenchmen also made the trans-Atlantic voyage aboard English ships back to Nantes, France, to be paid. **Charles Duval**, *Concorde*'s pilot from Point Louis, was back by September 5, 1718, which was a quick turnaround if he was with the pirates at Beaufort. The return passage from the Americas to Europe generally took six to eight weeks. Chief Surgeon **Jean Dubois** (Dubou) from Gascony made it back to Nantes on October 21, 1718. It is not known how the rest of the Frenchmen fared, including carpenter **Rene Duval**, whose wife, Perinne Caset, picked up his pay on July 13, 1718.[21]

Even less is known of the Africans aboard at the time of the ship's sinking, except that 60 were reported as leaving Beaufort with Thache and others. Africans apparently played varying roles aboard *Queen Anne's Revenge*; some were sold or given as

Under the marker buoy lies what remains of *Queen Anne's Revenge*.
(Courtesy of the North Carolina Department of Natural and Cultural Resources)

"gifts" by the pirates. Others served Thache directly, such as the four oarsmen with the pirate captain when he robbed plantation owner William Bell on the Pamlico River late one night.[22] Of Thache's crew captured at Ocracoke, five, **Richard Stiles**, **James Blake**, **James White**, **Thomas Gates**, and Thache's bodyguard, **Caesar**, were listed as Africans; they were tried as free men during the ensuing trial at Williamsburg and convicted. It is uncertain, however, if they were indeed hanged for their crimes.

For three centuries, Tar Heels from the Old North State have claimed title to the brief period when pirates ruled the seas of colonial America; some even proudly tout pirate heritage in their bloodlines. Whether you want to admit it or not, if your roots reach back to colonial Carolina, you may indeed be related to someone who was there in June 1718 when two ships were abandoned at Beaufort Inlet. If so, more than likely your ancestor isn't listed above but could be one of the many who, after being cast ashore, quietly faded into undocumented history, moving on to make an honest living, raise a family, and avoid the violent fate of their notorious pirate captain.

With the discovery of *Queen Anne's Revenge*, popular lore now has a tangible counterpart to guide current generations through this formative period in their history. As scientific work continues on the shipwreck site and in the conservation laboratory, and as artifacts are put on public display in museums, there are many ways you can engage in this exciting discovery project. Find out more just ahead.

CHAPTER EIGHT

The Legacy of the Sunken Prize

Blackbeard's Queen Anne's Revenge

On March 3, 1997, after more than three months of secrecy and planning since the *QAR* discovery, Governor James B. Hunt made a pronouncement. "It looks as if the graveyard of the Atlantic yielded one of the most exciting and historically significant discoveries ever located along our coast. The state of North Carolina is working to protect the site and will do everything we can to that end. We look forward to the day when all North Carolinians can see these exciting artifacts for themselves."[1]

With that announcement, attention was drawn to North Carolina and the quintessential soul of piracy, Edward Thache, aka Blackbeard, for his flagship had finally surfaced after 300 years. Now it seems the whole wide world is watching. Media coverage has been continuous since announcing the shipwreck's discovery, including many spots on major television shows, such as NBC's *Today Show*, *National Geographic Today*, and ABC's *Good Morning America*, which broadcast live from the ocean floor at the *QAR* site as we dove and answered question from host Joan Lunden back in New York. The excitement generated by this novel experiment was so high that it seemed we had put an astronaut on Saturn!

More in-depth coverage has come from North Carolina's UNC-TV through their IQ series, BBC

via the Discovery Channel, an episode of *Deep Sea Detectives* on the History Channel, and others, including one program made for Italian television. Most coverage has aired and re-aired continuously. Articles in newspapers and magazines now run in the thousands, with circulation around the globe. They include the *New York Times*, the *British Times*, the *Atlanta Journal*, the London *Times*, *National Geographic*, *American Airlines Magazine*, *Smithsonian Magazine*, the *Christian Science Monitor*, and many more. Staff members have made hundreds of presentations to school and civic groups and written articles for general audiences. At the other end of the spectrum, research generated from the *QAR* project has resulted in dozens of research papers presented at professional meetings for archaeologists, conservators, and geologists, as well as subsequent scholarly articles. Interest in any aspect of the shipwreck recovery project is newsworthy, and reports are widely read. This phenomenon of public enthusiasm continues to amaze us and provide the impetus for top-notch science and research, while simultaneously accommodating everyone's interest.

Truth be told, one of the most satisfying moments for us, however, was when our work was featured on Jon Stewart's highly popular *Daily*

Good Morning America from the *QAR* site. (Courtesy of the North Carolina Department of Natural and Cultural Resources)

A successful cannon recovery. (Courtesy of the North Carolina Department of Natural and Cultural Resources)

Show on June 15, 1999. The host made light of our pronouncement that pieces of *QAR*'s surviving wood hull dated to the early eighteenth century, which supported it being Blackbeard's ship "or any other ship lost at that time." Stewart joked that at 38 years of age, Blackbeard, like many other men, named his ship "Workaholic or Daddy's Toy." It was a funny piece that raised awareness for our project; however, it also highlighted the fact that in those early days, while almost everyone seemed to know of Blackbeard, although some confused the real person with the mythical Bluebeard, the name of his ship, *Queen Anne's Revenge*, was relatively unknown. That may have been in part because the pirate's version of the ship's name was seldom mentioned in eighteenth-century reports during the six months he sailed it. Long-standing anonymity for the ship was just cause for us to want to set the record straight and educate the public regarding *Queen Anne's Revenge* (ex. *Concorde*). After all, the primary focus of our investigation was squarely on the ship and what it stood for throughout its sailing career. Thus, the project officially became the *Queen Anne's Revenge* Shipwreck Project. The highlights we provide below exemplify the diverse and long-term programs associated with the project's educational outreach. While some programs have

come and gone, recovery at the *QAR* site continues and laboratory conservation of artifacts is ongoing. These will undoubtedly provide new and improved opportunities on the horizon for you to enjoy.

From the *QAR* Site: On the Surface, under the Waves, and Onshore

Since the *QAR* discovery, public attention has been heightened during each archaeological expedition to the site. We accomplish this by focusing media attention on the large artifact raising event, usually staged near the end of fieldwork. From 1997 through 2015, the recovery of 23 iron cannons, two anchors, and the sternpost have beckoned readers, listeners, and viewers to see what was going on in the coastal waters of North Carolina. Each time, the news seems to have spread farther and farther across the globe, quite literally to China. Those pirates have boundless allure!

All that attention puts intense pressure on us and our team to pull off successful and safe recovery events time and again, as the whole world watches. We knew that any major miscue while going "live" could be devastating for the project. These apprehensions were not unfounded, given difficulties that arose as Cannons C-2 and C-3, weighing 2,500 and 2,250 lbs., respectively, were fished out of the ocean on Wednesday, October 22, 1997. It was our first large artifact recovery, and here's how it went down, or rather, how they came up.

In the days immediately beforehand, we had worked industriously to excavate test units around the two cannons to free them from the seabed and move them to a staging area away from excavations for lifting. Cannon C-2 was successfully moved; however, time ran out on Cannon C-3, and our plan was altered to pull it up directly off the wreck site without the use of air-filled lift bags. This nearly ended in disaster.

The weather was not good on the day of the lift, but not quite bad enough to cancel the recovery operation. R/V *Dan Moore*, from Cape Fear Community College in Wilmington, arrived at the shipwreck site, and Captain Steve Beuth struggled to get the lumbering vessel in position as recovery divers Richard Lawrence, Leslie Bright, Mike Daniel, and Ray Giroux anxiously waited. Given the variables of wind, waves, and current, it was difficult for Beuth to gauge the exact spot to drop anchor, well away from the eighteenth-century debris field, to allow the vessel to drift back over the site. After an hour, a second attempt was made, and when that clearly failed, anchoring was abandoned and the vessel was tied directly to the mooring block at the north end of the site. However, there was concern that the vessel's size, combined with rough seas, would strain and possibly drag the one-ton cement block, which had not yet settled into the sandy bottom, having been deployed only a few weeks earlier.

Finally, the vessel drifted back over Cannon C-2, and Lawrence and Bright quickly entered the water, attached an inflatable lift bag to cargo straps that cradled the cannon, and began adding air. In these operations, the tricky part is to control the speed of ascent once the cannon begins to lift off the seabed. The closer to the surface it gets, the more the lift bag expands, which consequently accelerates the cannon's rise to the surface. Should it come up too

Cannon C-2 is brought onto the deck of R/V *Dan Moore*. (Courtesy of the North Carolina Department of Natural and Cultural Resources)

fast and right under the recovery vessel, it could punch a hole in the boat's bottom and cause another shipwreck! Luckily this didn't happen, as the lift bag and its precious cargo popped to the surface well clear of *Dan Moore*'s stern. The crusty relic was then pulled in closer, attached to the lifting crane's large hook, and soon rested on deck. After a few hearty hoorahs, the divers turned their attention to the second cannon and a much more difficult recovery.

Because the weather was deteriorating, the next recovery was attempted without lifting bags. *Dan Moore*'s hawser (heavy anchor line) holding it in place was pulled even tighter to position the vessel's stern over Cannon C-3. Daniel and Giroux took the lifting hook with them directly to the bottom and attached it to the cargo straps that wrapped the cannon. As the unwieldy artifact was reeled up and then broke the surface, it was obvious that part of the rigging had slipped; only the muzzle peeked above the waves, with the rest of its 8-ft. length dangling underneath. At the same time, *Dan Moore*'s stern was bouncing up and down in the water, raising the possibility that the butt of the cannon was dipping deep enough to slam into other wreckage on the bottom. It took every effort to hoist the bobbing, swaying, crusty cannon up and over the stern. And then, as the cannon was being lowered onto blocks, to everyone's surprise an eel

The Legacy of the Sunken Prize

popped out of the muzzle hole and indignantly slithered off the deck and back into the ocean.

Adding to the excitement of the moment, Captain Beuth realized his vessel was dragging the mooring block, quite possibly across the *QAR* site. He quickly ordered everything secured and the hawser released, thus allowing *Dan Moore* to drift off the site before getting under way and heading back to shore. Once at the dock, both cannons were lifted from ship to trailer and later hauled to the conservation laboratory. Everyone took a deep breath to relax and then time to celebrate. Thoughts continued to linger, however, over what damage may have been done to the *QAR* site. Fortunately, subsequent diver inspections showed that Cannon C-3 had not been bouncing uncontrollably on the bottom, and while the mooring block did move several hundred feet, it had skirted exposed wreckage. The initial large artifact raising was a success on all accounts, but it also provided us an important lesson on how quickly things can go wrong. Certainly, there have been a few more instances of flirting with danger, like when Cannon C-24 drifted away from the recovery vessel as attending divers nearly ran out of air. Quick action by Captain Julep Gillman-Bryan and her crew aboard UAB's *Snap Dragon II* helped avert disaster. Another time a wildly swinging Anchor A-1 nearly crashed into the side of *Dan Moore*, but deft maneuvering by the crane operator succeeded in bringing the unwieldy artifact safely to the deck.

Otherwise, publicized events have gone quite smoothly. Through it all, the *QAR* project received worldwide media coverage, and public visibility increased. When the heavily encrusted "Baby Bertha," Cannon C-22, was successfully recovered in May 2001, nearly 150 people were watching aboard a U.S. Army Reserve landing craft. Beginning in 2005 with recovery of Cannons C-15 and C-24, and for many of the subsequent large artifacts, we took public outreach one step further by putting them on temporary display soon after they reached shore. This was a way to let the public enjoy and marvel

A swinging recovery for Anchor A-1. (Courtesy of the North Carolina Department of Natural and Cultural Resources)

QAR "fresh catch," the 1-pounder cannon, C-22, with a thick layer of ballast stone, on view before being transported to the conservation lab. (Courtesy of the North Carolina Department of Natural and Cultural Resources)

at the "fresh catch" before sending it to the conservation lab for years of care. Those on hand to see these crusty objects in person realized that they were among the first to be gazing at eighteenth-century artifacts since Blackbeard and his crew last laid eyes on them as they left their sinking vessel. Some people came from as far away as Maryland just to witness the event and then drove back home.[2] The entire crowd was mesmerized by the size and crustiness of these massive objects. What

Dive Down!

Word spread quickly within the recreational diving community that the famed shipwreck was found. Soon divers clamored to descend on *Queen Anne's Revenge*, which not unexpectedly created a challenge for site managers.

The state's Department of Natural and Cultural Resources (NCDNCR), primarily the Underwater Archaeology Branch, was confronted by several conflicting priorities. First, because the *QAR* shipwreck was considered a state-owned public resource, there was always the belief that accessibility should be granted to everyone. Allowing access to recreational scuba divers, however, posed legitimate threats, both accidental and intentional, which could compromise the integrity of the site. Second, as recreational dive sites go, *QAR* was far from ideal and possessed its own challenges. In addition to low visibility, strong currents, and wave surge, the modest amount of wreckage showing above the seabed was heavily encrusted. What was wonderment to a trained archaeologist would be underwhelming to the average diver without ample contextual interpretation. Third, developing and administering a dive access program would require resources well beyond what was available to the state and outside any of its management priorities.

So the challenge was to develop a safe and manageable program that limited the site's exposure to potential damage, met NCDNCR's educational outreach goals, and was financially self-sustaining. Dive Down, a program developed by the Friends of *Queen Anne's Revenge*, the project's supporting nonprofit group, was created to meet those objectives.

In each session, participants were afforded two full days of immersive instruction, interpretation, and diving. The educational program consisted of four modules: Geology, History, Marine Ecology, and Archaeology. Each module, presented by a professional, placed the wreck site within its proper, multifaceted context. Dive Downers learned about Blackbeard and early eighteenth-century North Carolina maritime history, as well as how artifacts were documented, retrieved, and conserved. They were enthralled when permitted to practice various techniques firsthand on *QAR* sediments, where panning produced small flecks of pirate gold and other micro-artifacts. At the same time, a comprehensive dialogue was kept regarding the tenets of underwater archaeology, the sanctity of provenience, the importance of clear research objectives, and the complexities of site management decisions. Additionally, instructors explained aspects of the wreck site's physical environment, such as composition of seabed sediments, physics of wave action and prevailing ocean currents, and marine life habitat. The Dive Down program concluded with two dives, a practice dive on a nearshore shipwreck with similar conditions, followed by a supervised dive on the *QAR* site. This would not have been possible if North Carolina did not have a well-established recreational diving industry and requisite expertise, personnel, vessels, and equipment. Local dive professionals provided high levels of diver safety and logistical efficiency, as well as critical insurance and liability

176   *The Legacy of the Sunken Prize*

coverage. This allowed staff archaeologists to help divers recognize key features as they toured the *QAR* site. Participants paid a single fee to cover expenses, including instructor fees and dive charter costs. This setup provided fair compensation for Dive Down staff, ensured a quality product for the diving participants, and made the program financially self-sustaining.

Beginning in 2005 until 2009, when *QAR*'s exposed wreckage disappeared under protective sands, nearly 300 divers completed Dive Down. Participants reported very high levels of satisfaction, citing the program's uniqueness and its quality education. Davin Coburn, a diver from the 2009 season, commented, "As a diver, you can find an endless list of scuba destinations, vacations, holidays, and other spots for a back-roll entry. But no dive trip I've ever been on was as smartly integrated with the community and its surroundings as the *QAR* Dive Down program. For two days, our group met with historians, archaeologists, and scientists who told us about everything from pirate lore to regional marine geology. I felt a connection to the wreck 'pile' before I ever saw it in person—and it's a connection that remains today." Another successful outcome was the forging of lasting relationships between the recreational diving community and underwater archaeologists, which advanced a mutual appreciation, cooperation, and preservation for North Carolina shipwrecks, especially for the one Blackbeard lost centuries ago! Consequently, all those involved with Dive Down became valuable advocates for the *QAR* Shipwreck Project.

Participants in the *QAR* Dive Down program prepare to explore *Queen Anne's Revenge*. (Courtesy of the North Carolina Department of Natural and Cultural Resources)

they saw (and smelled!) was in stark contrast to the common perception of a pirate cannon brought from the depths of the ocean. It wasn't clean and ready to shoot, and no mermaid was seen clinging tightly to it.

Six identified iron cannons still remain on the seabed, as well as three anchors, the largest nearly 13 ft. long, all to be recovered sometime in the future. Perhaps you may be among the few to witness firsthand the next magnificent artifact on the day it reemerges from Blackbeard's flagship.

The *QAR* project's website, www.qaronline.org, was first developed to broadcast our daily reports during the 1997 expedition. As time moved on, the site expanded to provide background information, newsletters, conservation reports, research papers, and other related materials. In 1999, the site won the prestigious StudyWeb award as one of the best education sites on the World Wide Web. It has been especially useful in promoting public awareness during fieldwork and large artifact raising events. For instance, the typical number of visits to the *QAR* website jumped eightfold to over 12,000 during a single week in May 2005, when archaeological excavation and artifact recovery were in full swing. As can be expected, the explosion in social media over the past decade has greatly magnified the *QAR* project's worldwide exposure.

In 2000 and 2001 the *QAR* website also served as a conduit for a highly innovative Dive Live program, which was the creation of Bill Lovin of Marine Graphics and Rick Allen of Nautilus Productions.[3] *QAR* Dive Live provided live-streaming video and audio from the shipwreck using microwave technology broadcast to the Internet. As archaeologists worked underwater, school groups from around the country could log onto the Internet, watch them work, and ask questions about what they were doing in real time. It was cutting-edge technology in those days.

Questions posed during Dive Live were often simple: "Have you found any treasure like gold, or skeletons and pirate flags?" By taking these

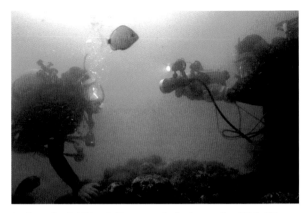

Archaeologist Kim Eslinger and photographer Rick Allen filming *QAR* Dive Live. Photograph by Julep Gillman-Bryan. (Courtesy of the North Carolina Department of Natural and Cultural Resources)

questions seriously and with enthusiasm, project researchers could steer the conversation to more in-depth aspects. Tools and techniques of underwater archaeology and the physical dynamics of the *QAR* site, as well as social and economic implications of piracy, were introduced and discussed. Shipwrecks, pirates, and Blackbeard "set the hook" with the Dive Live audience, and as project archaeologists spoke from their fantastic underwater world, concepts related to what, why, and how they worked were easy to convey. Adults were impressed also, especially teachers, who realized that Dive Live served as a virtual field trip, taking their students to places they would not otherwise be able to visit.

From the *QAR* Conservation Laboratory

At the *QAR* lab in Greenville, where amazing things are continuously discovered, public outreach has been a significant part of the staff's charge. *QAR* conservators Sarah Watkins-Kenney, Kimberly Kenyon, Courtney Page, and Erik Farrell, along with a crew of temporary staff, students, and volunteers, conduct monthly open-house tours, give lectures for professional and service groups, talk to school groups, and answer numerous media requests. In May 2013, they conducted an Inter-

The Legacy of the Sunken Prize

QAR chief conservator Sarah Watkins-Kenney (r) and team apply coating to a cannon while being filmed. (Courtesy of the North Carolina Department of Natural and Cultural Resources)

QAR Lab open-house event. (Courtesy of the North Carolina Department of Natural and Cultural Resources)

net broadcast dubbed *QAR* Project Web Live. The event included a conservation show-and-tell display, coupled with interviews and question-and-answer sessions with *QAR* conservators. Approximately 11,000 schoolchildren in fourth and eighth grades tuned in to the event.

Staff members, volunteer consultants, and research students also participated in the filming of an exciting program for a Smithsonian channel. The focus was the x-raying of six cannons that had not been cleaned since their recovery. As images appeared on the screen, everyone was delighted to see that four of the six were loaded, thus proving that

pirates aboard *Queen Anne's Revenge* were armed and ready!

Since 2005, staff at the *QAR* conservation laboratory in Greenville have invited the general public into their facility for an annual Open Day, as well as for group tours by appointment on a monthly basis. Visitors are guided by staff and volunteers to various stations throughout the conservation facility and are shown an assortment of artifacts from the shipwreck, ranging from small finds of pewter, lead shot, glass shards, and strands of rope to larger objects like cannons, cask hoops, and wooden pieces of the ship's hull. Collectively, these artifacts illustrate the different processes involved in conservation and the importance of each step.

As they enter during the open-house event, school-aged children are presented with a sheet of questions and sent off on a scavenger hunt. Some of the questions are deliberately simple: What is the name of the ship's pirate captain? Who works on artifacts in the lab? Where is the shipwreck? Others are more complicated: What is a trunnel? Where do finished objects go after the lab? And a trickier one: What can be shot out of a cannon? The obvious answer is a cannonball, but that only provides a part score, for pirates also shot iron bars, nails, and anything else handy. Maybe plan your visit to Greenville to see the *QAR* Conservation Laboratory and what artifacts are being discovered as the staff oh-so-carefully break apart those thousand concretions.

Looking for Pirates

For the enthusiast hoping to catch a glimpse of Blackbeard or looking for anything pirate-related, there is plenty to quench one's thirst, from former haunts in the Caribbean to pirate dealings all the way up the Atlantic seaboard to Rhode Island and Massachusetts, where Black Sam Bellamy lost his ship *Whydah*. Many places are more fabrication than real, that is, until one reaches North Carolina, where Blackbeard was known to have roamed.

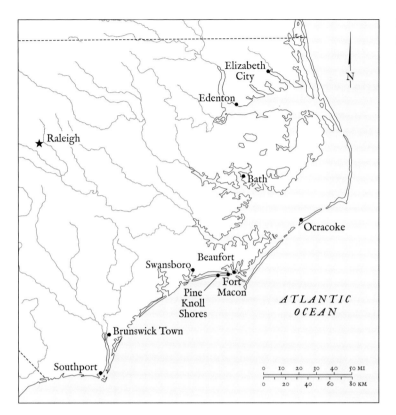

Places of interest related to Blackbeard and *Queen Anne's Revenge*

Elizabeth City

Edenton

Raleigh

Bath

Ocracoke

Beaufort

Swansboro

Fort Macon

Pine Knoll Shores

ATLANTIC OCEAN

Brunswick Town

Southport

N

| 0 | 10 | 20 | 30 | 40 | 50 MI |
| 0 | 20 | 40 | 60 | 80 KM |

If one is willing to explore the eastern parts of North Carolina, there are numerous places of interest and museums that feature pirates, as well as artifacts recovered from the *QAR* wreck site.

When arriving from the south, you might start in Charleston, the city Blackbeard and his men raided just before sailing into North Carolina waters. As you enter the Tar Heel State, the first stop should be the North Carolina Maritime Museum at Southport, which focuses on Stede Bonnet, Blackbeard's pirate partner in crime. Bonnet and his men were captured near Southport in the lower Cape Fear River, and as you read earlier, things didn't turn out so well for them. Heading north, you will pass Historic Brunswick Town, which was attacked by Spanish privateers in 1748, and then travel north and east through Swansboro, where Otway Burns lived. He was a noted American privateer during the War of 1812. As you continue, take an easterly turn at Cape Carteret onto Emerald Isle and con-

tinue north to the North Carolina Aquarium at Pine Knoll Shores, with its 50,000-gallon theme tank featuring replicas of *QAR* cannons and anchors as they rest on the seabed as schools of fish swim by.

From there, a short drive up the island brings you to Fort Macon State Park. While the fort postdates Blackbeard by more than a century, its ramparts provide a great vantage point from which to view what he faced while attempting to bring his large, cranky flagship through Beaufort Inlet. From there you can also assume the role of Captain Piner with a team of underwater archaeologists aboard R/V *Shellpoint* as they round the southern point of the inlet and assess sea conditions at the *QAR* wreck site just offshore. You can decide if it would be safe to work on the water or declare it unsafe and return to dock and spend the day ashore, much to the crew's disappointment.

The Legacy of the Sunken Prize

QAR tank at Pine Knoll Shores Aquarium.
(Courtesy of Mark Wilde-Ramsing).

QAR exhibit at the N.C. Maritime Museum, Beaufort.
(Courtesy of Mark Wilde-Ramsing)

Those who arrive from the north might want to begin in the nation's capital and visit the Smithsonian's Museum of American History, where artifacts from *Queen Anne's Revenge* provide real evidence for the exhibit On the Water: Pirates in the Atlantic World. It would certainly be appropriate to continue down through Williamsburg and the tidewater of Virginia, where some of Blackbeard's men were captured, tried, and reportedly hanged. Entering North Carolina along this route, you should pass through Elizabeth City. This area, which was settled well before Blackbeard arrived on

the scene, features the Museum of the Albemarle and a permanent exhibit of artifacts from *Queen Anne's Revenge*. The road south winds through Edenton, the colony's second capital, whose namesake, Governor Charles Eden, had one of his homes across the bay. Continue on to North Carolina's first capital, Bath, where Blackbeard and Governor Eden conducted "official" business and where the pirate captain reportedly married and lived for a brief time. The North Carolina Historic Site in Bath interprets the life and wild times when pirates roamed its streets. Traveling farther east, which includes a ferry ride across Pamlico Sound, brings you to Ocracoke Island, where Blackbeard established an outpost from which he could keep a watchful eye on ships going in and out of the colony as well as up and down the coast. In the shallows off Springer Point, Blackbeard and his crew were attacked by Royal Marines from Virginia, and his life came to a bloody end.

If coming in from the west, you could stop at the Museum of History in downtown Raleigh, where a cannon, a pewter plate, gold flakes, and other items from *Queen Anne's Revenge* are part of the permanent exhibit The Story of North Carolina. Regardless of how you travel through the state, the North Carolina Maritime Museum in Beaufort should be the final destination. As the primary repository of *QAR* artifacts, the museum's main gallery provides an in-depth look at the results of archaeological investigations and research conducted by the *Queen Anne's Revenge* Shipwreck Project.

With all the hoopla surrounding archaeological investigations, we have often wondered how effective the *QAR* project has been in educating the public amidst the Hollywood hype that surrounds all things pirates. We thought back to the beginning when most people didn't recognize *Queen Anne's Revenge*, but as the years have gone by we witnessed a real sea change. A prime example was the 2011 release of Disney's *Pirates of the Caribbean on Stranger Tides*, which featured not just Ian McShane as Blackbeard but his ship *Queen Anne's*

Revenge. What really tipped the scale of success in our minds, however, was when *Queen Anne's Revenge* was featured not once but three times on the iconic quiz show *Jeopardy*!

Jeopardy Show #6379—Thursday, May 17, 2012

Celebrity Jeopardy with comedian Lewis Black and journalists Clarence Page and Chuck Todd

Jeopardy Round: "Fade to 'Black,'" for $600

Answer: *Queen Anne's Revenge* was this pirate's ship.

Question: Who was Blackbeard?

Jeopardy Show #6821—Monday April 21, 2014

Double Jeopardy Round: "Less-than-Genteel Men of History," for $800

Answer: In the 1990s, divers off the Carolina coast found the wreck of the *Queen Anne's Revenge*, captained by this pirate.

Question: Who was Blackbeard (Edward Teach)?

Jeopardy Show #7144—Thursday, October 8, 2015

Double Jeopardy Round: "Mr. Peabody and Sherman," for $1,200

Answer: "I'm getting a little seasick aboard this pirate ship, the *Queen Anne's Revenge*, Mr. Peabody." "Yes, I too, Sherman, but it's this man's ship & in its own way . . . [chest opens] . . . quite bootyful."

Question: Who was Blackbeard?

Remarkable! With each show the value of the correct response increased in value. While the quiz show in itself may not be a true gauge of the impact of our work, we feel it does represent an ever-increasing awareness of what has been accomplished as a result of the *Queen Anne's Revenge* Shipwreck Project. For us, the experience has been

truly "bootyful" and out there for the whole wide world to see.

Edward Thache could not have foreseen the consequences his actions caused in today's world. By taking on the moniker Blackbeard, the pirate captain intimidated his fellow crewmen, maddened the authorities, and enamored a popular audience, then and now. In a way, we are grateful to Captain Thache for running his flagship aground on a June morning so long ago and that it remained hidden under the sand and waves. Since it was discovered two decades ago, the shipwreck site has been carefully explored, extensively excavated, and subjected to analysis by scores of researchers representing multiple disciplines. Through archaeology, all that brain power has been focused on the enticing evidence that survives from *Queen Anne's Revenge*. In the pages of this book, we have sought to connect various lines of inquiry related to the physical evidence, historical record, and local lore surrounding the pirate flagship and former French privateer and slaver. In this way, the intriguing time of Blackbeard and his band of pirates becomes vibrant. Voices have also been given to the other souls in their company—those free, kidnapped, and enslaved. None of us today can truly know what life was like so long ago when winds filled the expansive sails of the tall ships that moved people and cargo from one continent to another. Achieving a bit of archaeological perspective and respect for them, however, is possible and may give us a greater sense of who we are and where we came from.

Finally, if you haven't already figured it out, we now reveal our biggest secret of all: Archaeology is an intricate, intriguing, stimulating, mind-provoking, often slow, but mostly exciting and fulfilling kind of business. This is particularly true for archaeologists working underwater on a shipwreck, and not just any shipwreck, a pirate ship, and not just any pirate ship, but Blackbeard's Sunken Prize: *Queen Anne's Revenge.*

ACKNOWLEDGMENTS

The discovery and recovery of the shipwreck known as *Queen Anne's Revenge* has involved hundreds of people over the past twenty years. From the earliest magnetometer readings off the seafloor to the careful placement of conserved artifacts into public display cases, numerous individuals have given their time and expertise to this submerged archaeological project. Throughout the pages of this book we have attempted to recognize those involved, most of whom often received little or no compensation other than a sense of pride in having participated in an intriguing and exciting venture. Their names can be found within the text or photo captions, or in a table that provides a listing of researchers. We heap an extra scoop of gratitude on our vignette authors, who have greatly enriched our efforts: Richard Lawrence, Lynn Wood Mollenauer, Lindley S. Butler, David J. Bernstein, Charles R. Ewen, Joseph M. Wilde-Ramsing, Laura Kate Schnitzer, David T. Clark, and Lauren S. Hermley. We have not mentioned everyone, even by a long shot, and can only hope that those who have played a part will accept general ownership and take pleasure in our rendering of this world-class investigation of Blackbeard's flagship.

We specifically thank the Intersal team, who found Blackbeard's long-lost ship, and the North Carolina Department of Natural and Cultural Resources, whose personnel are charged with overseeing the management, protection, and development of this remarkable find. At the time of discovery, North Carolina Department of Natural and Cultural Resources secretary Betty Ray McCain and her deputy Jeffrey Crow were at the helm and enthusiastically embraced the *QAR* project. When state appropriations weren't forthcoming, Secretary McCain wasn't embarrassed to plunder and pillage adequate funding to keep the project afloat. Through the years, subsequent NCDNCR secretaries and their crews have sought to achieve the ultimate goal of preserving *Queen Anne's Revenge*. This required holding a steady course forward despite times when the *QAR* project was becalmed in the doldrums, shaken in violent weather, or under attack by pirates.

Of course, without funding and support outside of what was received from the North Carolina General Assembly, the *Queen Anne's Revenge* Shipwreck Project would have foundered and sunk. Support came from many folks who offered equipment and in-kind services along the way, such as the drywall contractor who heard about our need for containers to keep recovered small artifacts wet and subsequently sent us 500 five-gallon buckets! Parker Boats met a similar need for large artifacts by fiberglassing dozens of tanks for cannons, at no cost. Dollar donations arrived in different ways, such as the $600 tax return that was given because a concerned citizen felt the project needed it more than he did. No doubt, though, it was the major sponsors that propelled the *QAR* project forward when financial assistance was most needed.

National Park Service (Save America's Treasures)
Eddie & Jo Alison Foundation (Grady White)
Golden Leaf, Inc.
National Oceanic and Atmospheric
    Administration (National Marine Sanctuary
    Foundation)
Bucky & Wendi Oliver
The Cannon Foundation
Eric & Rita Bigham

Marion Stedman Covington Foundation
National Geographic Expedition Council
Price Family Foundation
Weyerhaeuser Company
Mary Biddle Duke Foundation
Tabitha McEachern
North Carolina Sea Grant
Archaeological Institute of America
Wachovia Foundation
Robert L. Luddy
Crystal Coast Tourism Authority
Friends of the NC Archives
Town of Morehead City
Town of Beaufort
Leon and Sylvia Sylvester
North Carolina Historical and Literary
   Association.

Most importantly, investigation of *Queen Anne's Revenge* has been and continues to be a project for the people, particularly the citizens of North Carolina. Some may even call it "homegrown." The story of this French privateer/slaver-turned-pirate ship is ours to share, but only because we have benefited from tremendous interest and enthusiasm along the way. We salute *all* efforts in support of the *Queen Anne's Revenge* Shipwreck Project, the results of which you have read about in the preceding pages. Now, in honor, we raise a toast to fair winds and following seas for the remainder of the project's journey.

For this book, we are most indebted to the editors and staff at the University of North Carolina Press for taking our nascent idea and encouraging us to make it into a story. With our limited experience of this kind, UNCP Editorial Director Mark Simpson-Vos, Associate Editor Jessica Newman, and Assistant Managing Editor Stephanie Wenzel were instrumental in guiding us along as we sought to construct our narrative with factual underpinnings, augmented with compelling images, to thoughtfully engage a broad public audience. We also thank the UNCP Board of Governors for greenlighting our literary venture.

We launched *Blackbeard's Sunken Prize* in January 2015, which puts the endeavor nearly three years in length. During that time, advice, guidance, and editorial comments were forthcoming from a host of friends and colleagues, most notably Lindley Butler, Beverly Tetterton, and Lee Herron. Visualizing key scenes in our story, we sought and received original renderings of *QAR* scenes from artists Virginia Wright-Frierson, Martin Peebles, and Bernie Case, literally trying to put ourselves, and thus our readers, into those specific moments in history. Their contributions are greatly appreciated.

Finally, we wish to express our gratitude to family and friends, who provided additional encouragement and support during this book journey: those who informally read bits and pieces of our drafts, those who listened to our frustrations and offered comfort and support, and those who simply prepared dinner and steered clear while we were busy on the computer. Most importantly, we are indebted to you for reading our story and sharing it with others who wish to know more about Blackbeard's flagship and the souls who sailed with him in the spring of 1718.

NOTES

Preface

1. Linda F. Carnes-McNaughton and Mark U. Wilde-Ramsing, "Preliminary Glassware and Bottle Analysis from Shipwreck 31CR314, *Queen Anne's Revenge* Site," Queen Anne's Revenge *Shipwreck Project Research Report and Bulletin Series*, QAR-R-08-02 (Raleigh: North Carolina Department of Cultural Resources, 2008), http://www.qaronline.org/reports/preliminary-glassware-and-bottle-analysis-shipwreck-31cr314-queen-annes-revenge-site.

2. Mark U. Wilde-Ramsing and Linda F. Carnes-McNaughton, "Blackbeard's *Queen Anne's Revenge* and Its French Connection," in *Pieces of Eight: More Archaeology of Piracy*, ed. Charles R. Ewen and Russell K. Skowronek (Gainesville: University Press of Florida, 2016), 15–56.

Chapter 1

1. Unpublished research from Lewis C. Forrest, Ayden, N.C., who has examined eighteenth-century primary-source documents and newspaper articles for the surname of Blackbeard and has found no fewer than 13 spellings of his name. While "Teach" was most often seen in media and literature, "Thatch," "Thach," and "Thache" equally appear in official eighteenth-century documents. Compelling genealogical evidence for Blackbeard's surname being Thache, which we have used throughout this book, is based on Charles Leslie, *A New History of Jamaica* (London, 1740), and brought to light in Baylus C. Brooks, "'Born in Jamaica, of Very Credible Parents' or 'A Bristol Man Born?' Excavating the Real Edward Thache, 'Blackbeard the Pirate,'" *North Carolina Historical Review* 92 (July 2015): 235–77.

2. A compelling case is made in Arne Bialuschewski, "Daniel Defoe, Nathaniel Mist, and the *General History of the Pyrates*," *Papers of the Bibliographical Society of America* 98 (March 2004): 21–38, that Nathaniel Mist, a former sailor, printer, and Jacobite journalist who was hounded by authorities for his political views, authored *A General History of the Robberies and Murders of the Most Notorious Pyrates* (London, 1724; reprinted in 1724, 1725, and 1726) under the pseudonym Captain Charles Johnson.

3. Johnson [Mist], *Pyrates*, 60.

4. Ibid., 57.

5. Mark U. Wilde-Ramsing and Richard W. Lawrence, *North Carolina Underwater Archaeology Branch Environmental Procedures* (Kure Beach: North Carolina Underwater Archaeology Branch, 2004), https://archaeology.ncdcr.gov/underwater-archaeology-branch/environmental-review/procedures.

6. Richard W. Lawrence, Leslie S. Bright, Dinah B. Hill, James A. Pleasants, and Mark Wilde-Ramsing, *Bath Harbor Survey: Report on the Activities of the 1979 Field School in Maritime History and Underwater Archaeology* (Kure Beach: North Carolina Underwater Archaeology Branch Publication, 1984); Ronald A. Thomas, *A Phase I Archaeological Survey 31BF115 and 31BF117 and a Phase II Archaeological Survey 31BF115 Texas Gulf, Bath Creek, North Carolina* (Newark: MAAR Associates Inc., 1987).

7. Claude V. Jackson III, *Historical and Archaeological Investigations of a Federal Period Vessel Near Oriental, North Carolina* (Kure Beach: North Carolina Underwater Archaeology Branch Publication, 1992), https://archaeology.ncdcr.gov/underwater-archaeology-branch/survey-inventory-reports.

8. For more on UAB, see Richard W. Lawrence, "Forty Years beneath the Waves: Underwater Archaeology in North Carolina," in *The Archaeology of North Carolina: Three Archaeological Symposia* (Raleigh: North Carolina Archaeological Council Publication No. 30, 2011), 12.1–18, http://www.rla.unc.edu/NCAC/Publications/NCAC30/index.html.

9. *The Tryals of Major Stede Bonnet and other Pirates, viz . . . Who were all condemn'd for Piracy . . . At the Admiralty Sessions held at Charles-Town in the Province of South Carolina, on Tuesday the 28th of October, 1718. And by several Adjournments continued to Wednesday the 12th of November, following. To which is Prefix'd An Account of the Taking of the said Major Bonnet, and the rest of the Pirates* (London: Benjamin Cowse, 1719), 48.

10. Ibid., 3.

11. *The Trials of Eight Persons Indited for Piracy [etc.]*, Massachusetts Court of Admiralty (Boston: Printed by B. Green, for John Edwards, 1718; reprint, Ann Arbor: Text Creation Partnership, March 2005), 11, http://quod.lib.umich.edu/e/evans/N01688.0001.001/1:6?rgn=div1;view=fulltext (May 28, 2017).

12. Johnson [Mist], *Pyrates*, 60

13. Ibid., 61.

14. Ibid., 57.

15. Baylus C. Brooks's archival research on Edward Thache Jr. (Blackbeard) in the Register General's Department of Spanish Town, Jamaica, provided critical information to confirm his genealogical link. In his article (Brooks, "'Born in Jamaica'") he connects various pieces of existing research regarding Thache's life based on supporting evidence from Johnson [Mist], *Pyrates*; Arne Bialuschewski, "Blackbeard off Philadelphia: Documents Pertaining to the Campaign against the Pirate in 1717 and 1718," *Pennsylvania Magazine of History and Biography* 2 (April 2010): 165–78; and Colin Woodard, *The Republic of Pirates: Being the True and Surprising Story of Caribbean Pirates and the Man Who Brought Them Down* (Orlando: Harcourt, 2007).

16. *Records of the Executive Council, 1664–1734*, vol. 7, *The Colonial Records of North Carolina*, 2nd series, ed. Robert J. Cain (Raleigh: Division of Archives and History, 1984), 85.

17. *Minutes of the Provincial Council of Pennsylvania from the Organization to the Termination of the Proprietary Government*, vol. 3, *Containing the Proceedings of Council from May 31st, 1717 to January 23d, 1735–6* (Harrisburg: Theophilus Fenn, 1840), https://archive.org/stream/minutesprovinci05coungoog#page/n62/mode/2up, 54 (June 4, 2017).

18. Colin Woodard, "The Last Days of Blackbeard: An Exclusive Account of the Final Raid and Political Maneuvers of History's Most Notorious Pirate," *Smithsonian*, February 2014.

19. *Minutes of the Provincial Council of Pennsylvania*, 58.

20. Jennifer Steinberg, "The Last Voyage of the Slave Ship *Henrietta Marie*," *National Geographic*, August 2002.

Chapter 2

1. John Garland Newton, O. H. Pilkey, and J. O. Blanton, *An Oceanographic Atlas of the Carolina Continental Margin* (Raleigh: North Carolina Department of Conservation and Development, 1971).

2. *The Tryals of Major Stede Bonnet and other Pirates, viz . . . Who were all condemn'd for Piracy . . . At the Admiralty Sessions held at Charles-Town in the Province of South Carolina, on Tuesday the 28th of October, 1718. And by several Adjournments continued to Wednesday the 12th of November, following. To which is Prefix'd An Account of the Taking of the said Major Bonnet, and the rest of the Pirates* (London: Benjamin Cowse, 1719); *Calendar of State Papers: Colonial America and West Indies*, August 1717–December 1718, National Archives, United Kingdom Government Records and Information Center, London; *Colonial and State Records of North Carolina, Minutes of the North Carolina Governor's Council*, vol. 2 (May 27, 1719), 341–49; Captain William Brand (HMS *Lyme*), "Letter to Secretary to Admiralty, July 12, 1718," PRO-ADM 1/1472 (Public Record Office in London, copy held in the N.C. State Archives); Captain Vincent Pearse (HMS *Phoenix*), "Details from February 23, 1718 to June 3, 1718," PRO-ADM 1/2282 (Public Record Office in London, copy held in the N.C. State Archives); "Captain Thomas Smart (HMS *Squirrel*) to Secretary to Admiralty, 1718 June 20," PRO-ADM 1/3815 (Public Record Office in London, copy held in the N.C. State Archives); *Boston News-Letter*; London's *Post Boy*.

3. Modern scholars have begun to shine a bright light on the period of piracy from 1715 to 1726 through extensive research in the archives throughout Europe and the New World. Of note are Marcus Rediker, *Between the Devil and the Deep Blue Sea: Merchant Seamen, Pirates, and the Anglo-American Maritime World, 1700–1750* (Cambridge: Cambridge University Press, 1987); David Cordingly, *Under the Black Flag: The Romance and the Reality of Life among the Pirates* (New York: Random House, 1995); Lindley S. Butler, *Pirates, Privateers, and Rebel Raiders of the Carolina Coast* (Chapel Hill: University of North Carolina Press, 2000); Benerson Little, *The Sea Rover's Practice: Pirate Tactics and Techniques, 1630–1730* (Washington, D.C.: Potomac Books, 2005); Colin Woodard, *The Republic of Pirates: Being the True and Surprising Story of the Caribbean Pirates and the Man Who Brought Them Down* (Orlando: Harcourt, 2007); and Peter T. Leeson, *The Invisible Hook: The Hidden Economics of Pirates* (Princeton: Princeton University Press), 2009.

4. Wilson Angley, *An Historical Overview of the Beaufort Inlet–Cape Lookout Area of North Carolina* (Raleigh: North Carolina Division of Archives and History, 1982).

5. Jacques Ducoin, *Compte Rendu de Recherches dans les Archives Francaises sur le Navire Nantais La Concorde Capturé par des Pirates en 1717* (Raleigh: North Carolina Division of Archives and History, 2001); Jacques Ducoin, *Barbe-Noire et le Négrier La Concorde* (Grenobles: Glénat, 2010).

6. Jean Mettas, *Répertoire des Expéditions Négrières Francaises au XVIII Siécle*, ed. Serge Daget (Paris, 1978); Jean Boudriot, *Traite et Navire Negrier, l'Aurore, 1784: Collection Archeologie Navale Francaise* (Paris: Editions Ancre, 1984); Jean Boudriot and Hubert Bertia, *The History of the French Frigate, 1650–1850* (East Essex, England: Jean Boudriot Publications, 1993).

7. Charles Mesnier, "A letter from the Intendant of Martinique describing the capture of *La Concorde*," December 10, 1717, AN Col C8a (8A) 22 (171) F 447, Centre des archives d'outre-mer, Aix-en-Provence, France.

8. Ducoin, *Compte Rendu de Recherches*; Ducoin, *Barbe-Noire*.

9. Jean Le Roux, Commander, *Concorde*, "Déclaration de retour de *La Concorde*," Annexe XIII: B 4575 folio 19 à 24, 28 & 33v, November 3, 1711, Archives départementales de Loire-Atlantique, Nantes, France.

10. Mettas, *Répertoire des Expéditions Négrières Francaises*, 16, 37.

11. The number of cannons aboard *Concorde* when it was captured by pirates is unclear. In their depositions upon returning to France, Captain Dosset reported that *Concorde* was equipped with 14 cannons, while Lieutenant Ernaut stated there were 16 guns. See Pierre Dosset, "Deposition for Verification and Addendum to the Deposition of Lieutenant Ernaut regarding *La Concorde de Nantes* Plundered and Taken by the Pirates," Folia 90v & s, October 13, 1718, and Francois Ernaut, "Deposition regarding *La Concorde de Nantes* Plundered and Taken by Pirates," Folia 56v & s, April 17, 1718, both in Série B 4578, Archives départementales de Loire-Atlantique, Nantes, France.

12. Mathew Munson, letter recorded in *Calendar of State Papers: Colonial America and West Indies*, vol. 29, #635, July 5, 1717, National Archives, United Kingdom Government Records and Information Center, London.

13. The mortality rate aboard *Concorde*, 20 percent of the crew and 12 percent of Africans, highlights the well-documented dangers of the business for slave ship officers and crew. See Rediker's *Between the Devil and the Deep Blue Sea*, 46–47.

14. Lindley Butler, "Blackbeard's Revenge," *American History* 35 (August 2000): 20.

15. Richard Joy, "Deposition regarding *New Division* Boarded by Pirates sworn to Charles Payne of Governor William Hamilton's office," Public Record Office 152/12, copy held in the National Archives, United Kingdom Government Records and Information Center, London, November 30, 1717.

16. Christopher Taylor "Deposition Regarding *Great Allen* Attacked and Burned by Pirates," Fort-Royal in Martinique, AN Col C8A 24 f 80 & 84–45, M. de Pas de Feuquières, February 12, 1718, Centre des archives d'outre-mer, Aix-en-Provence, France (translation provided by Lynn Mollenauer, University of North Carolina, Wilmington, September 1, 2016).

17. Henry Bostock, "Deposition regarding *Margaret* Seized and Plundered by Pirates contained in a letter from Governor William Hamilton," *Calendar of State Papers, Colonial Series: America and the West Indies*, vol. 30, #298, iii, January 6, 1718, National Archives, United Kingdom Government Records and Information Center, London, 1–2.

18. *Tryals of Major Stede Bonnet*, 9.

19. *Boston News-Letter*, November 11, 1717.

20. Fireships were sacrificial vessels, usually older ships that were loaded with explosives and sailed within close range of the enemy, then detonated for maximum damage. See William Faulkner, *An Universal Dictionary of Marine: or A Copious Explanation of the Technical Terms and Phrases Employed in the Construction, Equipment, Furniture, Machinery, Movements, and Military Operations of a Ship* (1780; reprinted as *Faulkner's Marine Dictionary*, New York: Augustus M. Kelley, 1970), 124.

21. Turtlers are the ships of Spanish fishers who target marine turtles; most favored were green turtles, for their meat. For an explanation of the importance turtles played in the lives of Caribbean pirates, see Alexander Oliver Exquemelin, "On the Account: The Lives of Buccaneers of the Caribbean, by One of Their Number," in *The Mammoth Book of Pirates*, ed. Jon E. Lewis (London: Constable and Robinson, 2006), 83–96.

22. *Tryals of Major Stede Bonnet*, 45.

23. Captain Charles Johnson [Nathaniel Mist], "A General History of the Robberies and Murders of the Most Notorious Pyrates, From their First Rise and Settlement in the Island of Providence to the Present Year," in *Key Writings on Subcultures 1535-1727: Classics from the Underworld*, vol. 4 (London: George Rutledge & Sons, 1927; reprint, London: Rutledge, 2002).

24. Robert Johnson, Governor of South Carolina, *Calendar of State Papers, Colonial Series: America and the West Indies*, vol. 30, #556, June 18, 1718, National Archives, United Kingdom Government Records and Information Center, London.

25. Taylor "Deposition regarding *Great Allen*," 2.

26. "A list of His Majesty's Ships and Vessels Employed, and to be Employed, at the British Governments and Plantations in the West Indies," in Captain Charles Johnson [Nathaniel Mist], *A General History of the Robberies and Murders of the Most Notorious Pyrates*, reprint of the 3rd edition with introduction by David Cordingly (London: Conaway Maritime Press, 1725), 12–13.

27. Johnson [Mist], *Pyrates*, 60.

28. *Concorde*'s Muster Roll, Marine 337, 120 J 337, Archives départementales de Loire-Atlantique, Nantes, France, from Ducoin, *Barbe-Noire*, 166–73, and Ernaut, "Deposition regarding *Concorde*," 1–5.

29. Ernaut, "Deposition regarding *Concorde*," 1–5.

30. Taylor, "Deposition regarding *Great Allen*," 2.

31. *Tryals of Major Stede Bonnet*, 48.

32. Jerome S. Handler, "On the Transportation of Material Goods by Enslaved Africans during the Middle Passage: Preliminary Findings from Documentary Sources," *African Diaspora Archaeology Newsletter*, December 2006.

33. *Tryals of Major Stede Bonnet*, 45.

34. Phillip Masters, "Transcriptions of Articles Pertaining to the Golden Age of Piracy, Jul. 01, 1715—Jun. 20, 1719 (all dates are old calendar)" (unpublished manuscript, North Carolina Underwater Archaeology Branch, Kure Beach, November 2005), 1–21.

35. Johnson [Mist], *Pyrates*, 60.

36. Bostock, "Deposition regarding *Margaret*," 1.

37. *Tryals of Major Stede Bonnet*, 8.

38. Ibid.

39. "Report by the Board of Trade of Great Britain Concern-

ing General Conditions in North Carolina, September 08, 1721," *Colonial and State Records of North Carolina*, 2:419.

40. Ibid.

41. William Hutchinson, *A Treatise on Naval Architecture founded upon Philosophical and Principles, towards Established Fixed Rules for the Best Form and Proportional Dimensions in Length, Breadth and Depth, of Merchants Ships in General, and also the Management of them to the Greatest Advantage, by Practical Seamanship; with Important Hints and Remarks relating thereto, especially both for Defense and Attacks in War at Sea, from Long Approved Experience* (1794; reprint, Annapolis: United States Naval Institute, 1969), 205.

42. Butler, *Pirates, Privateers, and Rebel Raiders*, 5; "Report by the Board of Trade of Great Britain," 2:419.

43. *Tryals of Major Stede Bonnet*, 45.

44. Ibid., 19.

Chapter 3

1. For more information on ocean inlet physiography, see Miles O. Hayes, "General Morphology and Sediment Patterns in Tidal Inlets," *Sedimentary Geology* 29 (1980): 139–56; Richard A. Davis Jr., "Barrier Island Systems—a Geologic Overview," in *Geology of Holocene Barrier Island Systems*, ed. Richard A. Davis (New York: Springer-Verlag, 1994), 1–46; and Janok P. Bhattacharya and Roger G. Walker, "Deltas," in *Facies Models—Responses to Sea Level Change*, 3rd. ed., ed. Roger G. Walker and N. P. James (St. Johns, Newfoundland: Geological Association of Canada, 1992), 157–76. For information specific to North Carolina, see Stanley R. Riggs, William J. Cleary, and Stephen W. Snyder, "Influence of Inherited Geologic Framework upon Barrier Beach Morphology and Shoreface Dynamics," in *Marine Geology* 126 (1995): 213–34.

2. J. J. Fisher, "Geomorphic Expression of Former Inlets along the Outer Banks of North Carolina" (M.A. thesis, University of North Carolina, 1962), 1–102.

3. Richard W. Lawrence, "An Overview of North Carolina Shipwrecks with an Emphasis on Eighteenth-Century Vessel Losses at Beaufort Inlet," *Queen Anne's Revenge Shipwreck Project Research and Bulletin Series*, QAR-R-08-01 (Raleigh: North Carolina Department of Cultural Resources, 2008), http://www.qaronline.org/reports/overview-north-carolina-shipwrecks-emphasis-eighteenth-vessel-losses-beaufort-inlet.

4. John T. Wells and Jesse E. McNinch, "Reconstructing Shoal and Channel Configuration in Beaufort Inlet: 300 years of Change at the Site of *Queen Anne's Revenge*," *Southeastern Geology* 40 (February 2001): 11–18.

5. "Annual Reports, Morehead City Harbor, N.C.," 1904–94, Wilmington District, U.S. Army Corps of Engineers.

6. Allison Suggs, "Channel Movements over Wreckage Site 31CR314: Final Project for Youth Advocacy and Involvement Internship" (unpublished manuscript, North Carolina Underwater Archaeology Branch, Kure Beach, 2004), https://www.qaronline.org/reports/channel-movements-over-wreckage-site-31cr314-final-project-youth-advocacy-and-involvement.

7. Neils Lindquist, "Age Estimate for a Coral Collected from the *Queen Anne's Revenge*" (unpublished manuscript, Institute of Marine Sciences, University of North Carolina, Morehead City, 1998).

8. Jesse E. McNinch, John T. Wells, and Thomas G. Drake, "The Fate of Artifacts in an Energetic, Shallow-Water Environment: Scour and Burial at the Wreck Site of *Queen Anne's Revenge*," *Southeastern Geology* 40 (February 2001): 19–27; Arthur C. Trembanis and Jesse E. McNinch, "Predicting Scour and Maximum Settling Depths of Shipwrecks: A Numeric Simulation of the Fate of Queen Anne's Revenge," *Proceedings of Coastal Sediments '03* (Clearwater Beach: ASCE Press, 2003).

9. Jesse E. McNinch, John T. Wells, and Arthur C. Trembanis, "Predicting the Fate of Artefacts in Energetic, Shallow Marine Environments: An Approach to Site Management," *International Journal of Nautical Archaeology* 31 (April 2006): 1–20.

10. D. M. Ludlam, *Early American Hurricanes, 1492–1870* (Boston: American Meteorological Society, 1963); Ivan R. Tannehill, *Hurricanes: Their Nature & History*. (Princeton: University Press, 1958).

11. Mark U. Wilde-Ramsing and Wayne Lusardi, "Management Plan for North Carolina Shipwreck 31CR314, *Queen Anne's Revenge*" (North Carolina Underwater Archaeology Branch, Kure Beach, 1999), http://www.qaronline.org/reports/management-plan-north-carolina-shipwreck-31cr314-queen-anne%E2%80%99s-revenge.

12. The origins of the Hearse Song are unknown; it was popular during World War I, being sung by British and American troops. Its popularity continued through the twentieth century in children's verse. There are many different verses and lines, some of which we have used here.

Chapter 4

1. Richard W. Lawrence, "Forty Years beneath the Waves: Underwater Archaeology in North Carolina," in *The Archaeology of North Carolina: Three Archaeological Symposia* (Raleigh: North Carolina Archaeological Council Publication No. 30, 2011), 12.1–18, http://www.rla.unc.edu/NCAC/Publications/NCAC30/index.html.

2. Salvage of Abandoned Shipwrecks and Other Underwater Archaeological Sites, North Carolina General Statutes, Raleigh, 1967, chap. 121, article 3.

3. "Designation of Protected Area for Shipwreck Site 0003BUI and the Artifacts Related Thereto under Authority Set forth in 7 NCAC 04R.1009," signed Betty Ray McCain,

Secretary, North Carolina Department of Cultural Resources, Raleigh, March 3, 1997.

4. Mark Wilde-Ramsing, "Assessment Plan for Underwater Archaeology Branch site 003BUI" (unpublished manuscript, North Carolina Underwater Archaeology Branch, Kure Beach, 1997).

5. Mark Wilde-Ramsing and Wayne Lusardi, "Management Plan for North Carolina Shipwreck 31CR314, *Queen Anne's Revenge*" (North Carolina Underwater Archaeology Branch, Kure Beach, 1999), https://www.qaronline.org/reports/management-plan-north-carolina-shipwreck-31cr314-queen-anne%E2%80%99s-revenge.6. For further reading on the goals of archaeology, see Matthew Johnson, *Archaeological Theory: An Introduction* (Oxford: Blackwell, 1999).

7. Richard W. Lawrence and Mark Wilde-Ramsing, "In Search of Blackbeard: Historical and Archaeological Research at Shipwreck Site 0003BUI," *Southeastern Geology* 40, no. 1 (February 2001): 1–9.

8. Jay Barnes, *North Carolina's Hurricane History*, 4th ed. (Chapel Hill: University of North Carolina Press, 2013).

9. Chris Southerly, "*Queen Anne's Revenge* Shipwreck Project 2004 Photo Mosaic Expedition Summary," *www.qaronline.org* (Raleigh: N.C. Department of Natural and Cultural Resources), http://www.qaronline.org/reports/spring-2004-photo-mosaic-expedition-summary.

10. Mark U. Wilde-Ramsing, "A Stratified Site Sampling Research Plan for the 2005–2006 Investigations and Recovery at North Carolina Archaeological Shipwreck Site 31CR314" (North Carolina Underwater Archaeology Branch, Kure Beach, 2006), https://files.nc.gov/dncr-qar/documents/files/32-Spring-2006-Recovery-Plan.pdf.

11. Plans, daily field logs, and summary reports on *QAR* field activities from 1997 through 2011 at http://www.qaronline.org/reports/qar-research/field.

Chapter 5

1. Mark Wilde-Ramsing and Wayne Lusardi, "Management Plan for North Carolina Shipwreck 31CR314, *Queen Anne's Revenge*" (North Carolina Underwater Archaeology Branch, Kure Beach, 1999), http://www.qaronline.org/reports/management-plan-north-carolina-shipwreck-31cr314-queen-anne%E2%80%99s-revenge.

2. George F. Bass, "Cape Gelidonya: A Bronze Age Shipwreck," *Transactions of the American Philosophical Society* 57 (1967): 8.

3. Wendy Welsh and Mark Wilde-Ramsing, "Final Report on Peering into a Pirate's Trove: A Proposal to Conduct High Definition Radiography on Concretions from the Queen Anne's Revenge Shipwreck Site. National Geographic Expeditions Council Grant No. EC0259–05" (North Carolina Underwater

Archaeology Branch, Kure Beach, 2008), http://www.qaronline.org/reports/final-report-peering-pirates-trove-proposal-conduct-high-definition-radiography-concretions.

4. Sarah Watkins-Kenney, Kimberly Kenyon, Erik Farrell, and Courtney Page, "Conservation Plan 2015–2018 for Wet Storage and Wet Treatment of Artifacts Recovered from *Queen Anne's Revenge* Shipwreck Site (31CR314)" (unpublished manuscript, *QAR* Conservation Laboratory, N.C. Department of Natural and Cultural Resources, Greenville, 2015), 20.

5. Barbara A. Bianco, Christopher R. DeCorse, and Jean Howson, "Beads and Other Adornments," in *New York African Burial Ground Archaeology Final Report* (2006), 382–418; Eric Edwards, "Rethinking Pitt-Rivers," 2014, Pitt Rivers Museum, Oxford, England, web.prm.ox.ac.uk//objectbiographies (September 12, 2017) on manilas from West Africa.

Chapter 6

1. Reverse osmosis (RO) is a water treatment method for removing impurities, including ions, molecules, and larger particles, from drinking water by forcing it through a semipermeable membrane. Conservators extract sea salts contained in artifacts by submerging them in RO water, which is periodically checked and replaced. When the salinity in the RO water no longer contains salt drawn from the artifact, treatment is complete.

2. Historian Jacques Ducoin was contracted by the North Carolina Department of Cultural Resources to answer key questions about *Concorde* and its taking by the English pirate Edward Thache, which resulted in Ducoin's 2001 manuscript "Compte Rendu de Recherches dans les Archives Francaises sur le Navire Nantais La Concorde Capturé par des Pirates en 1717" (North Carolina Department of Cultural Resources, Division of Archives and History, Raleigh); Ducoin's research was also published in his *Barbe-Noire et le Négrier La Concorde* (Grenobles: Glénat, 2010).

3. Lee A. Newsom and Regis B. Miller, "Wood Species Analysis of Ship's Timbers and Wood Items Recovered from Shipwreck 31CR314, *Queen Anne's Revenge* Site," Queen Anne's Revenge *Shipwreck Project Research Report and Bulletin Series*, QAR-R-09-01 (Raleigh: North Carolina Department of Cultural Resources, 2009), https://www.qaronline.org/reports/wood-species-analysis-ships-timbers-and-wood-items-recovered-shipwreck-31cr314-queen-annes; Michael G. Baillie, "Final Report on Dating *QAR* Timbers" (manuscript, School of Archaeology/Palaeoecology, North Carolina Underwater Archaeology Branch, Kure Beach, 2002), https://www.qaronline.org/reports/final-report-dating-qar-timbers.

4. David D. Moore and Mike Daniel, "Blackbeard's Capture of the Nantaise Slave Ship *La Concorde*," *Tributaries* 11 (2001): 62; David H. Roberts, ed. and trans., *Eighteenth-Century Ship-*

building: *Remarks on the Navies of the English & the Dutch from Observations Made at Their Dockyards in 1737 by Blaise Olivier, Master Shipwright of the King of France* (Rotherfield, East Sussex, England: Jean Boudriot Publications, 1992).

5. Analysis of *QAR* textiles was completed; see Runying Chen, "A Preliminary Analysis of Plant Fiber Artifacts from Shipwreck 31CR314," November 2006, Greenville (manuscript, North Carolina Underwater Archaeology Branch, Kure Beach); Louie Bartos, "David Steele's *The Art of Sail Making* & HMS *Victory*'s Fore Topsail," *Sea History* 111 (2005): 10–13; Adria L. Focht, "Blackbeard Sails Again? Conservation of Textiles from the *Queen Anne's Revenge* Shipwreck" (independent study report, Department of Anthropology, East Carolina University, Greenville, N.C., May 2008).

6. Linda F. Carnes-McNaughton and Mark U. Wilde-Ramsing, "Preliminary Glassware and Bottle Analysis from Shipwreck 31CR314, *Queen Anne's Revenge* Site," Queen Anne's Revenge *Shipwreck Project Research Report and Bulletin Series*, QAR-R-08-02 (Raleigh: North Carolina Department of Cultural Resources, 2008), http://www.qaronline.org/reports/preliminary-glassware-and-bottle-analysis-shipwreck-31cr314-queen-annes-revenge-site.

7. Shanna Daniel, "The Seat of Ease: Sanitary Facilities from Shipwreck 31CR314, *Queen Anne's Revenge* Site," Queen Anne's Revenge *Shipwreck Project Research Report and Bulletin Series*, QAR-B-09-02 (Raleigh: North Carolina Department of Cultural Resources, 2009), https://www.qaronline.org/reports/seat-ease-sanitary-facilities-shipwreck-31cr314-queen-annes-revenge-site.

8. Similar interior hull patching has been reported on Spanish wrecks the Emmanuel Point ship (1559) and the English ship *Whydah* (1717). On the Molasses Reef wreck (early sixteenth century) several lead stock sheets were found tied into a bundle with a single hole through each sheet as part of the carpenter's repair kit; see Thomas J. Oertling, "The Molasses Reef and Highborn Cay Wrecks: Two Early Sixteenth Century Hulls," in *Underwater Archaeology Proceedings from the Society for Historical Archaeology Conference*, ed. James Delgado (Ann Arbor: Braun-Brumfield, 1988), 119; A large rolled lead sheet on the *Whydah* was also identified as stock material for making patches; see Christopher E. Hamilton, "Final Report of Archaeological Data Recovery: The *Whydah* Shipwreck Site WLF-HA-1" (Whydah Joint Venture and U.S. Army Corps of Engineers, South Chatham, Mass., 1992).

9. Mechanical jacks have been found on the English slave ship *Henrietta Maria* (1700) and on several of the 1715 Spanish fleet ships in Florida.

10. John E. Callahan, J. William Miller, and James R. Craig, "Ballast Stones from North Carolina Shipwreck 003BUI, the *Queen Anne's Revenge*: Hand Specimen, X-Ray, Petrographic,

Chemical, Paramagnetic, and 40K-40Ar Age," *Southeastern Geology* 40, no. 1 (2001): 49–57; John E. Callahan, J. William Miller, and James R. Craig, "Ballast Stones of the Queen Anne's Revenge," poster/presentation at *QAR* Lab Open House, April 2012.

11. Early French settlements in the Caribbean were in Hispaniola, where the western part was Saint-Domingue (today's Haiti); others whose names are the same today are Martinique and Grenada.

12. Mark U. Wilde-Ramsing and Joseph M. Wilde-Ramsing, "Report on 'IHS Maria' Bell Recovered from 31CR314," *Bell Tower* 66, no. 4 (2008).

13. The preliminary analysis of the second bell was provided by email from Joaquín Díaz, Fundación Joaquín Díaz, Valladolid, Spain, to Joseph Wilde-Ramsing, October 10, 2016 (unpublished document on file at the QAR Conservation Lab, Greenville, N.C.).

14. For additional information on styles of anchors, see Betty Nelson Curryer, *Anchors: An Illustrated History* (London: Chatham Publishing, 1999).

15. A review of items most often taken by pirates based on 14 incidences reported in the *Boston News-Letter*, 1716–18, reveals that during 6 of those occasions ship's equipment (sails, rigging, anchors, etc.) was confiscated; see Phillip Masters, "Transcriptions of Articles Pertaining to the Golden Age of Piracy, Jul. 01, 1715—Jun. 20, 1719 (all dates are old calendar)" (unpublished manuscript, North Carolina Underwater Archaeology Branch, Kure Beach, November 2005).

16. Robert Smith and Ruth Brown, "Report No. 082—QAR Bronze Signaling Gun," January 23, 2007, Yorkshire, U.K. (manuscript, North Carolina Underwater Archaeology Branch, Kure Beach); Ruth Brown, "Bronze Signaling or Saluting Gun, Second Report (No. 090)," 2007, Yorkshire, U.K. (manuscript, North Carolina Underwater Archaeology Branch, Kure Beach), https://www.qaronline.org/reports/bronze-signalling-or-saluting-gun.

17. Anthony Kennedy and Wendy Welsh, unpublished study on keratin/horn chemical analysis, 2012 (on file at the *QAR* Conservation Laboratory, Greenville, N.C.).

18. The lead fasteners are intriguing in that they have been found on two other British shipwrecks of this era (the 1717 *Whydah* and the 1711 HMS *Feversham*) and were excavated from an early 1600s well in the colonial settlement of Jamestown. In each of these contexts the tiny objects were identified as fasteners used on either leather, wood, horn, or a combination of all three, such as decorative studs on upholstered chairs or trunks, or horse tack. See Wendy Welsh, "Lead Studs from Shipwreck 31CR314: *Queen Anne's Revenge*," Queen Anne's Revenge *Shipwreck Project Research Report and Bulletin Series*, QAR-B-08-01 (Raleigh: North Carolina Department of

Cultural Resources, 2009), https://www.qaronline.org/reports/lead-studs-shipwreck-31cr314-queen-annes-revenge-site, and Merry Outlaw, Curator at Jamestown Rediscovery, 2016 personal communication.

19. Intact example of a gimbal lamp is on exhibit at the National Museum of the United States Navy, Washington, D.C. An online source for the example is from St. Etienne, France. Three gimbal oil lamps were discovered on the 1629 *Batavia* shipwreck, where they were found in the gunpowder room; see Jeremy N. Green, *The Loss of the Verenigde Oostindische Compagnie retourschip Batavia . . . Western Australian 1629: and Excavation report and catalogue of Artefacts*, BAR International Series 489 (1989): 76–77.

20. Interestingly, these types have also been found on the 1717 *Whydah* wreck; see Hamilton, *Whydah*.

21. Wayne R. Lusardi, "The Beaufort Inlet Shipwreck Artifact Assemblage," in *X Marks the Spot: The Archaeology of Piracy*, ed. Russell Skowronek and Charles E. Ewen (Gainesville: University Press of Florida, 2006), 207–8.

22. Ibid.

23. Keith C. Wilbur, *Pirates and Patriots of the Revolution: An Illustrated Encyclopedia of Colonial Seamanship* (Old Saybrook, Conn.: Globe Pequot Press, 1973), 59–65.

24. William Pearce, "Heaving of the Lead," *Hartford-Bridge or the Skirts of the Camp* (London: T. N. Longman, 1793), 17–18.

25. Wilbur, *Pirates and Patriots*, 59–65.

26. Sarah Watkins-Kenney, "Note on Sounding Leads Recovered from *QAR* on August 19, 2013" (unpublished report, *QAR* Conservation Laboratory).

27. Douglas Bryce, *Weaponry from the* Machault, *an 18th-Century French Frigate*, Studies in Archaeology, Architecture, and History (Ottawa: Parks Canada, 1984), 43.

28. Thomas Roth, personal communication to Wendy Welsh, June 8, 2004, regarding marks on Cannon C-19.

29. Ruth Brown and Robert Smith, *Report No. 047, Iron Gun 173 QAR* (Kure Beach: North Carolina Underwater Archaeology Branch, 2005); Nathan Henry, "Analysis of Armament from Shipwreck 31CR314, *Queen Anne's Revenge* Site," Queen Anne's Revenge *Shipwreck Project Research and Bulletin Series*, QAR-B-09-01 (Raleigh: North Carolina Department of Cultural Resources, 2009), http://www.qaronline.org/reports/analysis-armament-shipwreck-31cr314-queen-annes-revenge-site.

30. Brown and Smith, *Report No. 047*; Henry *Analysis of Armament*, 10–12.

31. John M. Kenney, Department of Physics, East Carolina University, personal communication to Mark Wilde-Ramsing, September 16, 2016, regarding gunpowder residue.

32. Lusardi, "Beaufort Inlet Shipwreck Artifact Assemblage," 202–4.

33. Chen, "Preliminary Analysis of Plant Fiber Artifacts from Shipwreck 31CR314," 18–19; H. R. Mauersberger, ed., *Matthews' Textile Fibers: Their Physical, Microscopical, and Chemical Properties* (New York: Wiley, 1947).

34. Nathan C. Henry, "*Queen Anne's Revenge* Iron Shot Report," Queen Anne's Revenge *Shipwreck Project Research and Bulletin Series*, QAR-B-11-01 (Raleigh: North Carolina Department of Cultural Resources, January 2009), http://www.qaronline.org/reports/iron-shot-shipwreck-31cr314-queen-annes-revenge-site.

35. Ruth Brown, "*QAR* Breechblocks: Preliminary Report (No. 122)" (North Carolina Department of Cultural Resources, Raleigh, January 2009), http://www.qaronline.org/reports/qar-breechblocks.

36. Lusardi, "Beaufort Inlet Shipwreck Artifact Assemblage," 207–8.

37. Museum of Galileo Institute and Museum of Science, Florence, Italy, http://catalogue.museumgalileo.it/gallery/Compasses.html, examples 652,3706 for comparison.

38. John Seller, *The Sea Gunner* (London: H. Clark, 1691), 158, for description on gunner's manual.

39. Francois Ernaut, "Deposition regarding *La Concorde de Nantes* Plundered and Taken by Pirates," Série B 4578, Folia 56v–57v, April 17, 1718, Archives départementales de Loire-Atlantique, Nantes, France; *Concorde*'s Muster Roll amended by Captain Dosset, July 22, 1718, Marine 120 J 337 Folia 53, Archives départementales de Loire-Atlantique, Nantes, France.

40. Dr. Lee Newsom, Flagler University (formerly of Pennsylvania State University), 2011 personal communication concerning the results of her wood species identification for both the *QAR* and La Belle knife handles.

41. Reference for Louis XV image on weapons: David Leyoden and Michel Petard 2010 personal communication (emails). Though the exact origin of this block is not certain, a similarly decorated sword guard was recovered from the *Machault* shipwreck, which shows a Romanesque or draped bust of a male, possibly a monarch. Reference and *Machault* sword image, see Catherine Sullivan, *Legacy of the* Machault*: A Collection of 18th-Century Artifacts*, Studies in Archaeology, Architecture, and History (Ottawa: Parks Canada, 1986), 99. See Bryce, *Weaponry from the* Machault, 30–31, for photograph and discussion of embossed sword guard.

42. Two pommel capstans matching this one have been recorded. One was purchased by/for a museum from an eBay seller (who described it as English, ca. 1680s–1690s, but without provenance data), and the second pommel was excavated from the battlefield site of Ackia, a French and Indian War site where French marines fought Chickasaw warriors in 1736. See Steven D. Smith, James B. Legg, Brad Lieb, Charles Cobb, Chester Depratter, and Tamara S. Wilson, *Ackia and*

Okla Tchitoka: Defining Two 1736 Battlefields of the French-Chickasaw War, Tupelo, Mississippi (Columbia: South Carolina Institute of Archaeology and Anthropology, 2013), 76–78.

43. A law was passed in England in 1637 that required all weapons to be inspected and test-fired by the Gunmaker's Company and once by the gun maker. Both the V and the GP were altered in 1672 and again in 1702. Information on gun marks came from Lusardi, "Beaufort Inlet Shipwreck Artifact Assemblage"; Claude Blair, *European & American Arms, C.1100–1850* (New York: Bonanza Books, 1962), 116–17; and George C. Neumann, *Battle Weapons of the American Revolution* (Texarkana, Tex.: Scurlock, 1998), 14.

44. M. L. Brown, *Firearms in Colonial America* (Washington, D.C.: Smithsonian Institution Press, 1980) 153; George C. Neumann, *Battle Weapons*, 43; T. M. Hamilton, review of "A History of Gunflints" by John Witthoft, *Historical Archaeology* 2 (1968): 116–17. One nearly identical serpentine sideplate was shown on a restored Queen Anne dog-lock musket, from www.Pirate Brethren.com 2015. Sometimes referred to as sea serpents, they were also popular on firearms used by pirates, indicated by several found on the 1717 *Whydah* shipwreck; see Hamilton, *Whydah*, 251–64.

45. Neumann, *Battle Weapons*, 199.

46. George D. Moller, *American Military Shoulder Arms*, vol. 1, *Colonial and Revolutionary War Arms* (Boulder: University Press of Colorado, 1993), 305–11.

47. Wilbur, *Pirates and Patriots*, 70.

48. T. M. Hamilton, *Colonial Frontier Guns* (Chadron, Nebr.: Fur Press, 1980), 83; Moller, *American Military Shoulder Arms*, 310, 314; Neumann, *Battle Weapons*, 46, 200.

49. Typically this portable multipurpose tool kit was suspended by a small chain or thong attached to a musketeer's crossbelt. Worms were also equipped with a threaded extractor used to remove lead shot from the barrel. See George C. Neumann and Frank J. Kravic, *Illustrated Encyclopedia of the American Revolution* (Texarkana, Tex.: Scurlock, 1975), 264. It is useful to note that several silver (or white brass) gun worms and vent picks were also found on the 1717 *Whydah* shipwreck, which overall contained a greater abundance of weaponry and parts, which was expected, given the violent nature of its demise; see Hamilton, *Whydah*, 254.

50. J. Ned Woodall, "Gunflints and Other Lithic Artifacts from Shipwreck 31CR314, *Queen Anne's Revenge* Shipwreck Site," Queen Anne's Revenge *Shipwreck Project Research Report and Bulletin Series*, QAR-B-04-01 (Raleigh: North Carolina Department of Cultural Resources, 2004), https://www .qaronline.org/reports/gunflints-and-other-lithic-artifacts-31cr314-queen-annes-revenge-site.

51. Bag shot was found loaded within a cannon recovered from the pirate ship *Whydah*; see Hamilton, *Whydah*, 238–39.

52. T. M. Hamilton, "Firearms on the Frontier: Guns at Fort Michilimackinac, 1715–1781," *Reports in Mackinac History and Archaeology*, no. 5 (Ottawa: National Historic Parks and Sites Branch Parks Canada, 1976), 35.

53. Nathan Henry, "Ship's Armament," draft report, August 29, 2006 (unpublished report, North Carolina Underwater Archaeology Branch, Kure Beach), 16–17.

54. Of special research interest are numerous lead shot, once rounded, that have been purposefully modified or reformed by whittling into elongated drumlike shapes or exhibit chew marks (by humans, pigs, or rodents), impact marks, rifling marks, hemispherical banding, or dimpling. Some of these oddities were created by how the shot was packaged and fired (e.g., hail shot from a cannon or buck-and-ball shot from a musket). Various methods of blasting lead shot from fired cannons or muskets, such as "hail-shot" or "buck and ball," could result in the misshaped lead pieces. Understanding the internal and external ballistics of these cannons and muskets will help future archaeologists better determine the multiple causes of such deformities and combat actions among pirates (D. F. Harding and Glenn Foard in personal communication with Myron Rolston, 2016).

55. Newsom and Miller, "Wood Species Analysis," 9.

56. Hamilton, *Whydah*, Appendix IV, from De Lussan 1699:86–87, Ken Kinkor 1992 study.

57. Captain Charles Johnson [Nathaniel Mist], *A General History of the Robberies and Murders of the Most Notorious Pyrates* (London, 1724; reprint, New York: Lyons Press, 1998), 56.

58. Information on the condition of *Concorde* crew at the time of capture: Moore and Daniel, "Blackbeard's Capture of the Nantaise Slave Ship *La Concorde*," 14–30; Ernaut, "Deposition regarding *Concorde*"; Pierre Dosset, "Deposition for Verification and Addendum to the Deposition of Lieutenant Ernaut regarding *La Concorde de Nantes* Plundered and Taken by Pirates," Série B 4578, Folia 90v & s, October 13, 1718, Archives départementales de Loire-Atlantique, Nantes, France; Charles Mesnier, "A letter from the Intendant of Martinique describing the capture of *La Concorde*," December 10, 1717, AN Col C8a (8A) 22 (171) F 447, Centre des archives d'outre-mer, Aix-en-Provence, France.

59. Summary information on the blockade of Charleston harbor: South Carolina Court of Vice-Admiralty, *The Tryals of Major Stede Bonnet and other Pirates, viz . . . Who were all condemn'd for Piracy . . . At the Admiralty Sessions held at Charles-Town in the Province of South Carolina, on Tuesday the 28th of October, 1718. And by several Adjournments continued to Wednesday the 12th of November, following. To which is Prefix'd An Account of the Taking of the said Major Bonnet, and the rest of the Pirates* (London: Benjamin Cowse, 1719), iii–iv;

Robert Johnson, letter from Gov. Robert Johnson, South Carolina, June 18, 1718, Calendar of State Papers, Colonial Series: America and West the Indies, vol. 30, #556A, National Archives, United Kingdom Government Records and Information Center, London; extract of several letters Carolina, August 19, 1718, Calendar of State Papers, Colonial Series: America and the West Indies, vol. 39, #660; and Richard Lawrence, "Preliminary Observations on British and American Documents Concerning the Activities of the Pirate Blackbeard, March 1717 to June 1718" (manuscript, North Carolina Underwater Archaeology Branch, Kure Beach, 2008), https://www.qaronline .org/reports/preliminary-observations-british-and-american-documents-concerning-activities-pirate.

60. Lusardi, "Beaufort Inlet Shipwreck Artifact Assemblage," 135–47.

61. Philippe Boucaud, November 2011 personal communication with Shanna Daniel re: identification of pewter makers' marks on the syringe, cyster, and pewter porringer (on file at the *QAR* Conservation Laboratory, Greenville, N.C.).

62. Various sources on history of clystering as medical practice, on land and sea: J. K. Crellin, "Domestic Medicine Chests: Microcosms of 18th and 19th Century Medical Practice," *Pharmacy in History* 21, no. 3 (1979): 122–31, published by the American Institute of Pharmacy; Zachary B. Friedenberg, *Medicine under Sail* (Annapolis, Md.: Naval Institute Press, 2002); Jonathan Charles Goddard, "The Navy Surgeon's Chest: Surgical Instruments of the Royal Navy during the Napoleonic Wars," *Journal of the Royal Society of Medicine* 97 (2004): 191–97; Kay K. Moss, *Southern Folk Medicine, 1750–1820* (Columbia: University of South Carolina Press, 1999); *The Pirate Surgeon's Journals: Golden Age of Piracy*, http://www.pirate surgeon.com; *Pirate Medicine: Pestilence and Pain during the Golden Age of Piracy on Pirates of the Caribbean, Fact and Fiction*, http://Pirates.Hegewisch.net/Pestilence 2011); Cindy Vallar, ed., "Pyrate Surgeons," *Pirates and Privateers: The History of Maritime Piracy*, May–July 2007; Guy Williams, *The Age of Agony, the Art of Healing, 1700–1800* (Chicago: Academy Chicago, 1986); and John Woodall, *The Surgions Mate* (London: Edward Griffin, 1617).

63. Boucaud, 2011 personal communication with Daniel; Philippe Boucaud, August 2017 personal communication with Linda Carnes-McNaughton stating that upon further examination the letter F is seen in front of CANU, which he describes as a "yet unidentifiable member of the family." He had previously attributed this mark to Pierre CANU.

64. For information about maker's marks and source on weight sets, see Bruno Kisch, *Scales and Weights: A Historical Outline* (New Haven: Yale University Press, 1965); Diana Crawford-Hitchins, 2009 and 2011 personal communication with Wendy Welsh re: identification of marks on nested weight

sets (on file at the *QAR* Conservation Laboratory, Greenville, N.C.).

65. Comparative data on galley pot residues from the *La-Belle* shipwreck: James E. Bruseth and Toni S. Turner, *From a Watery Grave: The Discovery and Excavation of LaSalle's Shipwreck, LaBelle* (College Station: Texas A&M University Press, 2005).

66. Boucaud, November 2011 personal communication with Daniel.

67. The 1717 muster roll for *Concorde*'s voyage lists crewmen Charles Duval, pilot, and Rene Duval, carpenter, both of whom were forced to join the pirates aboard *Queen Anne's Revenge*; see Marine 120 J 337 Folia 53, Archives départementales de Loire-Atlantique, Nantes, France.

68. For a history of needles as surgical tools, see John Kirkup, *The Evolution of Surgical Instruments: An Illustrated History from Ancient Times to the Twentieth Century* (Novato, Calif.: Norman, 2006).

69. Alexandre Olivier Exquemelin, *The Buccaneers of America: A True Account of the Most Remarkable Assaults Committed in Late Years upon the Coast of the West Indies by the Buccaneers of Jamaica and Tortuga both English and French* (1684; reprint, London: Routledge, 1924).

70. Henry Bostock, "Deposition regarding *Margaret* Seized and Plundered by Pirates contained in a letter from Governor William Hamilton," *Calendar of State Papers, Colonial Series: America and the West Indies*, vol. 30, #298, iii, January 6, 1718, National Archives, United Kingdom Government Records and Information Center, London.

71. See Johnson [Mist], *Pyrates*, 60.

72. For the source and date for A DARBY iron cookpots, see Nancy Cox, "Imagination and Innovation of an Industrial Pioneer: Abraham Darby," *Industrial Archaeology Review* 12, no. 2 (1990): 127–44; *The Cookpot That Changed the World* (Spurlock Museum of World Cultures of Illinois, 2013); and "Abraham Darby and The Dynasty of Iron Founders" (Abraham Darby Academy, Telford, Shropshire, England, 2013).

73. Linda F. Carnes-McNaughton, "Brick and Tile Analysis from *QAR* Shipwreck Site," Queen Anne's Revenge *Shipwreck Project Research Report and Bulletin Series*, QAR-B-07-03 (Raleigh: North Carolina Department of Cultural Resources, 2007), https://www.qaronline.org/reports/brick-and-tile-31cr314-queen-annes-revenge-shipwreck-site; Gregory A. Waselkov, *Old Mobile Archaeology* (Tuscaloosa: University of Alabama Press, 1999); and Kathleen Deagan, *Artifacts of the Spanish Colonies of Florida and the Caribbean, 1500–1800* (Washington, D.C.: Smithsonian Institution Press, 1987).

74. Linda F. Carnes-McNaughton, "Ceramic Assemblage Analysis from Shipwreck 31Cr314, *Queen Anne's Revenge* Site," Queen Anne's Revenge *Shipwreck Project Research Report and*

Bulletin Series, QAR-R-08-03 (Raleigh: North Carolina Department of Cultural Resources, 2008), https://www.qaronline.org/reports/qar-shipwreck-ceramic-assemblage-analysis-queen-annes-revenge-shipwreck-project.

75. Ibid.

76. Pewter flatware discussion in Hamilton, *Whydah*, 355–60; U.K. Pewter Society, www.pewtersociety.org (September 13, 2017).

77. David D. Moore and Corey Malcolm, "Seventeenth-Century Vehicle of the Middle Passage: Archaeological and Historical Investigations on the *Henrietta Marie* Shipwreck Site," *International Journal of Historical Archaeology* 12 (2006).

78. On the "B s A" mark on pewter flatware, see Lusardi, "Beaufort Inlet Shipwreck Artifact Assemblage," 135–47.

79. Phillip E. Playford, "A Story of Two Plates," in *Voyage of Discovery to Terra Australis: by Willem De Vlamingh in 1696–97* (Perth: Western Australian Museum, 1998), 51–60.

80. L. M. Bickerton, *English Drinking Glasses, 1675–1825* (Aylesbury: Shire Publications, 1984); R. J. Charleston, *English Glass and the Glass Used in England, ca 400–1940* (London: Allen and Unwin, 1984); Linda F. Carnes-McNaughton and Mark U. Wilde-Ramsing, "Preliminary Glassware and Bottle Analysis from Shipwreck 31CR314, *Queen Anne's Revenge* Site," Queen Anne's Revenge *Shipwreck Project Research Report and Bulletin Series*, QAR-R-08-02 (Raleigh: North Carolina Department of Cultural Resources, 2008), https://www.qaronline.org/reports/preliminary-glassware-and-bottle-analysis-shipwreck-31cr314-queen-annes-revenge-site.

81. Bickerton, *English Drinking Glasses*.

82. Ivor Noel Hume, *Guide to Artifacts of Colonial America* (1969; reprint, New York: Knopf, 1978).

83. Mark U. Wilde-Ramsing and Linda F. Carnes-McNaughton, "Blackbeard's *Queen Anne's Revenge* and Its French Connections," in *Pieces of Eight: More Archaeology of Piracy*, ed. Charles R. Ewen and Russell K. Skowronek (Gainesville: University Press of Florida, 2016), 40–41.

84. For a description of French flacons and contents, see Jane E. Harris, "Eighteenth-Century French Blue-Green Bottles from the Fortress at Louisbourg, Nova Scotia," in *Studies in Material Culture Research*, ed. Karlis Karklins (Ottawa, Canada: Society of Historical Archaeology, 2000).

85. Simon Moore, *Spoons, 1650–1930* (Buckinghamshire, U.K.: Shire Publications, 1987); Michael Snodin, *English Silver Spoons* (London: Charles Letts Books, 1982); Perry Foster and Cynthia Foster, *English Flatware Patterns of the 18th and 19th Centuries* (1998; online publication from Argentum, the Leopard's Head Antiques); Colonial Williamsburg Foundation, Collections Catalog, item 1988–124, cannon-handled basting spoon made by Lawrence Jones of London, 1699–1700.

86. Kimberly M. Smith, "Comparative Analysis of Cask Material from Late Sixteenth through Early Nineteenth Century Shipwrecks" (M.A. thesis, Department of Anthropology, East Carolina University, 2009).

87. Lyle M. Stone, *Fort Michilimackinac, 1715–1781: An Archaeological Perspective on the Revolutionary War* (East Lansing: Museum of Michigan State University and Mackinac Island State Park, 1974), 177–79.

88. For pirates' behaviors and keeping ample spirits, see David Cordingly, *Under the Black Flag: The Romance and the Reality of Life among the Pirates* (New York: Random House, 1995), 93, and *The Pirate Hunter of the Caribbean: The Adventurous Life of Captain Woodes Rogers* (New York: Random House, 2011), 224, 225; Daniel Lenihan, "Rethinking Shipwreck Archaeology," in *Shipwreck Anthropology*, ed. Richard Gould (Albuquerque: University of New Mexico Press, 1983), 51; and Marcus Rediker, *Between the Devil and the Deep Blue Sea: Merchant Seamen, Pirates, and the Anglo-American Maritime World, 1700–1750* (Cambridge: Cambridge University Press, 1987), 192–93.

89. Hamilton, *Whydah*, 437.

90. Wilbur, *Pirates and Patriots*, 52–55.

91. Linda F. Carnes-McNaughton, "Tobacco Pipe and Tool Analysis from 31CR314, *Queen Anne's Revenge* Shipwreck Site," Queen Anne's Revenge *Shipwreck Project Research Report and Bulletin Series*, QAR-B-07-04 (Raleigh: North Carolina Department of Cultural Resources, 2007), https://www.qaronline.org/reports/tobacco-pipe-and-tool-analysis-31cr314-queen-annes-revenge-site.

92. Ibid.

93. Stone, *Fort Michilimackinac*, 244. For general information on fishing hook leader lines, see Denis Diderot, *A Pictorial Encyclopedia of Trade and Industry, 1713–1784*, 1st ed. (Mineola, N.Y.: Dover, 1959), plate 54 (no page number), and Wilbur, *Pirates and Patriots*, 50.

94. Peter Throckmorton, *The Sea Remembers: Shipwrecks and Archaeology from Homer's Greece to the Rediscovery of the Titanic* (New York: Smithmark, 1997), 99.

95. For button study and comparative chart, see Stanley South, "Analysis of Buttons from Brunswick Town and Fort Fisher," *Florida Anthropologist* 18, no. 2 (1964): 113–33.

96. Deerfield example of passementerie button in personal items online catalog, http://1704.deerfield.history.museum/list/artifacts/personal.do.

97. Stone, *Fort Michilimackinac*; Sullivan, *Legacy of the Machault*.

98. For comparative notes on size and function of buckles, see Stone, *Fort Michilimackinac*, 25–44.

99. For buckles, styles, and dating, see Ross Whitehead, *Buckles, 1250–1800* (Essex, U.K.: Greenlight Publishing, 1996).

100. Geoff Egan, email correspondence with Sarah Watkins-Kenney on lead cloth seal, October 30, 2007 (on file at the *QAR* Conservation Lab, Greenville, N.C.).

101. "The History and Symbolism of Pearl Jewelry," Brilliant Earth webpage, www.brilliantearth.com (February 21, 2016).

102. On Atlantic pearls, see ibid.

103. Dosset, "Deposition for Verification and Addendum to the Deposition of Lieutenant Ernaut."

104. Martha J. Ehrlich, "Akan Gold from the Wreck of the *Whydah*," in Hamilton, *Whydah*, Appendix 1.

105. Christopher R. DeCorse, *An Archaeology of Elmina: Africans and Europeans on the Gold Coast, 1400–1900* (Washington, D.C.: Smithsonian Institution Press, 2001).

106. For information about trade relations in the Gold Coast region of Africa, see Martha J. Ehrlich, "Early Akan Gold from the Wreck of the *Whydah*," *African Arts* 22, no. 4 (August 1989): 52–57. In her article, Ehrlich outlines the history of gold trade among African tribal groups during the 1600s–1800s and the rise of gold jewelry in the form of specially made beads, headpieces, and scepters among tribal leaders. Later, beads were used as trade currency among all levels of slave traders. To identify styles of beads through time, she referred to journals and drawings (charts) made by French commercial slave-trade agent Jean Barbot into the West Africa region in 1678–1712. Gold jewelry among the Akan peoples (leaders such as "Chiefs and Queenmothers") indicated wealth and status, highlighting fashion, religion, and commemoration.

107. Common among the African tribes of the Gold Coast was the worship of the sun, symbolized by their penchant for gold jewelry and offerings, personal adornment, and fashion. For the enslaved Africans on board a ship bound for the Americas, the gold-colored beads offered to them by traders may have placated them in the absence of their pure gold, taken by pirates and used as currency. Of the glass beads so far recovered from the *QAR* shipwreck, over 70 percent are gold-colored and heavily patinated.

108. Jerome S. Handler, "On the Transportation of Material Goods by Enslaved Africans during the Middle Passage: Preliminary Findings from Documentary Sources," *African Diaspora Archaeology Newsletter*, December 2006.

109. Ehrlich, "Akan Gold from the Wreck of the *Whydah*," in Hamilton, *Whydah*; Kenneth Kidd and Martha A. Kidd, "A Classification System for Glass Trade Beads for the Use of the Field Archaeologists," in *Proceedings of the 1982 Glass Bead Conference*, ed. Charles F. Hays III (Rochester, N.Y., 1982), on color type IIa17, Bright Yellow Gold.

110. Barbara A. Bianco, Christopher R. DeCorse, and Jean Howson, "Beads and Other Adornments," in *New York African Burial Ground Archaeology Final Report* (2006), 382–417.

111. Hamilton, *Whydah*, 335, after Timothy F. Garrard,

Akan Weights and the Gold Trade (Bristol, U.K.: Longman, 1980), 107.

112. Moore and Malcolm, "*Henrietta Maria*," 20–38.

113. Erik Goldstein (Colonial Williamsburg) and David Moore (North Carolina Department of Cultural Resources), unpublished correspondence on silver coin (on file at the *QAR* Conservation Lab, Greenville, N.C.).

114. Deagan, *Artifacts of the Spanish Colonies*, on assayer's mark and date.

115. Dosset, "Deposition for Verification and Addendum to the Deposition of Lieutenant Ernaut."

116. Franklin H. Price, "More Than Meets the Eye: A Preliminary Report on Artifacts from the Sediment of the Site 31CR314, *Queen Anne's Revenge*, an Eighteenth-Century Shipwreck off Beaufort Inlet, North Carolina," *Southeastern Archaeology Journal* 35, no. 2 (August 2001): 155–69.

117. Kisch, *Scales and Weights*.

118. Ibid., 134.

119. Crawford-Hitchins, 2009 and 2011 personal correspondence with Welsh.

120. Ibid., for mark on square weight for three pennyweight; a weight identical to this one was found on the *Whydah* wreck, see Hamilton *Whydah*, 213–14.

121. Eric Sloane, *Eric Sloane's America* (New York: Promontory Press, 1956), 32–33.

122. Timothy Guisewhite, land surveyor, 2012 personal communication on tallies and chains (on file at the *QAR* Conservation Lab, Greenville, N.C.).

Chapter 7

1. William J. Broad, "Sea May Have Yielded a Piece of Pirate Lore," *New York Times*, March 4, 1997, http://www.nytimes.com/1997/03/04/us/sea-may-have-yielded-a-piece-of-pirate-lore.html (June 3, 2017).

2. Mark U. Wilde-Ramsing and Charles R. Ewen, "Beyond Reasonable Doubt: A Case for *Queen Anne's Revenge*," *Historical Archaeology* 46 (Spring 2012): 110–33.

3. George L. Miller, Patricia Samford, Ellen Shlasko, and Andrew Madsen, "Telling Time for Archaeologists," *Northeast Historical Archaeology* 29 (2000) 1–22; P. R. G. Hornsby, R. Weinstein, and R. Homer, *Pewter: A Celebration of the Craft, 1200–1700* (London: Museum of London, 1989).

4. *The Tryals of Major Stede Bonnet and other Pirates, viz . . . Who were all condemn'd for Piracy . . . At the Admiralty Sessions held at Charles-Town in the Province of South Carolina, on Tuesday the 28th of October, 1718. And by several Adjournments continued to Wednesday the 12th of November, following. To which is Prefix'd An Account of the Taking of the said Major Bonnet, and the rest of the Pirates* (London: Benjamin Cowse, 1719), 8.

5. Keith Muckelroy, *Maritime Archaeology* (Cambridge: Cambridge University Press, 1978) 160–65; James P. Delgado, ed., *Encyclopedia of Underwater and Maritime Archaeology* (London: British Museum Press, 1997), 57–59.

6. Robert E. Lee, *Blackbeard the Pirate: A Reappraisal of His Life and Times* (Winston-Salem: John F. Blair, 1974), 122.

7. G. K. Zipf, *Human Behavior and the Principle of Least Effort* (Cambridge: Addison-Wesley, 1949); also see Vincent M. La Motta and Michael B. Schiffer, "Formation Processes of House Floor Assemblages," in *The Archaeology of House Activities*, ed. Penelope M. Allison (London: Routledge, 1999) 19–29.

8. The song "The John B Sails" originated in the West Indies and was first transcribed in Richard Le Gallienne, "Coral Islands and Mangrove-Trees," *Harper's Monthly Magazine*, December 1916, 81–90. It also appeared in Carl Sandburg, *The American Songbag* (1927; reprint, New York: Harcourt Brace Jovanovich, 1990). There have been numerous verses and different titles, such as "Sloop John B," which was made popular in song by the Kingston Trio (1958) and the Beach Boys (1966).

9. Captain William Brand (HMS *Lyme*), *Letter to Secretary to Admiralty. July 12, 1718*, PRO-ADM 1/1472) Public Record Office in London, copy held in the N.C. State Archives).

10. Colin Woodard, "The Last Days of Piracy: An Exclusive Account of the Final Raid and Political Maneuvers of the Most Notorious Pirate," *Smithsonian*, February 2014.

11. Captain Charles Johnson [Nathaniel Mist], *A General History of the Robberies and Murders of the Most Notorious Pyrates* (London, 1724; reprint with an introduction by David Cordingly, New York: Lyons Press, 1998), 62.

12. "The Taking of Teach the Pirate, 1719," Founders Online, National Archives, last modified July 12, 2016, http://founders .archives.gov/documents/Franklin/01-01-02-0007. The original source is Leonard W. Labaree, ed., *The Papers of Benjamin Franklin*, vol. 1, *January 6, 1706, through December 31, 1734* (New Haven: Yale University Press, 1959), 7. National archivists add that "the second ballad which Franklin wrote and hawked through the streets of Boston was 'a Sailor Song on the Taking of Teach or Blackbeard the Pirate.'" This may have been written in March 1719, after the *Boston News-Letter* carried a full account of the last fight and death of Captain Edward Teach on November 22, 1718.

13. Kevin P. Duffus, *The Last Day of Black Beard the Pirate: Within Every Legend Lies a Grain of Truth* (Raleigh: Looking Glass Productions, 2008).

14. Johnson [Mist], *Pyrates*, 62.

15. Anthony Cracherode, *Report to the Lord Commissioners of His Majesty's Treasury in Reference to the Petition for Pirate Bounties, Calendar of Treasury Papers, 1556–7—[1728]: 1720–1728* (London: Longmans, Green, Reader, and Dyer, 1889), 134–39.

16. Philip Howard, "Living amidst 250 Years of Howard Family History," *Outer Banks Magazine*, June 2016.

17. James Adair, *The History of the American Indians; Particularly Those Nations adjoining to the Missisippi, East and West Florida, Georgia, South and North Carolina, and Virginia: Account of Origin, Language, Manners, Religious & Civil Customs, Laws [etc.]* (London: published for Edward and Charles Dilly, London 1775). Partially reprinted in "The Hydes of Northampton County," *North Carolina Genealogy Society Journal*, May 1994, 144.

18. Johnson [Mist] *Pyrates*, 313–24.

19. *Tryals of Major Stede Bonnet*, 1–48.

20. *Weekly Journal*, or *Saturday's-Post* 287, April 25, 1724. Provided by Lewis C. Forrest, Ayden, N.C. (May 25, 2015).

21. Pierre Dosset, "Deposition for Verification and Addendum to the Deposition of Lieutenant Ernaut regarding *La Concorde de Nantes* Plundered and Seized by the Pirates Including Wages Paid and Ship Log," Série B 4578, Folia 90v, October 13, 1718, Archives départementales de Loire-Atlantique, Nantes, France.

22. Lee, *Blackbeard the Pirate*, 145–46.

Chapter 8

1. Mark Wilde-Ramsing and Wayne Lusardi, "Management Plan for North Carolina Shipwreck 31CR314, *Queen Anne's Revenge*" (North Carolina Underwater Archaeology Branch, Kure Beach, 1999), http://www.qaronline.org/reports/ management-plan-north-carolina-shipwreck-31cr314-queen-annes-revenge-site.

2. Mark Wilde-Ramsing, "Mystery Man from Maryland," *Queen's Report: Update from the Queen Anne's Revenge Shipwreck Project* 5, no. 2 (Summer 2005), http://www.qaronline .org/reports/volume-5-number-2-summer-2005.

3. Kimberly Eslinger and Mark Wilde-Ramsing, "Live from Morehead City, It's *Queen Anne's Revenge*," Queen Anne's Revenge *Shipwreck Project Research Report and Bulletin Series*, QAR-B-08-02 (Raleigh: North Carolina Department of Cultural Resources, 2002), http://www.qaronline.org/reports/ live-morehead-city-its-queen-annes-revenge.

INDEX

F

Farrell, Erik, 178

Faunal analysis, 129. *See also* Bone

Firearms, 113, 114, 116–20, 161, 194n43, 194n49; gunflints, 118–19, 138; powder scoop, 119, 138

Fishing, 31, 96, 104, 130, 140

Food. *See* Sustenance and cooking

Fort Macon, N.C., 41, 108; State Park, 56, 59, 67, 180. *See also* United States Coast Guard Station Fort Macon

Fort Michilimackinac, 139–40

Frames. *See* Hull and fasteners

France, 30, 94, 97, 130, 163, 170; and slave trade, 22–23, 98; goods manufactured in, 86, 93, 101, 118, 126–27, 133, 134, 137, 145, 151, 157, 161; monarchy of, 126. *See also* French

Freeman, Chris, 41

French, 20, 81, 86, 101, 134, 141; privateer, 1, 90–91, 183, 186; slave trade, 3, 20–21, 22–23, 25, 151; colonial settlements, 21, 22–23, 25, 32, 131–33, 139, 140, 143; frigate, 21, 158; monarchy, 29, 115; measurements, 78, 92, 102, 106, 110, 131; manufactured goods, 93, 96, 115, 117–18, 121, 122, 124, 126, 132–33, 135, 141, 157, 161–62; surgeons, 96, 101, 123, 125, 133, 136, 143, 162, 164. See also *Concorde*; France

Frigate, French, 21, 24–26. See also *Concorde*

G

Gaming pieces, 139

Geodynamics LLC, 41

Geology. *See* Marine geology

George I (king of England), 19, 26, 136, 155, 157

German, 110. *See also* Germany

Germany, 101, 133, 151, 157. *See also* German

Ghana, Africa, 149

Gillman-Bryan, Julep, 58, 68, 175

Giroux, Ray, 174

Glass, 62, 78, 105, 141, 179. *See also* Beads: glass; Bottles; Glass containers; Stemware; Window glass and caming

Glass containers, 51, 78, 136. *See also* Bottles, Stemware

Global Positioning System (GPS), 54, 57, 60

Gloucestershire, England, 12

Gold, 19, 34, 37, 61, 62, 77, 78, 81, 90, 142–43, 145–47, 150–52, 157, 159, 160, 161, 176, 181. *See also* Akan jewelry

Goldsmith's Company Assay Office, 152

Gradiometer survey, 63–64

Grapnel, 100

Great Allen, 29, 32, 163

Grenada, 22, 98, 163

Grenades, 113, 120–21; bottles as improvised grenades, 121, 137

Gunflints. *See* Firearms

Gunpowder, 107–9, 118, 138

Gunter, Edmund, 102, 152

H

Hands, Israel, 26, 167

Harriot, David, 26, 33, 36, 170. See also *Adventure*

Harvey, Paul, 166

Henrietta Marie, 14, 134

Henry, Nathan, 76, 107

Hermley, Lauren, 176–77

Hispaniola. *See* Saint-Domingue

Historical archaeology, 8, 14–15, 68–69, 88–89

Hobhouse, Richard, 26

Honduras, Bay of, 26, 28

Horn. *See* Lantern; Sword

Hornigold, Benjamin, 13, 142

Howard, William, 36, 168

Hull and fasteners, 47, 51, 64–65, 89–92, 157, 173. *See also* Sternpost

Hull patches, lead, 51, 94, 159. *See also* Caulking

Hunt, James B., 57, 172

Hurricanes, 47, 66; Bonnie, 40, 46, 64; Dennis, 58, 65; Floyd, 58, 65; Irene, 65; Isabel, 66; Ophelia, 66

Hyde, Richard, 168

I

Inlet, coastal, 41–42; bar, 10, 35–36, 42, 44, 158. *See also* Beaufort Inlet

InterOcean S-4A electromagnetic current meter, 40, 46

Intersal, Inc. LLC, 1, 55, 58

Interspiro Divator Mark II (AGA), 59

Ireland, 19, 91, 169

Italy, 132, 151, 157

J

Jack, lifting. *See* Mechanical jack

Jamaica, 13, 26, 169

Jane, 38

Jeopardy, 183

Jewelry, 145–49, 157. *See also* Akan jewelry

Johnson, Captain Charles. *See* Mist, Nathaniel

Johnson, Robert, 28

Jones Bay, R/V, 59

Joy, Richard, 26

Jules César, 21

K

Kangxi region, China, 133

Keg tap, 138–39

Keith, William, 13

Kenyon, Kimberly, 81, 178

Kettle. *See* Cookpots

Kidd, Captain, 68

P

Page, Courtney, 79, 178

Pardon, 9, 10, 28, 30–31, 35, 38–39, 166, 169. *See also* Act of Grace

Pearl, 145–46

Pelican III, 6, 58

Pell, Ignatius, 8–10, 17, 26, 32–33, 68, 169–70

Pennsylvania State University, 90

Pestle. *See* Mortar

Pewterware, 77, 89, 138, 157, 159; dishes (plates and chargers), 51, 62; London pewterers, 134–35. *See also* Clyster; Spoon; Syringe

Philip V (king of Spain), 150

Piner, Tom, 58, 68, 70–72, 180

Pins. *See* Apparel

Pipes, tobacco, 32, 139–40, 157

Piracy, 11–12, 15, 30–31, 35, 38–39, 68, 178, 188n3, 196n88; trials for, 10–11, 36, 167–69; "pirates consent," 36. *See also* Blackbeard; Bonnet, Stede; Hornigold, Benjamin; Kidd, Captain; Thache, Edward; Vane, Charles

Pirates: members of Blackbeard's crew, 166–68; members of Bonnet's crew, 169–70. *See also* Caesar; Hands, Israel; Howard, William; Hyde, Richard; Richards, Lieutenant; Virgin, Henry

Pirates of the Caribbean on Stranger Tides (Disney), 181

Pissdale, 94

Pistol. *See* Firearms

Plank. *See* Hull and fasteners

Pola Palekh, 42

Porringer, 126–27, 129, 134–35, 162

Portugal, 22, 169

Portuguese, 21, 22, 81

Powder scoop. *See* Cannon (gunner's) tools; Firearms

Price, Franklin, 151

Princess, 32

Protestant Caesar, 26

Purifoy, Joe, 58

Q

QAR Dive Down, 176–77

QAR Dive Live, 59

QAR Project Web Live, 179

Quebec City, Canada, 133

Queen Anne's Revenge (archaeological site), 8, 15, 51, 158; discovery of, 2, 6–7, 14, 20, 172; value of, 20, 165; environmental setting of, 40–41, 46; site formation processes (deterioration), 43–51, 58, 158–59; damage to from dredging, 45; preservation of in situ, 48–49; early dives on, 52–53; identification of, 60, 62, 154–58, 173; abandonment of, evidence of, 160, 163–64. *See also* Beaufort Inlet shipwreck

Queen Anne's Revenge (pirate ship): battleship, flagship, x–xi, 3, 8, 13, 29, 37, 120; loss of, 10, 17, 20, 33, 39–40, 45, 158, 160, 165; name origin of, 19; lore about, lack of, 22; Caribbean cruise of, 26–28; armament of, 29, 37, 105, 179, 189n11; life aboard, 29–34, 154, 160–61; wrecking and abandonment of, 36–37, 42–43, 150, 163. *See also Concorde*

Queen Anne's Revenge Conservation Lab, xi, 58, 73, 75–78; X-radiography (x-ray), 15, 77, 79, 84–85, 107, 179; artifact processing, 71–73, 77–80, 164, 191n1; wet storage, 74–75; early conservation efforts, 76–77; artifact analysis, 80–85, 88–90, 97; tours for the public, 178–79. *See also QAR* Project Web Live

Queen Anne's Revenge Shipwreck Project, x–xi, 3; media coverage of, 16, 173, 175–76, 178, 183; planning of, 53–58, 62, 171; site security for, 56–57; funding for, 58, 76; recovery operations of, 58–73, 75, 77, 164, 174–75; gradiometer survey of, 59, 63–64; website of, 178. *See also QAR* Dive Down; *QAR* Dive Live

Queen Anne's War, 21, 25

Queen's University, Northern Ireland, 91

Quillon block, 115

R

Radiocarbon dating, 155

Ranger, 38

Revenge, 26–29, 36, 163. *See also Royal James*

Richards, Lieutenant, 26

Roatan, 26

Rogers, Woodes, 30, 35

Rope, 29, 47, 92–93, 103–4, 108, 110, 112, 113, 140, 149, 179

Rose Emelye, 13, 166

Royal James, 10, 36, 168. *See also Revenge*

S

Sails and rigging, 47, 49, 90, 92–93, 157; disabling of, 105, 109, 161. *See also* Rope

Saint-Domingue, 22, 98

Saintonge wares, 133, 161

Salter, Edward, 26, 30, 167

Salvador, 1, 54

Scale weight, 151–52, 161; coin weight, 19, 151–52, 157; nested weight, 88, 101, 125–26

Schnitzer, Laura Kate, 112–13

Scissors, 127

Scotch pine, 91

Scotland, 19, 169

Scour-burial process, 46–49

Sea Hawk, R/V, 58

Seaman's Vade Mecum, 122–23. *See also* Medical treatment

Shackleford Banks, 41, 43, 45

William III (king of England), 19

Williamsburg, 38, 167, 181

Wimble, James (1738 Map), 43–44, 52

Window glass and caming, 93, 157

Wyer, William, 26

X

X-radiography. See *Queen Anne's Revenge* Conservation Lab

Z

Zipf's principle of least effort, 164. See also *Queen Anne's Revenge* (archaeological site): abandonment of, evidence of